Faces of Kentucky

Faces of Kentucky

James C. Klotter
and
Freda C. Klotter

THE UNIVERSITY PRESS OF KENTUCKY

Publication of this volume was made possible in part
by a grant from the National Endowment for the Humanities.

Scholarly publisher for the Commonwealth,
serving Bellarmine University, Berea College, Centre
College of Kentucky, Eastern Kentucky University,
The Filson Historical Society, Georgetown College,
Kentucky Historical Society, Kentucky State University,
Morehead State University, Murray State University,
Northern Kentucky University, Transylvania University,
University of Kentucky, University of Louisville,
and Western Kentucky University.
All rights reserved.

Editorial and Sales Offices: The University Press of Kentucky
663 South Limestone Street, Lexington, Kentucky 40508-4008
www.kentuckypress.com

09 08 07 06 05 5 4 3 2 1

Library of Congress Cataloging-in-Publication Data
Klotter, James C.
   Faces of Kentucky / James C. Klotter and Freda C. Klotter.
       p. cm.
   Includes bibliographical references and index.
   ISBN 0-8131-2336-4 (hardcover : alk. paper)
   1. Kentucky—History—Textbooks. 2. Kentucky—Social life and
customs—Textbooks. 3. Kentucky–Biography—Textbooks.
   I. Klotter, Freda C., 1946–   . II. Title.
   F451.3.K58 2005
   976.9—dc22
                                                        2005014251

ISBN   978-0-8131-2336-3

This book is printed on acid-free recycled paper meeting
the requirements of the American National Standard
for Permanence in Paper for Printed Library Materials.

Manufactured in China.
 Member of the Association of
American University Presses

To our grandchildren

Table of contents

✦ **Introduction**   **xiii**

✦ **Chapter 1   Frontiers—Then and Now**   **1**

The Past   3
Writing about the Past   4
Native Americans in Kentucky   7
Paleoindians, 10,000 B.C.–8,000 B.C.   8
Archaic Period, 8,000 B.C.–1,000 B.C.   9
Woodland Period, 1,000 B.C.–A.D. 1000   10
Late Prehistoric Period, A.D. 1000–1750   12
The Great Dying   12
The Name "Kentucky"   14

✦ **Chapter 2   Starting a State**   **15**

The First West   17
The First Explorers   20
What They Found   22
Coming to Kentucky   25
Settling a State   27
Daniel Boone   32
Hard Times   35
Choices   36
The End of the Frontier   41
Statehood   41

✦ Chapter 3   Different Kentuckys   45

The People of Kentucky	46
Kentucky Homes	48
The Land	49
Climate	53
Geographic Regions	53
Jackson Purchase	55
Pennyroyal (or Pennyrile)	58
Western Coal Fields	59
Bluegrass	59
Mountains (Eastern Coal Fields)	59
Cultural or Human Regions	60
Appalachia (Eastern Kentucky)	61
Northern Kentucky	62
Bluegrass	63
South-Central Kentucky	65
Louisville	67
West Kentucky	70
Jackson Purchase	72
Regionalism	72
Kentucky Names	74

✦ Chapter 4   The Government of Kentucky   75

Government	76
The Kentucky Constitution	76
Change	78
Levels of Government	79
Branches of Government	79
The Executive Branch (the Governor)	82
The Judicial Branch (the Courts)	85
The Legislative Branch (the General Assembly)	87
The Legislators	87
Passing a Law	90
The Mystery of "Honest Dick" Tate	91

★ **Chapter 5 — Living in Kentucky** — **93**

Daily Life — 94
Clothes and Fashion — 97
Food — 99
Work — 103
Health — 106
Fun and Games — 109
Basketball — 115
Religion — 117

★ **Chapter 6 — From Statehood to the Civil War** — **125**

Slavery — 126
Slave Life — 129
Freedom — 131
Antislavery — 135
Key Political Leaders — 136
Three Kentucky Presidents — 139

★ **Chapter 7 — The Civil War and the End of a Century** — **145**

The Brothers' War — 147
On the Battlefield — 149
Guerrillas — 153
Results of the War — 155
From the End of the Civil War to the Start of a New Century — 158
Feuds and Murders — 160

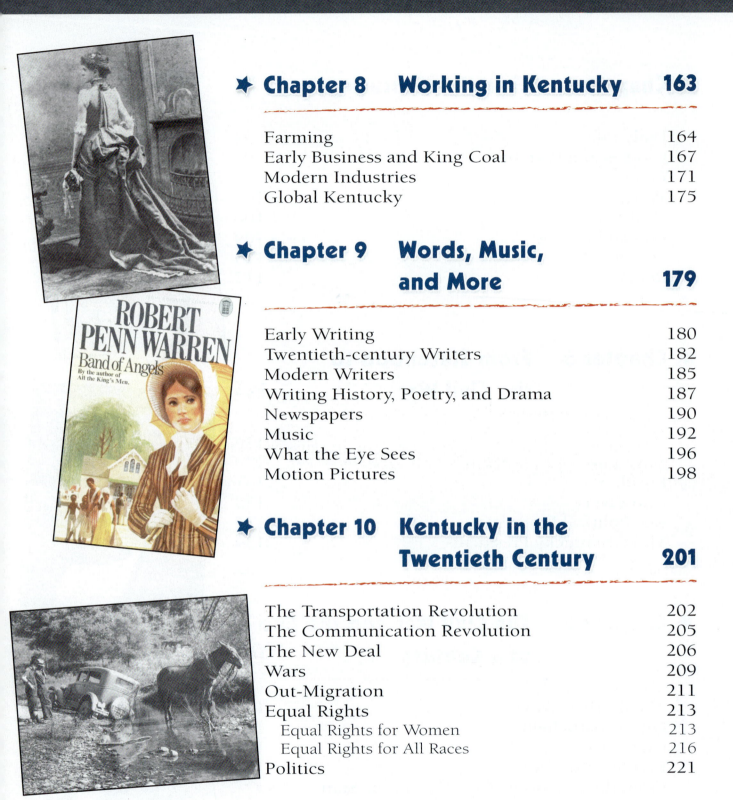

✦ **Chapter 8   Working in Kentucky   163**

Farming   164
Early Business and King Coal   167
Modern Industries   171
Global Kentucky   175

✦ **Chapter 9   Words, Music, and More   179**

Early Writing   180
Twentieth-century Writers   182
Modern Writers   185
Writing History, Poetry, and Drama   187
Newspapers   190
Music   192
What the Eye Sees   196
Motion Pictures   198

✦ **Chapter 10   Kentucky in the Twentieth Century   201**

The Transportation Revolution   202
The Communication Revolution   205
The New Deal   206
Wars   209
Out-Migration   211
Equal Rights   213
   Equal Rights for Women   213
   Equal Rights for All Races   216
Politics   221

✦ Chapter 11   Going to School   225

Early Kentucky Schools   226
Life in School   227
Special Schools   233
Schools in the Twentieth Century and Beyond   235
Colleges and Universities   239
Going to College   242

✦ Chapter 12   Today and Tomorrow in Kentucky   245

A Typical Kentuckian   246
Saving Parts of the Past   247
Future Issues   248
Your Future   251

Appendixes   253

Additional Sources for Research   267

Acknowledgments   269

Credits   270

Index   277

Introduction

This book is for people who want to learn more about Kentucky. Young people, especially, need to know about the history and lifestyles of many countries. We all should understand the cultures of China, Brazil, India, France, South Africa, and dozens and dozens of other parts of the world. The United States, of course, is important for those of us who live here. Finally, we all should know what has shaped our state and local area, and what continues to shape them now.

Well-informed, well-educated citizens must understand *all* parts of our world—the international, national, state, and local. This book can help us learn about Kentucky and its cities and counties. It is there where it starts for all of us.

The title of this book, *Faces of Kentucky,* has several meanings. First of all, it refers to the people of the state. Kentucky people present many different faces to the world. They may be young or old, male or female, rich or poor. The people in the state may live in a city or in the country. They may come from very different backgrounds. Some may work in a factory; others may work on a farm. They may do different things for fun, may believe differently, and may act in different ways. In short, there really are many faces across Kentucky.

The title also speaks of Kentucky's various geographical faces. Our state is a place of high hills and low swamps, of forests and flat land, of roads and rivers, and of much else. The land shows us many faces. The people on the land do, too. This is their story, about their land.

Faces of Kentucky tries to show all aspects of the state. It tells about history, geography, economics, government, and more. Many of these words are explained later in the book. New words appear in special type **like this** as vocabulary words.

In almost all the chapters, two other features are found. There are sections that give the actual words written or spoken by people of an earlier time. Those primary documents can help us better understand what took place then, and why. The chapters also have sections called "Kentucky Faces." In those sections, a person's life is told in more detail. The story of a real person can make the facts and explanations come alive. The more general "faces" of Kentucky are changed into personal faces for you.

We also have used examples from cities and counties across the state. About 100 of the state's 120 counties are included. You might recognize a description or a place name and wish to find out more about a person who lived in your part of Kentucky or an event that took place near you.

Finally, we have asked you questions here and there. Some we answer; some we do not. We hope that the questions will cause you to think—about how things were in the past, or about why they are as they are now, or about how things might be in the future.

Now that we have said all that, it is time to find out more about Kentucky, *your* Kentucky.

chapter 1

Frontiers—
Then and Now

One meaning of the word *frontier* is a border between places. But those borders can be very different at different times.

Dr. Story Musgrave of Kentucky went into space as an astronaut in 1983 on a space shuttle. Though he was born outside the state, he learned to fly in Lexington and considered Kentucky his home. He went on five more shuttle trips. Once he helped repair a space telescope. Another time he walked in space. When he retired, no other person had ever gone on more space flights.

Musgrave was not the only astronaut from Kentucky. Terry Wilcutt was born in Russellville, went to high school in Louisville, and got a college degree in Bowling Green. He taught math in high school for a time. Then he became a space shuttle pilot and took part in four flights. Once he linked up with the space station.

Astronaut Story Musgrave in space, with Earth in the background.

Both men traveled thousands of miles in just a few days. Both saw things that few others had seen. Both were filled with wonder as they left their world for the unknown of space. But when they faced that unknown future and the frontier of space, they simply were doing what humans have done for thousands of years.

Think about the feelings of the first human who stepped on the soil of what is now Kentucky. Exactly when that event happened, and who that person was, is unknown. But that first person (one of a group that we now call Indians or Native Americans) started a process of people living here, one that still goes on. The first Kentuckian could travel only a few miles on foot each day. Yet as that person looked over this untouched land, he or she likely felt the same way those astronauts did many thousands of years later. That person saw a new place that no other had seen. That man or woman faced a new frontier. That human looked to a fresh future.

Many, many years later, some people from Europe came to what seemed to them a New World. They called it America. Just think how it would be today if a space shuttle suddenly came upon an unknown new planet and found that it had humans already living on it. That was what it was like when the Europeans came to America and later to Kentucky. They found humans they did not know even existed. The Indians, of course, had the same reaction. These people from across the ocean were new to them too.

European explorers soon made their way to Kentucky. They found a land that filled them with excitement. Like the Indians before them, they wanted to live here. They also sought a new life on this new frontier. Although living thousands of years apart, the first Indians and the first European explorers, and even those astronauts from Kentucky, all shared the same human feelings about the places they saw.

Today, if you want to travel to places that no one has seen before, you may have to go into space, as astronauts Musgrave and Wilcutt did. But many frontiers still exist on Earth. The spirit of those earlier people is part of our life too. After all, change

Astronaut Terry Wilcutt

happens all the time. Your future may involve another meaning of the word *frontier*. It can also mean discovering new learning and the outer boundaries of knowledge. Your frontiers may be of the mind. You may make discoveries in science or medicine, or invent new ways of doing things, or write books that cause people to think in new ways, or do so much more. Different frontiers still await new explorers.

★ The Past ★

People who study the past are explorers too. Like those who came to Kentucky many years ago, they want to find out about something. Indians, explorers, astronauts—all sought to solve the mystery of what was out there on the frontiers of Kentucky or in the frontiers of space. Students of the state's written record are called historians. They are like detectives trying to solve mysteries. Historians want to solve mysteries of the past.

Why are the past and its mysteries important? Why should we study history?

First of all, think about what you did today. When you got up, you already knew the way to the bathroom and to the kitchen and to your school. At lunch, if you saw food you knew you liked, you did not have to taste it to find out whether it was good. You had learned these things early in life. They had become part of your own history. You do not have to discover the same facts again every day.

History is like that. If we learn what other people did before us, then we do not have to relearn what they learned. We do not have to repeat their mistakes. We can find out what worked for them. The historical record is really our only guide to how humans acted. It can thus help us in our lives.

If you got up each morning and did not know where to go or what to eat, you would have to learn those things over and over again. You could not do much, and you would make many mistakes before you found out what you needed to know. If people in a state or a nation did not know their history, it would be like a person who had to relearn all of life's lessons every day. History is important.

History is also about real people and real events. The things you read about in this book actually happened. Many of the things you see on television or in the movies are made up. But here you will find true stories of persons who had to face real problems. Sometimes they made mistakes. We should see that and try not to make the same mistakes again. At other times they acted as heroes with courage, in matters big and small. We should use those actions as our ideals, and their lives as models for our own actions. So you see, history is not just about the past but can help shape our future.

⋆ Writing about the Past ⋆

Everyone can be a historian. How would you write a history of your grandparents? You might first want to talk to them and let them tell you about their lives. That is called oral history. Where else could you find out about them? You could ask other people what they know. You could go through family photographs or even old letters that may have been saved. Reading through old city and county newspapers may reveal stories about your grandparents. If their school had a yearbook, you could look up things about them there. Any land or house they bought would be listed in records in the courthouse. Finally, you could take all you had found and write their history.

In doing those things, you would be acting as a historian. You would be solving any mysteries and explaining your grandparents' lives to others.

Research can occur at places like the Thomas D. Clark Center for Kentucky History in Frankfort, or in a local library. (Note the map of Kentucky that is part of the floor in this picture.)

At the end, you likely would have learned things you did not know before—about them and about yourself.

The work historians do to get ready for writing history is called research. Generally, there are two different kinds of research. One is working with what are called primary sources; the other is using secondary sources. **Primary sources** were written or spoken at the time, by the persons directly involved, or are remembered later by those who lived then. **Secondary sources** were written later, by people trying to explain what happened to others. For example, if your grandparents told you directly about something in their lives, what would that be—a primary or secondary source?

Most of the books and newspapers we read are secondary sources. History books, encyclopedias, and magazine articles are based on research and written by someone trying to tell the story of an event or a person. These sources help us learn about the past and its peoples. The best way, though, is to do research in primary sources so you are the historian yourself.

Look at the two sources below about the explorer Daniel Boone:

From an encyclopedia written seventy-six years after Boone's death:

"He was five feet ten inches in height and of robust and powerful proportions."

From an interview with Daniel Boone's son:

"My father, Daniel Boone, was five feet, eight inches tall and had broad shoulders. . . . His usual weight was about 175 pounds."

How are they different? Which one is the better source?

Just because something is published in a book does not mean that it is correct. You should explore, search out, and discover what you think is the truth by doing your own research. After you look at primary sources, perhaps you will re-write what others have said is the history of something or someone.

But what happens when no letters, newspapers, or other written primary sources exist? How then do we re-create the past? In fact, that is the situation for most of the years humans have lived in Kentucky. Trying to tell their story is more difficult. If you have no written records and no one to interview, how do you find out about the peoples of the past?

Persons who try to do that are called **archaeologists.** Archaeologists study ancient or original people by looking at what the people left behind—stone tools, bits of pottery, pieces of clothes, burial places, skeletons, and even trash pits.

Archaeologists at work.

If someone looked at your family's trash, what could they find out about you? By examining the trash of the past, archaeologists can discover what people ate by looking at the animal bones or shells they threw away. They might find bits of broken jars and be able to see how the people stored food and other things. They could find old pieces of arrows and understand how the ancient people made weapons. Using such records, we can get a good idea of how people lived thousands of years ago.

Now that we know how archaeologists find out about the past, let's see what they have found.

★ Native Americans in Kentucky ★

Are Native Americans really native to America? Have they always been in America and Kentucky? Thousands of years ago, the land and oceans were different, and people from Asia could walk across a land bridge to what is now Alaska. From there they slowly spread over America. Perhaps some also came by small boats across the Pacific Ocean. So Native Americans traveled to America too, just as other people did, much later. Historians often also use the term *American Indians,* because Indians are not really native to America.

But whatever we now call them, the Indians found themselves in a new land, filled with animals that they could hunt—animals that could hunt them, too. Finally, one Indian—or perhaps a whole family—came to what we now call Kentucky, and the first humans walked this land.

That event probably happened at least twelve thousand years ago. One generation is said to be twenty years. A grandparent, a parent, and a child thus make up three generations. Native Americans lived in Kentucky long before any other groups came here. Six hundred generations of American Indians lived and died here before the first European explorers even came to America. In contrast, only a dozen or so generations have lived in Kentucky since the time of our first written history—some six hundred Indian generations and twelve others. To see it another way, look at the six-inch line below. If every inch stands for two thousand years of history, then how long have people other than Native Americans lived in Kentucky?

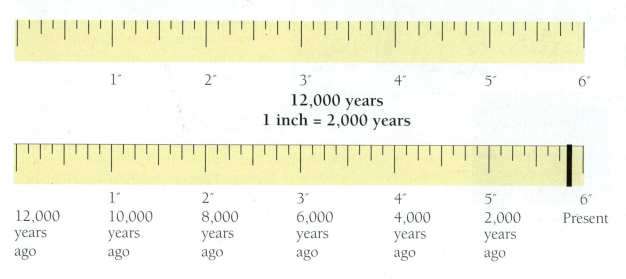

12,000 years
1 inch = 2,000 years

| 12,000 years ago | 10,000 years ago | 8,000 years ago | 6,000 years ago | 4,000 years ago | 2,000 years ago | Present |

Europeans have been in Kentucky only one-eighth of one inch on that scale—not very long.

But change takes place over time, even for the American Indians who lived here so long. Archaeologists have divided that twelve thousand years into four different periods, so let's look at each one.

★ Paleoindians, 10,000 B.C.–8,000 B.C. ★

The name *Paleoindian* refers to those original people who lived here a very long time ago. They came to Kentucky some twelve thousand years ago, in 10,000 B.C. or before. At that time, ice covered most of the northern part of the United States. In that ice age, Kentucky was much colder than today. Its trees looked like those in the far north do now. Large lakes also covered parts of the land.

Little is known about the Native Americans who walked the land then. Animals that no longer exist were all around them, including huge mammoths and mastodons (ice-age elephants). The Indians hunted for food, using sharpened stone points on spears. They stayed in small camps of a few dozen people. With no houses, they used rock shelters or anything they could find in nature. Overall, they lived a hard, simple, short life. Probably no more than five thousand people called Kentucky home.

Their lives were very different from ours today. Still, they had the same human feelings that we have. They saw people being born and others dying. They loved and hated. They understood pleasure and pain. They laughed and cried.

Early Indians lived in small, family-sized groups and moved a lot.

They knew happiness and sorrow.

They were not all alike, just as people now are not all alike. Some had different ideas or spoke different languages. Sometimes they lived at peace with each other. At other times they fought. We may not know that much about them, but we do know that they started the process of humans living in Kentucky.

Native Americans hunted the mammoths that roamed Kentucky at one time. They used the skin for protection from the cold and the meat for food.

★ Archaic Period, 8,000 B.C.–1,000 B.C. ★

A century lasts for one hundred years. The Archaic Period went on for about seventy centuries. It is the longest period of Native American life in Kentucky.

During that time, the land changed, becoming more like it is today. The ice age ended. The inland seas went away, and modern rivers started to flow. The population increased, and people did not move around as much. For food, they killed deer, elk, beaver, birds, and turtles. They also gathered nuts and ate river mussels. They cooked all their food using heated stones.

The Archaic people also invented new weapons for hunting. The **atlatl** (see picture on page 10) allowed them to throw their spears a longer way. They made stone axes as well and used them to build dugout canoes.

Near the end of the Archaic Period, a small change in what they did started what would be a major change over the years. The American Indians in Kentucky began to grow squash—both for food and as a container. They began what would slowly become farming—and a new way of life.

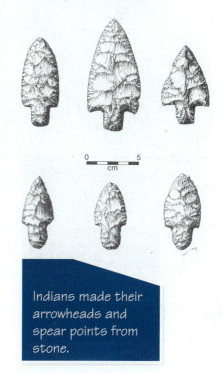

Indians made their arrowheads and spear points from stone.

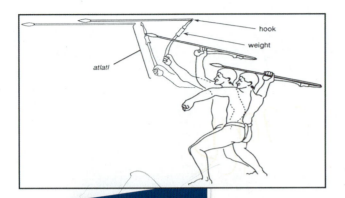

The atlatl helped Indians throw their spears farther.

A favorite target was the deer.

★ Woodland Period, 1,000 B.C.–A.D. 1000 ★

For two thousand years, change took place gradually. People still mostly hunted for food and only added sunflowers and a few other plants to what they grew. The two major inventions were pottery and a new weapon.

Some Native Americans placed their dead in large earthen burial mounds.

Woodland Indians in the eastern and central part of Kentucky began making pottery around 1,000 B.C. Having bowls and pots allowed them to cook directly over a fire. In that simple society, however, it took five hundred more years for pottery-making to reach parts of western Kentucky. Later, around A.D. 800, a new weapon came to Kentucky. It was the bow and arrow. It spread rapidly, and Native Americans soon used it for both fighting and hunting.

During this time, the Indians' lifestyle was becoming more complex. They used axes to cut trees and clear land, which changed their environment. Objects found in burial mounds (the Indians' graves) show that they had a strong belief in life after death.

A Woodland Indian

We do not know if he even had a name. Sometime around two thousand years ago, Native Americans entered Mammoth Cave to dig minerals they found there. They did not know it was one of the largest cave systems in the world. They did know it was very big and very dark.

An Indian man got up one morning, put on a brief piece of clothing, and left his camp for the cave. Perhaps he saw his mate making barrel-shaped pots as he was leaving. Perhaps others tending sunflowers in the fields watched him go. We don't know. We do know that he lit some reeds to use as torches and went three miles into Mammoth Cave. He was high on a ledge, digging some minerals and placing them in a pouch, when a rock fell on him. He could not get away.

The cool air in the cave preserved his body for centuries. About seventy years ago, some people finally found the Woodland Indian. He still reminds us of our link to those who lived and died before us.

The Mississippian Indians of the western part of Kentucky lived in large towns, with big earthen pyramids.

But the biggest change came at the end of the Woodland Period. Native Americans began to grow maize (corn). Corn, potatoes, tobacco, and tomatoes were all American crops unknown to Europeans. Only Indians grew them, and those crops created a new, farming life in the next period of time.

⋆ Late Prehistoric Period, A.D. 1000–1750 ⋆

Before the Europeans came to Kentucky, Native Americans lived in a kind of fort. Their forts looked a lot like those the settlers later built.

Corn-based farming produced more food, and that helped cause a rapid increase in the number of Indians. They built larger villages. With more people, towns formed and powerful chiefs ruled. Trade expanded all the way to the Great Lakes. But such growth brought different groups more in contact with each other. Violence grew.

Differences between regions within Kentucky became greater as well. In the western part, the **Mississippian Culture** included large villages of more than one thousand people. The towns had walls around them for protection. At the center were tall, flat-topped earthen pyramid platforms and a central, open plaza for sports and events. Around the plaza, people built houses with pole frames, sun-baked mud walls, and grass roofs. Colorful pottery and rich decorations displayed the skill of those who lived there.

In the east, a simpler society existed. Indians of the **Fort Ancient Culture** had smaller villages and no central platform mounds. They did use wooden walls for protection against others. Generally, they had simpler pottery and a less developed lifestyle.

But whether in the eastern part of the state or in the western, Native American life was about to face its greatest change and greatest challenge.

⋆ The Great Dying ⋆

In 1492, Christopher Columbus came to what others from Europe later called the New World. Soon they called it America. At that time, thousands of Indians lived in Kentucky.

But two hundred years later, English explorers to Kentucky found few tribes living here. By the 1750s, only two Native American towns seemed to

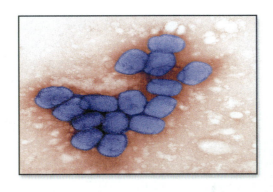

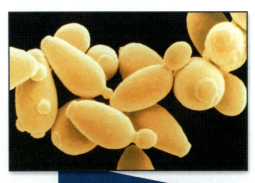

be left, outside of far western Kentucky. One was Lower Shawneetown on the Ohio River in Greenup County. In 1751, it had some twelve hundred people, but floods caused its residents to leave soon after. Another town was called Eskippakithiki, in Clark County. Indians left this town also, and it later burned. When the first wave of European settlers came to Kentucky a few years later, they found no Native Americans living in the land. Why?

If historians solve mysteries, this is a history mystery waiting to be solved. Here was rich farmland with plenty of animals. Here was a place where American Indians had lived in large numbers for thousands of years. Here was a good land. Why were the Indians gone by the 1760s?

The first part of the answer concerns what we can call the beginning of Kentucky's historical period. Written records allow us to understand better what happened. Those records show that various European explorers—from Spain, France, and England—first came in small numbers to Kentucky. They brought with them various items that they traded for furs. But the settlers did not know they carried something else—disease.

One person wrote that the Europeans won Kentucky from the Indians not by guns but by simply being there. He meant that the diseases that came with the Europeans killed many more Native Americans than any weapons or wars. Long before settlers arrived, invisible pioneers in the form of germs swept across Kentucky. Indians had never had contact with those diseases before, and their bodies could not resist them. The "Great Dying" resulted.

Across America and across Kentucky, millions died. Some say that half of all Native Americans were killed by the diseases. Others think as many as four out of every five died.

Like an invisible wave, disease spread. It killed people and caused others to flee from the unknown cause of death. Kentucky became almost vacant for a time. Those who did not

Land such as this may have caused Indians to call the area Kentucky—"a place of fields" or a "meadowland."

die had been weakened, in many ways. The deaths of those who told the stories from generation to generation left the tribes without a history. Many tribes lost their leaders. They had fewer people to resist the new European forces. Land went unused because no one was left to farm it. When explorers came to Kentucky and met Indians, they faced a people very unlike those of a century before. Native Americans still claimed Kentucky as a hunting land. Settlers would meet them there, and conflict followed. But the earlier effect of disease on the Indians made it an uneven fight from the start.

★ The Name "Kentucky" ★

Native Americans left their mark on Kentucky in many ways. Perhaps the clearest example is in the name itself. The exact origins are uncertain. One version is that *Kentucky* came from an Indian word *Kenta-ke,* meaning "a place of fields," or "a level place," or "meadowland." Another source says it came from a different tribe's name for the area—*Ken-tah-teh.* That meant "tomorrow" or "land of tomorrow."

Whatever the exact meaning, European explorers took what they heard and changed it to fit their language. As early as the 1750s, the land was called Kentucky.

Later, some would say that the name meant "Dark and Bloody Ground." It never meant that. But an Indian chief once said that when settlers would try to go there they would find a dark cloud hanging over the place and that attempts to settle it would end in bloodshed. The peaceful "meadowland" or "land of tomorrow" would indeed soon be known as a place of conflict.

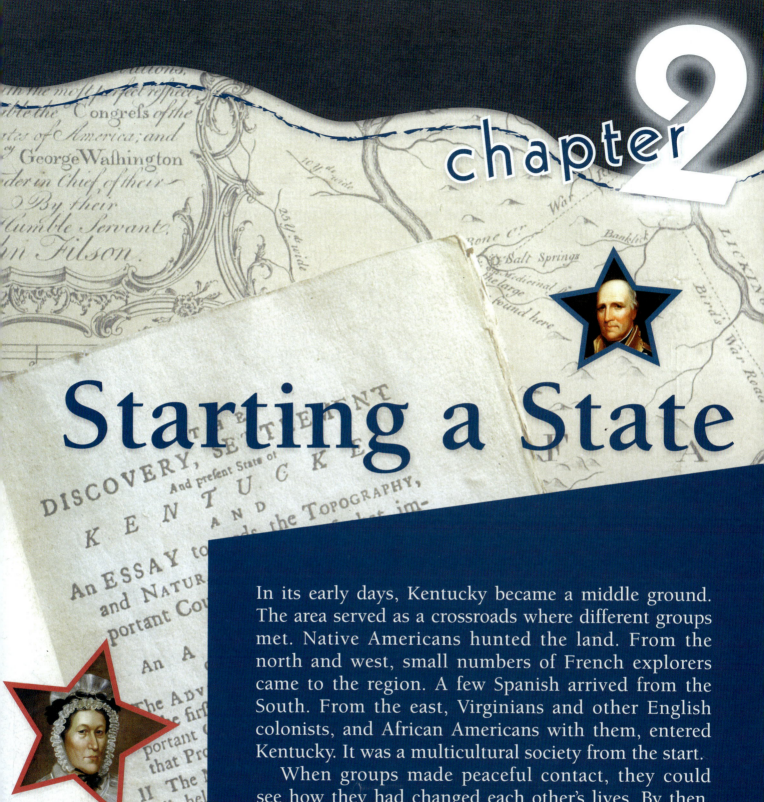

chapter 2

Starting a State

In its early days, Kentucky became a middle ground. The area served as a crossroads where different groups met. Native Americans hunted the land. From the north and west, small numbers of French explorers came to the region. A few Spanish arrived from the South. From the east, Virginians and other English colonists, and African Americans with them, entered Kentucky. It was a multicultural society from the start.

When groups made peaceful contact, they could see how they had changed each other's lives. By then, Indian villages with their cabins and walls looked very much like English forts. Indians and Europeans wore similar clothes on the frontier. All used the Native American moccasin. They combined European clothing with Indian items. Quickly the native people started using the rifle more and the bow and arrow less.

There were not clear divisions among the different groups of people. Just as the English fought the French, different Indian tribes fought each other. Sometimes one tribe would support the French, while another would go with the English. As the Europeans divided, so did the Native Americans.

When they came together, they did so to trade. **Barter** formed the basis of their economy. The Europeans would bring cheap jewelry, metal goods, weapons, mirrors, strong drink, and more. The Indians would bring deerskins, beaver furs, or other things to trade. They would then talk back and forth, bartering, until they agreed on a trade.

Even though the two worlds—European and Indian— were much alike, they also differed. Those differences would make **conflict resolution** difficult. When the two peoples disagreed, each needed to try to compromise to avoid fighting. That was difficult. People often died when a compromise was not reached.

Europeans in Kentucky most often made contact with the Shawnee tribe of Indians. The Shawnee lived in Ohio and hunted and traded in Kentucky. They built houses about twenty feet long, covered in tree bark. From these homes men went to hunt and women went to farm. The Shawnee said that no one owned the land (see document 2.1). That idea caused part of the conflict.

The Shawnee raised their children to be tough. They tied babies to cradle boards to make sure they would grow straight and strong. The boards also left a flat spot on the backs of Shawnee heads. Shawnee mothers bathed their children in cold water every day, even in winter, to harden them. Overall, Shawnee women had much more freedom than women in English homes, and therefore some European women captured by the Shawnee did not want to return to their own people.

Because so many members of the tribe had died of disease, the Indians often adopted white captives into their tribes. They treated a captive as an equal part of the family. The settlers usually did not treat captured Indians in the same way.

But the major conflicts came over animals and land. Simon Girty was a white man who had switched sides to lead the Indians. He spoke to a group of tribes and told them why they should fight:

"The Indians from all the tribes have had a right to hunt and kill these wild animals.

DOCUMENT 2.1

Daniel Trabue came to Kentucky in 1785, when he was twenty-five years old. Later, near the end of his life, he lived in Columbia in Adair County. There he wrote down his memories of those early days. Here he tells about a talk he had with an Indian chief. It shows how the two groups held a different view of land. (Spelling has been changed to the way we spell now.)

This chief said to me: "What do you want to take Indian land from them for?"

I told him that we always bought their land and paid them for it.

He said he believed that the Great Spirit made all the people. He made all the land and it was the Great Spirit's land. And it was wrong for Indian or white man to say it was his land. This was a lie.

"Now," said he, "if Indian make house, it is Indian's house. If he make corn field, it is his, but the land is the Great Spirit's. But," said he, "the white man he marks off the land in the woods and say it is his land." Said he: "This is a lie. It is not his land. It is the Great Spirit's land."

"But Brothers, the Long Knives [the people from Virginia] have overrun your country and your hunting grounds—they have killed the deer and the buffalo, the bear and the raccoon.

"Unless you rise and [kill] their whole race, you may [say goodbye] to the hunting grounds of your fathers."

Because, at the same time, the English coming to Kentucky showed little desire to do anything other than take and occupy the land, conflict followed.

★ The First West ★

The different Europeans in North America—the French, Spanish, and English—had been in the land called Kentucky at various times. The English, however, would be the ones to settle the land. A century went by, though, from the time the first English came here before that happened. What made them delay?

Mary Ingles

Mary Draper Ingles may have been the first European woman in Kentucky. But she did not want to have that privilege.

In 1755, she had a house in a pretty part of frontier Virginia. No English settlers lived in Kentucky, and none would live there for twenty more years. At that time, Mary was twenty-three years old and had been married for six years. She had two sons—Thomas, age four, and George, a two-year-old—and was expecting a third child at any time. Then, on July 8, her happy life changed.

That day Indians raided her settlement. They killed several people and captured Mary Ingles and her sons. Three days after being taken, she gave birth to a girl. The next day she got on a horse with her baby and rode on. Not to do so would have meant death. The Native Americans took her to their camp in Ohio. There they took her sons away from her.

Three months later, the Indians and Mary Ingles went to Big Bone Lick, in what is now Boone County in northern Kentucky, to get salt for their use. They forced her to leave her daughter behind. Mary decided that this might be her only chance to escape, and she fled. She went through the wilderness for forty days.

Mary Ingles barely made it. Thorn bushes tore off most of her clothes. Her feet grew swollen and were cut. She had little food and became almost too weak to stand. Then, at last, Mary came to a cabin near her home. It had been nearly half a year since her capture. She was re-united with her husband, and they moved away from the frontier. Just days after they left, Indians attacked the house where they had been staying. The Indians killed or captured everyone there. Mary had almost become a prisoner again.

Mary and her husband had four more children. One day some people told her that her son Thomas, now seventeen years old, had been located. He lived with a Native American family and could no longer speak English. After thirteen years with the Indians, he did not want to leave. Finally he did return to her, but he never fully liked his new life. Mary never saw her daughter or her other captured son again. Deeply saddened, she never was the same person as before.

She lived to an old age, for the time. She died at eighty-three. So ended the life of the first non-Indian woman in Kentucky.

Part of the reason for the delay had to do with **geography.** Geography concerns the Earth's natural features and how the land is made. Look at the map (2.1) that shows some of the geography of Kentucky. Mountains form a barrier between the area farther east and Kentucky. Early explorers called those the "Endless Mountains." We now call them the Appalachian Mountains. It was very hard to go across them. Most people went around them and came into Kentucky through a

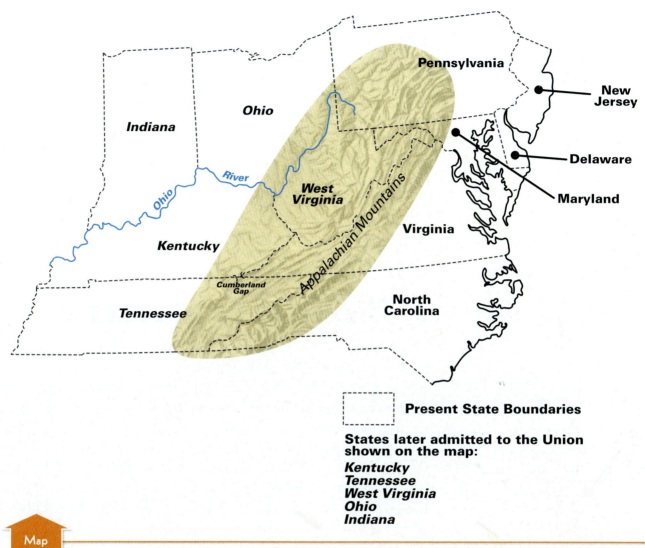

Indiana

Ohio

Pennsylvania

New Jersey

Delaware

Maryland

Ohio River

West Virginia

Appalachian Mountains

Virginia

Kentucky

Cumberland Gap

North Carolina

Tennessee

☐ Present State Boundaries

States later admitted to the Union shown on the map:
Kentucky
Tennessee
West Virginia
Ohio
Indiana

Map 2.1

The mountain barrier made it hard to get to Kentucky. Cumberland Gap gave people a way to get across the mountains.

break in the mountains. They called that entrance-way Cumberland Gap.

Look at the map again. The other way to get to Kentucky was to go down the Ohio River on a boat. Most people got off the boat at Maysville or Louisville or went up the Kentucky River and came to central Kentucky.

Either trip brought the English explorers into contact with the Native Americans who lived in Kentucky and who, later, just hunted here. The Indians were a second reason it took a long time for the English to settle in Kentucky. Conflict between the two groups made Kentucky a dangerous place.

A third reason was that the English had plenty of land where they were. But as more people came to America from

Europe over the years, they took more and more of that land, creating **scarcity**. New groups wanted land so that they too could farm and raise crops. The scarcity of land caused some to view Kentucky as a place where they could find land. Here they could fulfill their dreams.

Kentucky would become the first area to be settled outside of the thirteen English colonies. It was the first step westward for what became the United States. It had taken people more than a century to go just a few hundred miles inland from the ocean. Now, in just one more century, explorers and settlers would cover the whole continent. What took place in Kentucky set the stage for all later western movement. Kentucky became the First West.

⋆ The First Explorers ⋆

English explorers or hunters came to Kentucky a century before any Europeans settled in the area. Most of them left no record of their trips, but a few carved their names in the bark of trees to show that they had been here.

By the 1750s, some explorers began to write down what they saw on their trips. Christopher Gist and Thomas Walker were among the first to do so. (See document 2.2.) Traders had already been here to barter for furs. Then a group called Long Hunters came to Kentucky to get their own furs. Finally, people came just to look over the land, so that settlers later would know where the best places were.

All of those groups came on horseback or by boat. Many had slaves with them, so black and white alike came to Kentucky from very early times. The explorers and hunters wore shirts made of linen or hemp and covered their heads with broad-brimmed hats. Almost no one—not even Daniel Boone—wore a coonskin cap.

They could carry only a few things with them. In a blanket rolled up behind them on the horse, they might have some soap, a razor to shave with, some tobacco to smoke, and a bullet mold so that they could melt bullets they had shot and use them again. No stores existed in Kentucky. The explorers might also put a little food into their pack—coffee, flour, and sugar. Most of the time, they killed what they needed to eat—bears, buffalo, deer, turkeys, even swans.

After they made their way through Cumberland Gap or down the Ohio River, they went into the interior of Kentucky.

DOCUMENT 2.2

Two of the earliest written records of English explorers in Kentucky are those of Thomas Walker and Christopher Gist. Both men were sent to explore and find good land for others to claim as their own. Both kept journals of their trip.

Dr. Thomas Walker tells of finding Cumberland Gap and going into eastern Kentucky in 1750, where he and those with him built perhaps the first European cabin in Kentucky:

April 13th. We went . . . six miles to Cave [Cumberland] Gap, the land being level. On the south side is a plain Indian Road. On top of the Ridge are Laurel trees marked with crosses, others blazed and several figures on them.

23rd. We all crossed the [Cumberland] River . . . leaving the others to provide and salt some bear, build an house, and plant some corn.

Walker never got to the Bluegrass region, and he turned at last to cross back to Virginia.

Christopher Gist came down the Ohio River instead. He did go through northern and central Kentucky before returning to Virginia. He wrote in 1751:

Monday [March] 18—We turned from Salt Lick Creek to a Ridge of Mountains that made toward the Cuttaway River [Kentucky River], & from the top of the mountain we saw a fine level country as far as our eyes could behold.

Later he moved into the mountains of Kentucky, before leaving the state. He wrote:

Sunday [March] 24—We had but poor food for our horses & both we and they were very much wearied.

Monday [March] 25—We killed a Buck Elk and took out his tongue to carry with us.

Thomas Walker was one of the first to leave a written record of his trip to Kentucky. He is shown here carrying a hurt dog on his horse.

Once more the environment—the geography—shaped their actions. There they found the level land they sought to farm. They also wanted streams or rivers on or near their property, to provide water for themselves, their animals, and the land itself.

Once in Kentucky, those explorers and hunters found a very special land. They told others. The word *Kentucky* began to have a magical appeal.

★ What They Found ★

Early explorers called Kentucky "a new found Paradise," a heaven on earth, "the Garden of the West."

Animals were everywhere. Huge buffalo herds numbering a thousand or more roamed the land. A woman recalled a herd near Lexington: "The woods roared with their tramping, almost as bad as thunder." Daniel Boone said, "They were more frequent than I have seen cattle in the settlements." Those buffalo also made the first roads in Kentucky.

As the buffalo went from one place to another seeking the salt they needed, they moved in long lines. They took the easy way, going around mountains instead of over them. They

At one time, thousands of buffalo lived in Kentucky.

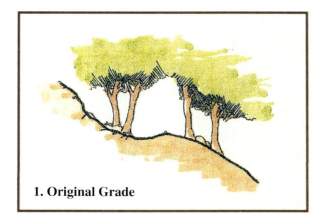

1. Original Grade

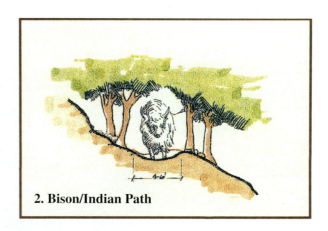

2. Bison/Indian Path

3. Indian/Explorer/Longhunter Path

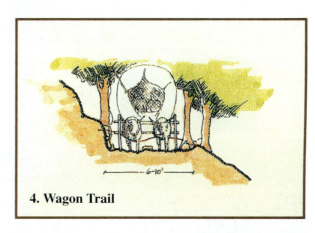

4. Wagon Trail

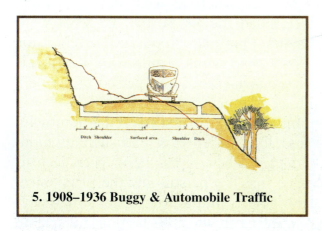

5. 1908–1936 Buggy & Automobile Traffic

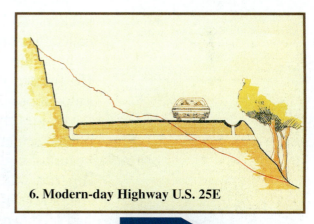

6. Modern-day Highway U.S. 25E

crossed rivers at the lowest water level. They cleared the area around them by eating plants as they walked. Year after year, century after century, they had traveled the same routes. They made large trails or *traces.*

Explorers told of one of those traces near Frankfort: "The buffalo trace at this point is 100 feet wide and in some places, the hoofs of buffalo have worn down the ground several feet." Another trace in Shelby County was forty feet wide and four

Buffalo trails served as the first roads. Later, people made those trails larger. These pictures show how those roads have changed over time.

Modern-day buffalo once more roam in the state.

feet deep. All across Kentucky, buffalo trails gave early explorers a road to follow. Many of the highways we travel today still follow parts of the buffalo traces, started thousands of years ago.

The buffalo was only one of the many animals in Kentucky. The area became a hunting ground without rival. One person said that a ten-mile square of forest would contain from 1 to 3 wolves, 2 or 3 panthers, 2 elk, 5 bears, 30 foxes, 200 turkeys, 400 deer and buffalo, and 10,000 squirrels. Later, settlers would go on all-day squirrel hunts. They killed 7,941 squirrels during one hunt; in another, in Madison County, 8,857 were killed. Many beavers, otters, and mink lived near streams. In forests, the animals chewed off small branches of trees and thinned out the woods as they tramped through them. Early hunters found they could move through the forests much more easily on the animal trails than in other places, as a result. The forests looked almost like parks at times.

Birds seemed to be everywhere as well. Ravens, woodpeckers, and parakeets filled the air. So too did what were called passenger pigeons. One man stood and watched for four hours while a flock of pigeons a mile wide flew over. He guessed that over *two billion* birds had passed by. Settlers killed those birds in huge numbers.

Besides the plentiful animals, the best thing that Kentucky offered settlers was land. One leader wrote, "a richer and more beautiful country than this, I believe has never been seen in America yet." He added that if a person saw the place once, "he never will rest until he gets in it to live." Later a man who had seen many parts of the earth wrote his friends and said he found in Kentucky "the richest land in the world." Another praised the tall grass, giant trees, and rich soil. In fact, those who first farmed the land said it grew twice as much as did the old, worn-out land back beyond the mountains. One writer even said, "This country is more temperate and healthy than the other settled parts of America."

Such words made Kentucky seem like a very appealing place. But the image and the reality were not always the same.

★ Coming to Kentucky ★

Having heard about the richness of this new place called Kentucky, settlers began to try to come here. That was a hard decision. First of all, it meant leaving a lot behind. Imagine that today you and all your family had to get into a small car and could take only the things you could fit in the trunk of the car. What would you take? What would you leave behind, never to see again?

The early settlers faced the same hard choice. If they came into Kentucky through Cumberland Gap, they had to walk the several hundred miles, or perhaps they took a horse or two. People came with few things. For most of them, the trip lasted at least four long and tiring weeks. They also faced the danger of being killed in an Indian attack or in an accident.

Settlers who set out for Kentucky from Pittsburgh, going down the Ohio River, could take a little more in their boats. Mary Dewees made her trip in a craft that was forty feet long, for example. River travel also got them here faster—in just one or two weeks. But the river way cost more, so poorer people could not take it. It also was more dangerous, because the river took you closer to the Indian towns north of the river.

If you left to go to Kentucky, it also meant that you would likely never again see your family or friends who did not go. It meant leaving a safe home for an unsafe one and leaving an easy life for a harder one, for a time at least. It meant going from what you knew to the unknown of Kentucky.

Cumberland Gap

But the promise of land and of a fresh start in a new place drove many settlers on. They wanted better lives for themselves and for their children when they grew up. They made the hard choice. They started out for Kentucky.

Some found what they sought. Others did not. Many had success. Many also never had—or could not keep—any land. Certain ones became leaders, and others found hardship or even death (see document 2.3).

DOCUMENT 2.3

Laurence Butler came down the Ohio River to Kentucky in 1784 and wrote to his friends, telling what he saw:

This river affords a vast quantity of freshwater fish; They have a kind that is called cat, which weighs upward of 100 weight. I remained at the Falls [Louisville] a few days and then traveled up the country to examine the land, which exceed anything I ever saw.

It is a fine country for horses. There is the greatest plenty of buffaloes, which serve for beef; and bears, which answer the same as bacon; and, as for wild turkeys, there is no end to them.

Thirteen years later, Gilbert Imlay published a book in which he told of the rich land:

Everything here assumes a dignity and splendour I have never seen in any other part of the world. Everything here gives delight.

But compare those views of Kentucky with these two. In the first, Daniel Trabue recalled the hard winter of 1779–1780:

The turkeys was almost all dead. People's cattle mostly dead. No corn. The people was in great distress. Many in the wilderness frostbit. Some dead. A number of people would be taken sick and did actually die from the want of solid food.

Another person wrote a letter from Harrodsburg and spoke of that same winter. (The spelling has been changed to modern forms.)

Unhappy settlers that set out late for this place still remain in the wilderness, having lost every horse and cow and whole families have perished on the road, while others escaping with the loss of their hands and feet and all the skin and flesh taken off their face by the excessive cold.

These are very different views of Kentucky. Were some views more correct than others? Were all correct? What do you think?

Those who did not come through Cumberland Gap to Kentucky came down the Ohio River in boats like this one.

Reading a Document

As you look at different documents throughout the book, you will be reading words of *primary sources*—people who were alive at the time they wrote about. These are clues to what happened in the past. If you read many primary-source documents, you can begin to put together the whole story.

As a person trying to solve the mystery of history, you should ask questions about each document—just like a detective. For example: Who wrote it? Was the person there, or did he or she just hear about what happened? When was it written? Was it written at the time of the event or later, when the person might have forgotten some of the facts? Why did the person write it? Did the writer want just to tell the story, or did he or she want to change it to make his or her role seem more important? Was the story written just for one person to see, or for a wide group?

Once you answer those questions, you can decide how good the source is and how much of it you want to believe.

★ Settling a State ★

Not all parts of Kentucky were settled at the same time. Large groups came first in the 1770s to central Kentucky, around Lexington, Frankfort, and Louisville. Over the next decade, the northern, south-central, and western regions were settled. By the 1790s, people were starting to live in eastern Kentucky. The most western parts of Kentucky did not have many people before the period of 1810–1819. So the frontier came at different times to different parts of Kentucky. It did not happen at one moment but during many. Geography caused some of that difference, with level areas being settled first. The Indian threat also made a big difference. No matter when people came to the frontiers in Kentucky, they all began to build homes out of a wilderness. Soon they would create a new state.

The first Kentucky frontier, and the first part of the region to be settled, was the central part of the Bluegrass. It would also be the scene of the bloodiest battles with the Native Americans who did not want to give up the land. In the first fifteen years of the English settlement of Kentucky, about 73,000 people came here. Another 1,500 or more died in conflicts with the Indians. In one year, just in Jefferson County,

Kentucky, 131 settlers were killed or captured—1 in every 8 people there. One person wrote, "We can hardly pass a spot, which does not remind us of the murder of a father, a brother, or a deceased friend." Native Americans probably said the same thing, for they had deaths as well. On the frontier, all the men and all the women were almost like soldiers. Every child helped them. Youth ended early on the frontier.

In such times of danger, strong leaders came forward. Their efforts helped to settle Kentucky and then make it safer for settlers. Brave and often fearless, those earliest leaders included James Harrod, Daniel Boone, Benjamin Logan, Simon Kenton, George Rogers Clark, and many more.

The tall and bearded James Harrod set up the first permanent English settlement in Kentucky. On June 16, 1774, he led a small group of men down the Ohio River and then up the Kentucky River. They started what they called Harrodstown, or Fort Harrod. We now call it Harrodsburg. The threat of Indians drove the settlers away. They came back the next year and did not leave.

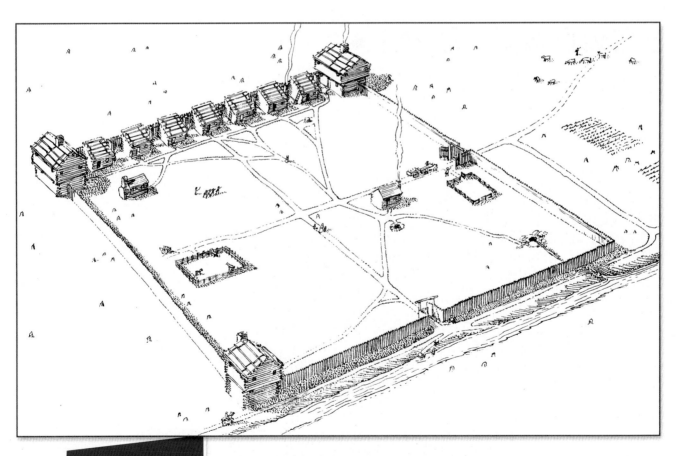

Fort Harrod

Harrod was born in Pennsylvania and grew up with little formal schooling. He did learn several Native American languages as well as French, while hunting in the area north of the Ohio River. His brother and several friends would die at the hands of Indians. But Harrod never hated Indians. In fact, many of the English leaders did not. They simply wanted to live in peace and hunt and farm. So too did the Indians. That the two groups could not resolve their conflicts and live together would have sad results.

Fort Harrod probably looked like this in frontier times.

In order to protect themselves, settlers at Harrodsburg and other places built forts. They were sometimes also called stations. Inside of the forts were log cabins about twenty feet square. The space between the logs was filled with clay. The floors were made of either wood planks (whose splinters might hurt bare feet) or just dirt. Chimneys made of stone, sticks, straw, and mud let the smoke out. Few cabins had windows. If they did have window spaces, they were either open or covered with greased paper. None had glass. It broke too easily and could not be brought to the frontier.

Fort Harrod was 264 feet square. It had walls made of oak tree trunks that were placed beside each other in the ground. Those walls were ten feet tall. At each corner of the fort, a larger blockhouse gave more protection if an attack came.

People did not like to live in forts and moved away as soon as it was safe. They had come to farm, not to fight. Forts were dirty. One person looked at the water supply near Fort Harrod and found that all kinds of things from the fort had made the water almost unfit to drink. Disease was common in forts. Also, the smell of horses and their waste and the odor of other animals filled the air. In the summer, dust and bugs came into the cabins. In the winter, mud covered the ground outside and smoke often stung people's eyes inside.

Forts were also crowded. Two years after it was built, Fort Harrod had 198 people. It was a small space for so many. One of every ten was African American, one of every four was a child, and about one of every three adults was a woman.

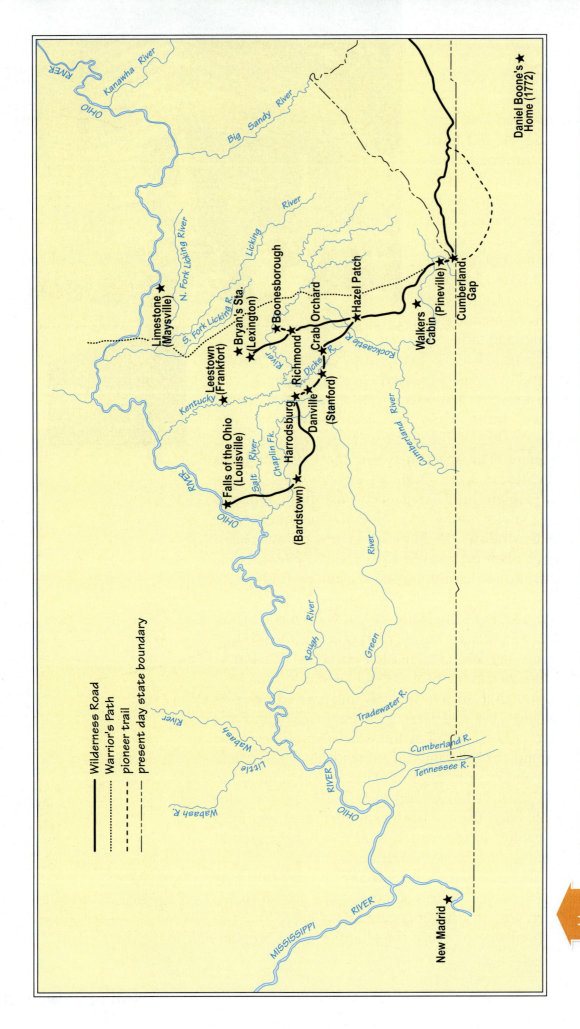

Map 2.2 The Wilderness Road led settlers to the forts and stations across central Kentucky.

Legend:
- Wilderness Road
- Warrior's Path
- pioneer trail
- present day state boundary

Locations:
- Daniel Boone's Home (1772)
- Cumberland Gap
- Walkers Cabin (Pineville)
- Hazel Patch
- Crab Orchard
- Boonesborough
- Bryan's Sta. (Lexington)
- Richmond
- Danville (Stanford)
- Harrodsburg
- Leestown (Frankfort)
- Limestone (Maysville)
- Falls of the Ohio (Louisville)
- (Bardstown)
- New Madrid

Rivers:
- OHIO RIVER
- Kanawha River
- Big Sandy River
- Licking River
- N. Fork Licking River
- S. Fork Licking R.
- Kentucky River
- Dicks R.
- Rockcastle R.
- Cumberland River
- Chaplin Fk.
- Salt River
- Rough River
- Green River
- Tradewater R.
- Little Wabash River
- Wabash R.
- MISSISSIPPI RIVER
- Cumberland R.
- Tennessee R.

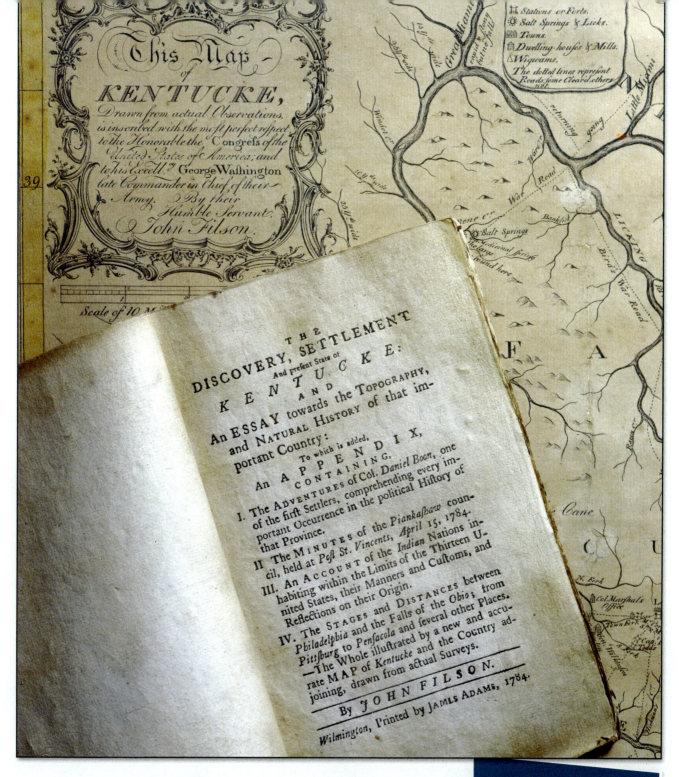

This Map of KENTUCKE, Drawn from actual Observations, is inscribed with the most perfect respect, to the Honorable the Congress of the United States of America; and to his Excell.ᵧ George Washington late Commander in Chief of their Army. By their Humble Servant, John Filson.

Scale of 10 M...

39

THE
DISCOVERY, SETTLEMENT
And present State of
KENTUCKE:
AND
An ESSAY towards the TOPOGRAPHY,
and NATURAL HISTORY of that im-
portant Country:
To which is added,
An APPENDIX,
CONTAINING,
I. The ADVENTURES of Col. Daniel Boon, one
of the first Settlers, comprehending every im-
portant Occurrence in the political History of
that Province.
II. The MINUTES of the Piankashaw coun-
cil, held at Post St. Vincents, April 15, 1784.
III. An ACCOUNT of the Indian Nations in-
habiting within the Limits of the Thirteen U-
nited States, their Manners and Customs, and
Reflections on their Origin.
IV. The STAGES and DISTANCES between
Philadelphia and the Falls of the Ohio; from
Pittsburg to Pensacola and several other Places.
—The Whole illustrated by a new and accu-
rate MAP of Kentucke and the Country ad-
joining, drawn from actual Surveys.
By JOHN FILSON.
Wilmington, Printed by JAMES ADAMS, 1784.

Stations or Forts.
Salt Springs & Licks.
Touns.
Dwelling-houses & Mills.
Wigwams.
The dotted lines represent
Roads some Cleard, others not.

They all served if an attack came. They all also moved outside the fort's prison-like walls as soon as they could.

One of the other major early settlements in Kentucky was first called St. Asaph's, then Logan's Fort after its leader. Now it is named Stanford. Though he did not start the settlement, Benjamin Logan soon guided it. A tall man with long, curly black hair, he said what he thought. Logan made some people mad by doing so. His skills as a leader kept the settlers alive in bad times, however.

John Filson's early book told of Kentucky. It included a map of the area and a history of Daniel Boone, which made Boone famous.

What are some words and spellings on this page that are different from modern-day ones?

★ Daniel Boone ★

The other major settlement in early Kentucky—and the second one to be built—was Fort Boonesborough. Daniel Boone, the most famous of the early pioneers, started it. But why is he so famous while others are not? Harrod set up the first fort, for example. Kenton lived a similar life.

Why Boone? He was important, first of all. More than that, however, a man named John Filson told Boone's story in the first book really written about Kentucky—*The Discovery, Settlement, and Present State of Kentucke.* Filson's book came out soon after Kentucky had been settled. It made Boone famous all over the world. Harrod, Kenton, Logan, and other leaders never got that kind of attention. Later, people would use Filson's book to write their own books about Boone's life. Much, much later, movies and a television series added to his fame.

Did Boone deserve so much fame? You can decide.

Daniel Boone was born of a Quaker family in Pennsylvania. The Quakers taught that people should live in peace, but Boone would end up being part of a violent time. He never went to school, but his son said Boone could "read, spell, and write a little." Boone learned well the lessons of the woods, though.

When he was twenty-one, Daniel married seventeen-year-old Rebecca Bryan. She probably never learned to read or write. No pictures of her exist. We do not know much about her. Tall, with jet-black hair and dark eyes, she had four children by the age of twenty and ten children overall. Later, she also raised six other children whose mother had died. When Boone left on his

Daniel Boone spent a winter alone in Kentucky. When other hunters came back in the spring, they heard him singing in the middle of a field.

Kentucky Faces

Simon Kenton

Simon Kenton could have been as famous as Daniel Boone. Once he even saved Boone's life. He lived a life almost as important. But no one wrote Kenton's story. He was largely forgotten for a long time.

Kenton was born in Virginia and never learned to read or write. At age sixteen, he fought a man and thought he had killed him. He changed his name to Simon Butler and ran away from home. Simon came to what is now Maysville, Kentucky, and planted the first corn grown by settlers north of the Kentucky River.

The tall and strong man helped protect the new settlements. He was captured by the Shawnee Indians at one time. They first tied him on a horse and ran it through the briars and branches in the woods, and he lived through that experience. Next they made him run the gauntlet. Two rows of armed Native Americans lined up, and he had to run through the space between them as they hit him. Many who ran the gauntlet did not survive. A black man had told him to run close to one side. He did that and lived. Before he finally escaped, he had to run the gauntlet more times and almost was burned at the stake.

After Simon got back to Kentucky, he found out that the man he thought he had killed was not dead after all. He now took back his old name of Simon Kenton and continued to explore in places others would not go. One man decided not to collect some money Kenton owed him. He wrote: "Too dangerous to go where Kenton is."

Later Kenton married and settled down. He and his wife had four children, before his wife died in a fire. He married her first cousin, and they had five more children.

Kenton moved to Ohio. Later he returned to Kentucky as an old man. He was put in jail for not paying some money he owed, but the authorities let the old pioneer go free the next year.

He died in Ohio in 1836, a forgotten hero in a distant land. Four years later, Kentucky named a county in his honor.

long hunting trips, Rebecca tended the crops and kept the family going. It took a strong woman to do all that.

Meanwhile, Boone started coming to Kentucky to hunt and get furs. He wore his long hair in Indian-style braids and dressed much like Native Americans did. One time he spent months alone in Kentucky, perhaps the only European in the whole area. A friend once asked him if he ever got lost. Boone said that he had not, but that he was once pretty confused for several days! Another time some Long Hunters (European hunters in search of furs) heard a strange sound. They found Boone lying on his back in the middle of a field, singing loudly. Boone loved nature and the openness of Kentucky.

An artist's picture of when Daniel Boone first viewed "the beautiful level of Kentucke."

Soon he led a group of settlers to the region. When he first tried to bring settlers in, some Indians killed one of his sons. He turned back. The next time he came, he had been hired by Richard Henderson to set up a fort. Henderson said he had bought a large part of Kentucky from the Indians and wanted people to settle that land. Later, his claim would not be accepted. Boone led a group through Cumberland Gap. They built a trail, later called the Wilderness Road, from there to the place where they started a fort. The fort on the Kentucky River would be called Boonesborough.

Daniel Walker was one of the men with Boone at that time. He recalled later what they felt. They saw what Boone called "the beautiful level of Kentucke." (Kentucky was later spelled with a *y* at the end instead of an *e*.) Said Walker: "A new sky seemed to be presented to our view. So rich a soil we had never seen before. We felt at a garden where there was no forbidden fruit." Two days later, however, reality struck. Indians killed two men in the group, one black and one white. Walker was wounded, and the others expected him to

A painter's view of how Boone led settlers through Cumberland Gap into Kentucky.

Notice the dog in this picture? Remember the picture on page 21 that showed Thomas Walker and his dogs? Why were dogs so useful in frontier Kentucky?

die. For twelve days they stopped to let him heal. He lived, and they then went on to set up Fort Boonesborough.

Once the three forts had been started, at Harrodsburg, Boonesborough, and Stanford, other people slowly started to arrive. It was not an easy trip nor an easy time.

★ Hard Times ★

William Whitley and his family left Virginia for Kentucky in the same year that the early forts were built. He told of going through the wilderness: "At times my wife would fall, horse and all, and at other times she and her children were all in a file tied together, for where one went, all must go. In that situation, we were 33 days in the wilderness. Had rain, hail, and snow." They came through safely. Whitley and his wife, Esther, built what has been called the first brick home in Kentucky. It still stands in Lincoln County. He died at the age of sixty-five, fighting for his country in the War of 1812. Soon after his death, Kentucky named a county in his honor.

Sarah Graham came to Kentucky five years after Whitley did. She was only seven years old. Later, a person asked her about that trip. She recalled that she had come with three

Photographs were not common until the 1840s. So paintings were the only way to capture a person's likeness. This is the only painting that was done of Daniel Boone while he lived.

had a big lead. That was the safe choice. The settlers might not catch the Indians, however, before the Indians crossed the Ohio River into safety.

The other choice would be to leave the trail. Boone thought he knew where the Native Americans were going. If he was right, he could take a shortcut and catch up with them. That choice was risky. If he was wrong, the girls would never be rescued. He might not see Jemima again. Following the trail was safer but might not work. A man with Boone later told what Boone did: "Paying no further attention to the trail, he now took a straight course through the woods, with increased speed, followed by the men in perfect silence."

Would Boone's risky choice work? They caught the Indians in Bath County and wounded two of them. The other three escaped. The girls were not harmed. When all were safe, everyone sat down and cried with joy. Boone's choice had been the right one.

Later when Daniel Boone was wounded defending Boonesborough, Simon Kenton carried him back toward the fort. Jemima Boone—the girl Daniel had saved—ran out to help bring her father to safety. She repaid what he had done for her.

A year and a half after that attack, Daniel Boone faced another hard choice. He and twenty-seven men had gone from the fort to get salt from the salty water that came out of the ground. Those places were called salt licks. The settlers needed salt to help preserve their meat, since they had no way to keep it cool for very long.

After Boone's daring gamble, he and his men rescued the captured girls.

While at the salt licks, Boone was seized by 120 Indians. He knew that his men could not defeat such a large force. They could fight but likely would be killed. Boone made the choice: he told them to surrender. They did what he said, but many of the men were angry with Boone. The Native Americans took Boone and the others into Ohio.

There Boone faced Chief Blackfish. The chief asked Boone if he had killed the chief's son earlier. Boone said that he had, then added: "But many things happen in war best forgotten." The Indians admired courage.

Kentucky Faces

Monk Estill

Many people said that they came to Kentucky for freedom. They wanted freedom of religion or freedom of political beliefs or freedom from poverty. The ability to choose freedom did not always extend to black Americans, though, because some of the settlers brought slaves with them.

One of those enslaved people was Monk. He stood about five feet, five inches tall and weighed two hundred pounds. In March 1782, some Indians attacked a place called Estill's Station, just south of Richmond, Kentucky. They captured Monk, but he tricked the Indians into thinking Estill's Station was better defended than it really was. The Native Americans left. Monk's owner, James Estill, and about twenty-five men followed the Indians. The two forces met near Little Mountain, named for the Indian mounds there. Today it is named Mt. Sterling.

In the fierce fight that followed, Monk yelled out where the Indians were. He finally escaped. However, James Estill and others were killed and the settlers had to retreat.

The battle became known as Estill's Defeat. Monk carried one of the wounded men back to the fort, more than twenty-five miles away. His new master freed him for his bravery.

Monk Estill was already the father of the first African American child born at Boonesborough. Now, as a free man, he had many more children and supported his family by making gunpowder. Monk Estill lived a long life. But the freedoms he won on the frontier went to very few other slaves.

After Daniel Boone's capture by the Shawnee Indians, they adopted him into the tribe.

Harrod, Kenton, Logan, and others, he is not praised enough.

Clark and many of the early settlers on that first frontier had come from Virginia. Kentucky was then part of Virginia. At first, all of Kentucky made up one county. Later several counties covered Kentucky, but still as part of Virginia. Kentuckians wanted their own state. In the middle of the Revolutionary War, when the nation sought freedom, Kentuckians asked for

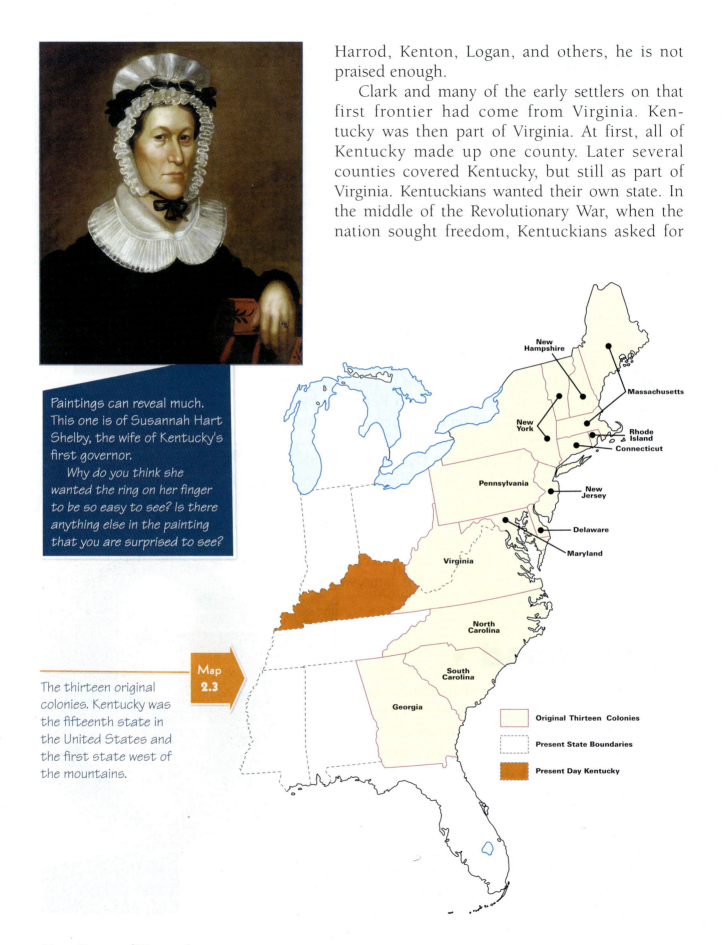

Paintings can reveal much. This one is of Susannah Hart Shelby, the wife of Kentucky's first governor.

Why do you think she wanted the ring on her finger to be so easy to see? Is there anything else in the painting that you are surprised to see?

The thirteen original colonies. Kentucky was the fifteenth state in the United States and the first state west of the mountains.

Map 2.3

New Hampshire
Massachusetts
New York
Rhode Island
Connecticut
Pennsylvania
New Jersey
Delaware
Maryland
Virginia
North Carolina
South Carolina
Georgia

Original Thirteen Colonies
Present State Boundaries
Present Day Kentucky

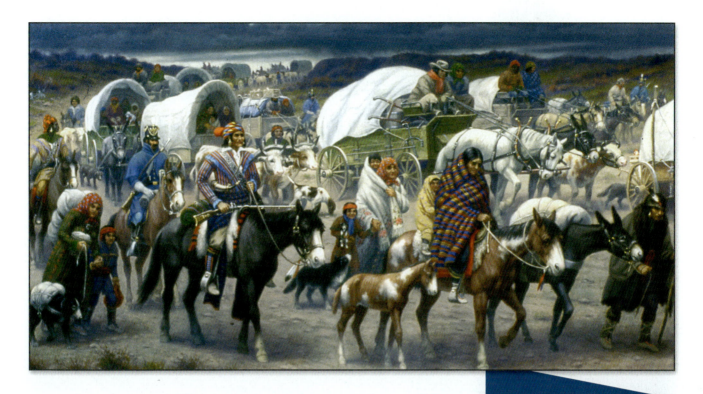

statehood. They based it on "that spark, which kindled the flame of Liberty."

Finally, on June 1, 1792, Kentucky became the fifteenth state in the new United States. It was the first state west of the mountains. The people chose as their first governor a man named Isaac Shelby. Of medium height and only a fair speaker, the forty-one-year-old Shelby was born in Maryland, had become a war hero, and had come to Lincoln County, Kentucky, at the end of the conflict.

He started from Danville that day in June, with horsemen around him, to go to the capital at Lexington. When he arrived, people fired rifles and cannon in the air to honor him. Then he took the oath of office as governor. Three days later, the people who were chosen to make the laws first met in a two-story log cabin.

Soon they decided where the capital would be located. Groups of people from various towns tried to get the honor, but Frankfort made the best offer. It offered land in town, money, and building materials—glass, nails, locks, stone, and timber. The new state had a new capital and now faced a new future.

A statue in Hopkinsville honors those Indians who died on the Trail of Tears.

What of those who lived for thousands of years in what was now the state of Kentucky? What happened to the Native Americans? By the time of statehood, most of them had been driven well beyond the borders of Kentucky.

The last large numbers of Indians went through the state much later, in 1838. They did not want to make that trip. The United States sent about sixteen thousand from the Cherokee Indian Nation on a twelve-hundred-mile journey to live in lands far away. Thousands of men, women, and children went through such towns as Hopkinsville, Princeton, and Paducah. In the cold of winter, most of the Indians walked the frozen roads. Of every four Native Americans who left their homes, one did not survive the trip. Some four thousand died. The tribe called it *Nunna-Da-Ul-Tsun-Y* or "the place where they cried." Others termed it the Trail of Tears.

The last, brief, major Indian presence in Kentucky was gone. But the frontier had ended long before that.

chapter 3

Different Kentuckys

A state is made up of both people and places. Let's look at each of those and see how they shaped Kentucky's past and are shaping its present.

Remember, when we talk about the past, we mean things that happened some time ago. For example, when you entered school for the first time, that became part of your own past. A state or a nation has its special past too, and studying that past helps us learn about its history.

★ The People of Kentucky ★

Kentucky now has about 4 million people living in it. That places it exactly in the middle of all the states in terms of population. Half of the states have a larger number of people, and half have fewer.

In the past, Kentucky did not have as many people as it does now. Soon after it became a state, about 221,000 men, women, and children called it home. It grew very fast at first. In fact, by 1840, Kentucky had become the sixth biggest state in the nation in population. Over the years, though, other states grew faster. So Kentucky is no longer one of the largest states.

Look at document 3.1. How long did it take Kentucky's population to double the first time? Once it reached 1 million people, about how many years did it take to get to 2 million, or from 2 million to the 4 million of today? Do you think it will grow as fast in the future? Why or why not?

People of different backgrounds make up Kentucky's population.

Who are these people who now live in Kentucky? Officially, of every one hundred people in the state, ninety-one are white, seven are black, and two are from other backgrounds—Asian, Indian, or other. People of Hispanic origin who live in Kentucky make up about two of every one hundred Kentuckians.

Two hundred years ago, Kentucky had a different population makeup. An **immigrant** is a person from another nation who comes to a place to live. The United States has been called a nation of immigrants. It is called that because everyone who settled the nation came here from other places—mostly Europe, Asia, or Africa. The new immigrants living in Kentucky now are just doing what other immigrants have done for hundreds of years. They are making a new home in Kentucky.

Kentucky had a more varied population in the past than it does now. After all, everyone in the new state was likely an immigrant or the

DOCUMENT 3.1

Population of Kentucky

1800 — 220,955	1920 — 2,416,630
1820 — 564,135	1940 — 2,845,627
1840 — 779,828	1960 — 3,038,156
1860 — 1,155,684	1980 — 3,660,324
1880 — 1,648,690	2000 — 4,041,769
1900 — 2,147,174	

child of an immigrant. At that time, of every one hundred Kentuckians, nineteen were African American. The rest came from European backgrounds. Of those from European backgrounds, about half had family ties to England, about one-fourth were from Scotland or Northern Ireland, about one in every ten was Irish, about one in twenty was German, and about one in twenty came from Wales. What do you know about your family's history?

If you lived in Kentucky right after it became a state, you would hear people speaking in a lot of languages or accents. A few Africans still spoke their native tongues. So too did some Germans. Even those speaking English might speak with a heavy Irish or Scottish accent. About fifty years after statehood, a large number of German and Irish immigrants came to Kentucky. They settled mostly in cities on the Ohio River. In Covington in Kenton County at that time, for example, more than one-fourth of the people had been born in another country. The same was true in Louisville. When immigrants speak in a different language today, it may seem strange to us, for we do not hear other languages as often. In the past, however, a variety of languages were commonly heard.

Kentucky is like the United States in being made up of people from many backgrounds. Many faces form the state.

★ Kentucky Homes ★

Where do these Kentuckians live? For most of the state's history, they lived in rural areas—that is, in small towns or on farms. Almost half of all people in Kentucky still live in such places. The state is much more rural than the nation as a whole. When you ask many Kentuckians where they live, they may not answer with the name of a town or city. Instead they will say that they live in a certain county. Why would they say that?

One of the reasons might be that Kentucky has so many counties. Counties make up a state just as the fifty states make up the United States. Kentucky has 120 counties. It has more counties than any other state except for two (Texas and Georgia). That means that some counties are very small. In physical size, Pike County has the most land and Gallatin County the least. In population, the smallest is Robertson County, which had only 2,266 people in the whole county in the year 2000. The largest in population is Jefferson County

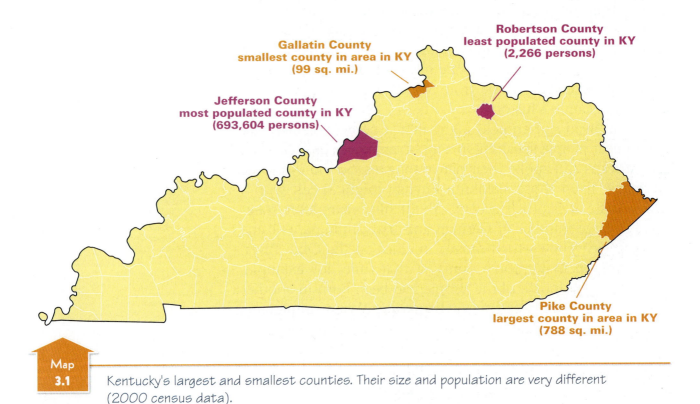

Gallatin County
smallest county in area in KY
(99 sq. mi.)

Robertson County
least populated county in KY
(2,266 persons)

Jefferson County
most populated county in KY
(693,604 persons)

Pike County
largest county in area in KY
(788 sq. mi.)

Map 3.1 Kentucky's largest and smallest counties. Their size and population are very different (2000 census data).

(Louisville) with 693,604. One in every six Kentucky counties has fewer than 10,000 people. In some rural areas, no large towns exist. Counties are the places people call home.

Some counties were created for good reasons, some for not-so-good ones. Often a new county was set up because people lived too far from the county seat, at a time when travel was slow. So they formed a new county. Sometimes people wanted to honor someone by naming a new county for that person. There were also counties that were divided into two because people did not get along with one another. Over the years, 120 counties were formed (see map 4.2). Some people think that number is too high. All agree that it would be very hard to reduce the number now by combining counties. Look in appendix 1. When was your county created? Who or what was it named for?

★ The Land ★

The geography of Kentucky shaped the land and its history, just as people did. We have already read about how in frontier times mountains forced people to come here through Cumberland Gap or down the Ohio River. Other physical features of the state have shaped Kentucky in various ways as well.

What is Kentucky like? How would you describe it? Is it a big state compared to other states? Is it long? Does it have high mountains? Are there many rivers? Is it hotter or colder than other states? What do you think?

In size, Kentucky is not a large state. It contains 40,395 square miles and ranks thirty-seventh among the fifty states in area. Look at map 8.1, which shows where Kentucky is in the United States. You can see that it has a good location, near the center of the nation. Many of the largest cities in America are close to Kentucky.

Kentucky is a fairly long and narrow state. From one end to the other, from Pike County to Fulton County, is 458 miles. Looking at it from north to south, its widest place is 171 miles. The highest point in the state is Big Black Mountain in Harlan County, which is 4,145 feet tall. The lowest point is on the Mississippi River, where Kentucky is 237 feet above sea level. There Kentucky touches one of the seven states which are around it. Map 7.1 shows those states.

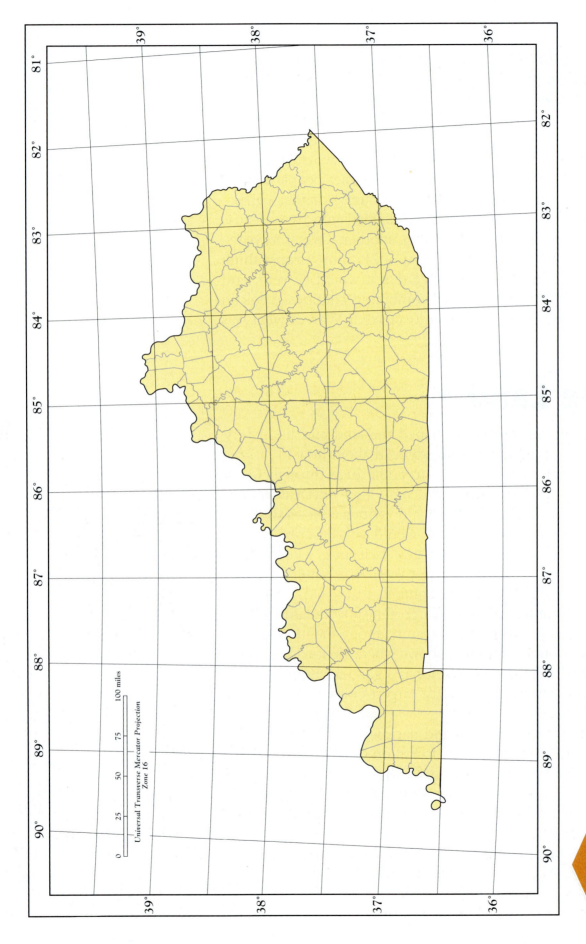

Map 3.2 Kentucky latitude and longitude. People find out where they are in the world by using latitude and longitude. What would be the numbers for where you live?

Universal Transverse Mercator Projection
Zone 16

0 25 50 75 100 miles

Kentucky's border was mostly formed by the time it became a state. Much of the border follows waterways. In fact, it is the only state that has rivers creating three sides of its boundary. The rivers that form Kentucky's borders are the Mississippi in the west, the Ohio in the north, and the Big Sandy and Tug Fork in the east. Mountains and a survey line complete the state borders.

Rivers do more than create Kentucky's borders. As you can see from map 3.3, Kentucky has many bodies of water. It has more streams and rivers that people can travel on than any other state except Alaska. Major rivers include the Ohio, Cumberland, Tennessee, Mississippi, Kentucky, Green, Licking, and others. They became early ways to travel and to take farm goods to market as well. The rivers provided water for people, crops, and animals. Towns and cities grew up near them. Those early rivers have changed over time. To help control flooding, dams have been built, and the dams have created large lakes in some places. Rivers still remain important for Kentuckians.

Rivers have not always been friendly to the people of the state, however. They overflowed during the great flood of 1937. Water covered many Kentucky towns. In some places it rained hard for almost three full days. The Ohio River rose fifty-seven feet higher than its usual level. Look at a river near you and just think what would happen if it went that high out of its banks. Where would all that water go?

The 1937 flood caused problems for cities all along the rivers. At Covington, water covered a third of the city. The flood spread over six of every ten houses in Louisville. People rode boats down Main Street. Thousands left their homes, which were covered in mud and water. At Paducah, almost the whole city lay under water. It looked like a ghost town. Water covered towns all along the Ohio River, even smaller towns. At Lewisport in Hancock County, 151 of the homes had water in them. Only 17 did not. The Kentucky River flooded over half of Frankfort. The water made it necessary to take prisoners out of the jails to keep them from drowning. All over Kentucky, people lost everything that they owned.

It was two years later that the greatest loss of lives in one flood took place.

During the Flood of 1937 in Louisville, high waters in front of the library made it appear that this statue was walking on water.

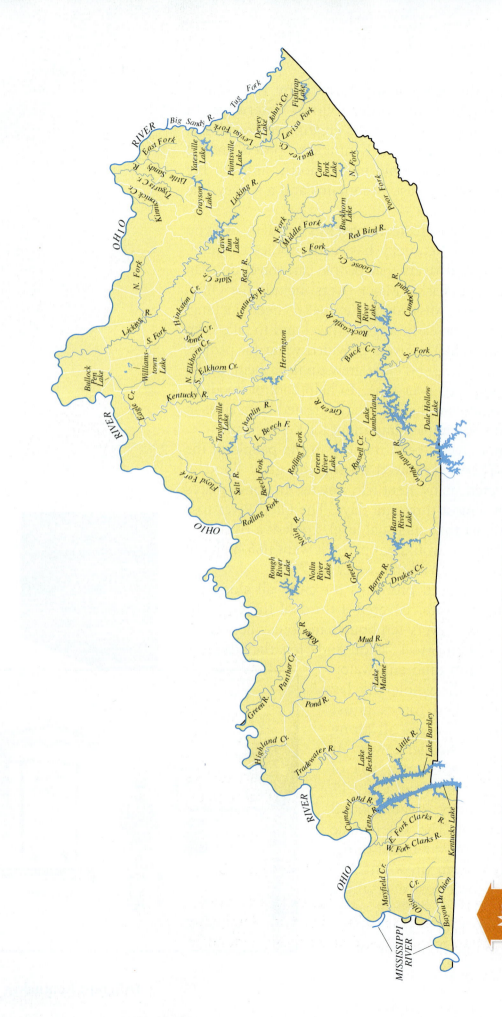

Kentucky's rivers and lakes. The rivers have played a major part in the development of the state. Which river is closest to you?

Map 3.3

A wall of water from a sudden storm flooded Breathitt and Rowan Counties in the eastern part of the state. It left about eighty people dead. Floods still remain a threat for parts of Kentucky, as one in 1997 showed.

Most of the time, rain is welcomed. A drought (when no rain falls) creates hard times as well. In 1930, there was a drought in Kentucky. Mayfield had no rain for a month, for example. Crops died, and the green grass turned brown. People were glad to see rain then. It makes crops grow and, in fact, allows us to live. Nature has many faces. It gives life and can take it away.

The 1955 flood waters almost covered up Governor Happy Chandler's political ad.

★ Climate ★

The temperature and the amount of rain and snow a place gets make up its climate. Due to its location, Kentucky has a moderate or temperate climate (see map 3.4). It has four distinct seasons. It does not usually have the extreme cold and deep snows of far northern states, nor the high heat of states in the Deep South. Temperatures seldom go below zero or above one hundred degrees. Snowfall amounts usually are small. Overall, rainfall and snowfall totals about forty-five inches per year.

Within the state, there are some differences in climate. For example, northern Kentucky temperatures tend to be about five degrees cooler than those in western Kentucky. A place such as Somerset, in the south-central part of Kentucky, may get ten more inches of rain per year than Covington, to the north. Average temperatures for the whole state go from the low thirties in January to the high seventies in July. Kentucky's climate allows a growing season of seven to eight months for crops every year.

★ Geographic Regions ★

Those who study geography often divide Kentucky into five (or six) areas or regions. Those are the Jackson Purchase, Pennyroyal (or Pennyrile), Western Coal Fields, Bluegrass, and Mountains

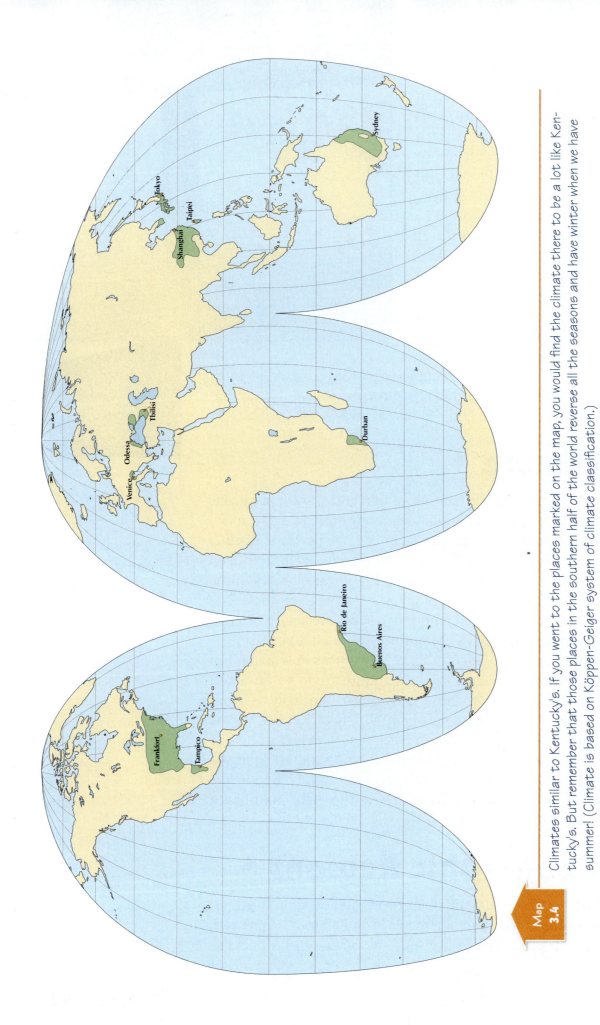

Climates similar to Kentucky's. If you went to the places marked on the map, you would find the climate there to be a lot like Kentucky's. But remember that those places in the southern half of the world reverse all the seasons and have winter when we have summer! (Climate is based on Köppen-Geiger system of climate classification.)

Map 3.4

(or Eastern Coal Fields). A very small region, called the Knobs, is now usually included in the Bluegrass.

The regions are based on common features of the land in each one. Look at map 3.6 and see which region you live in, and then see what each area is like in its landscape.

JACKSON PURCHASE

The Jackson Purchase is the newest and smallest region of Kentucky. Twenty-six years after Kentucky became a state, former Kentucky governor Isaac Shelby and future U.S. president Andrew Jackson bought the land in 1818 from the Chickasaw Indians for the United States. They paid the Native Americans three hundred thousand dollars, with payments spread over fifteen years. It was called the Jackson Purchase. Out of that area, eight Kentucky counties were created.

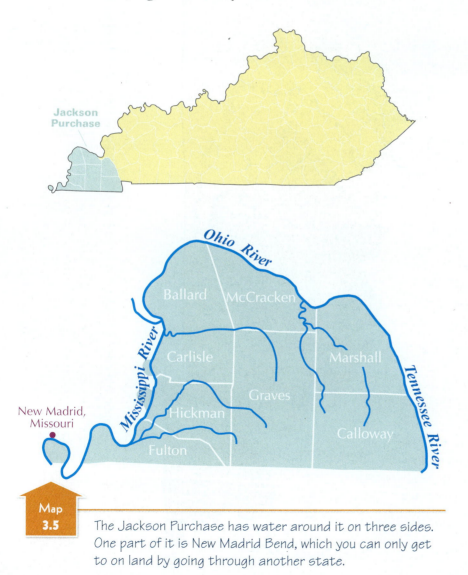

Map 3.5

The Jackson Purchase has water around it on three sides. One part of it is New Madrid Bend, which you can only get to on land by going through another state.

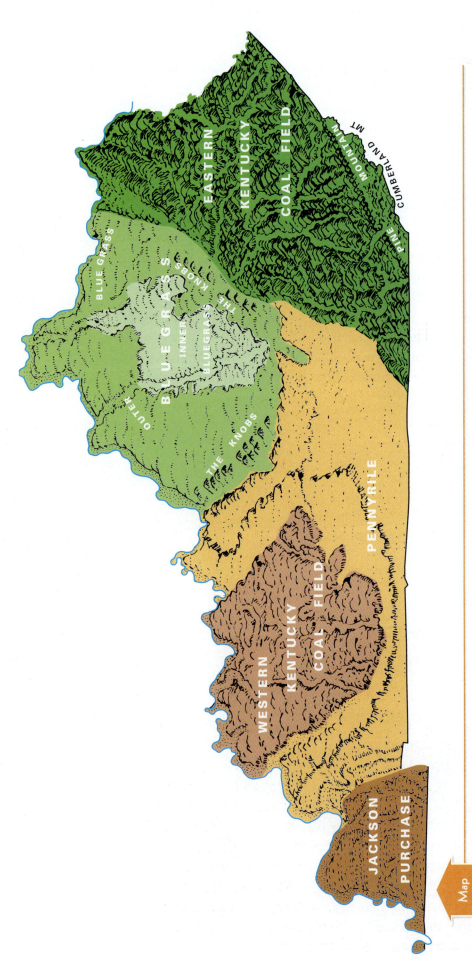

EASTERN
KENTUCKY
COAL FIELD

PINE CUMBERLAND MOUNTAIN MT

BLUE GRASS

BLUEGRASS

INNER BLUEGRASS

THE KNOBS

OUTER

THE KNOBS

PENNYRILE

WESTERN
KENTUCKY
COAL FIELD

JACKSON
PURCHASE

Map
3.6

Geographers divide Kentucky into several physical regions. Looking at Kentucky that way, where do you live?

DOCUMENT 3.2

Near Kentucky is New Madrid, Missouri. Over several months in 1811 and 1812, it was the center of perhaps the greatest earthquake ever to occur in the nation's history. The many quakes struck Kentucky very hard. Hundreds of miles away, walls cracked. The tremors caused bells to ring in churches as far away as Boston, Massachusetts. The Mississippi River flowed backward briefly. Luckily, western Kentucky was not heavily populated at the time, so not many people died. Scientists think another earthquake will occur in that area sometime in the future.

A man who was in the area at the time of the quake told what he saw:

We felt the shock of an earthquake, accompanied by a rumbling noise, resembling the distant firing of a cannon. The river was boiling, foaming, and roaring terrifically. Men, women, and children gave up in despair, some fainting, so great was their fear. The earth was in continual agitation, visibly waving as a gentle sea.

A few months later, another man wrote about what he found:

The surface of the ground was cracked in almost every direction and stood like yawning gulfs, so wide I could scarcely leap over them. [On] the shores of the river, the banks were cracked, trees broken off, and in many places acres of ground sunk down so that the tops of the trees just appeared above the surface of the water. All nature appeared in ruins.

Rivers form the borders of the Jackson Purchase on three sides—the Mississippi, Ohio, and Tennessee Rivers. Within the Purchase, a very small part of it is separated from the rest of the state by the waters of the Mississippi River. There are no bridges over that water, so that area can only be reached by going into Tennessee. That region is called New Madrid Bend. Overall, the Jackson Purchase area is the lowest part of Kentucky and has a lot of flat, fertile, river-bottom land. The Purchase is the part of Kentucky that is closest to the New Madrid Earthquake Fault Line. There in 1811 and 1812 a huge earthquake hit (see document 3.2). When it ended, a new lake had been formed. Reelfoot Lake in Fulton County, Kentucky, and in Tennessee, was made when water filled a great crack in the earth.

Kentucky Faces

Stephen Bishop

Stephen Bishop was born an enslaved person. When he was seventeen years old, his owner bought Mammoth Cave. Bishop became a guide through its dark depths. A year later his owner sold the cave—and Bishop—to another man.

Over the next few years, Bishop became the most popular guide for the cave. A witty, self-educated man, he knew history and knew how the cave had been formed. He also explored more of Mammoth Cave than any other person. The small but strong Bishop was the first to cross the Bottomless Pit, and he discovered many new parts of the cave. He also found some of the blind, eyeless animals that lived there in the total darkness.

Bishop guided visitors to these new wonders. They carried their small lamps that burned lard or oil to make a faint light in the huge cave. One visitor recalled "their lights chasing for a moment the shadows." In that cave, where there was no sunshine or rain or wind or any change in temperature all year long, they found "a world to itself."

Stephen Bishop's own world changed when his owner died. The owner's will said Bishop would be freed from slavery. Bishop had saved some money and bought land near the cave. He lived as a free man only briefly. He died a year later, at the age of only thirty-six. Bishop was buried near the entrance to the cave he loved.

An artist's re-creation of how Mammoth Cave explorer and guide Stephen Bishop might have looked.

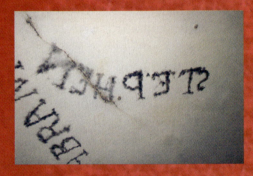

Bishop used the smoke from a torch to put his name on the ceiling of Mammoth Cave. But he did something tricky. *Do you know how you can read his name?*

PENNYROYAL (OR PENNYRILE)

The largest physical region of Kentucky is named for a small plant. More than one-fourth of Kentucky's counties lie in this area of the state. Probably the best-known natural feature of the Pennyroyal is Mammoth Cave, the longest underground cave system known in the world. Explorers have found so far some 340 miles of caverns. It became a U.S. National Park in 1941. This cave and others were created out of the limestone rock. Water flowed through cracks in the rock over a very long time, forming open places. Later, the water drained away, and caves were left.

WESTERN COAL FIELDS

This region got its name from the coal that lies under its surface. The mostly level land also offers good farming. Several rivers run through the Western Coal Fields as well.

BLUEGRASS

Kentucky is called the Bluegrass state. That name comes from the bluegrass that gives this region its name. In fact, though, bluegrass did not always grow in Kentucky. People brought the grass to America from England. Probably by accident, it started to grow in Kentucky very early. By the time Daniel Boone first came to Kentucky, bluegrass already had spread. It helped make the region such a good place for animals, because horses and cows grazed on it.

Bluegrass is really a dark green. Some people saw it and said it was blue-green and gave it its name. Now all over the world, people call it Kentucky bluegrass.

The physical Bluegrass region has rich farmland, rolling hills, and deep gorges on the Kentucky River. The outer parts have more hills. That area is called the Knobs.

The Kentucky River has created the beautiful Palisades area in central Kentucky.

MOUNTAINS (EASTERN COAL FIELDS)

This region is one of the largest in Kentucky. It is part of a mountain chain that goes from Georgia in the South to New York in the North. Here lie the highest parts of Kentucky. The forest-covered hills in the area do not leave much level land in the "hollows." Many state parks and a national forest have been created in the region because of the scenic beauty of the area. Natural Bridge is a rock formation high on a hill, while close to it Red River Gorge offers scenery and hiking.

Thousands of years ago the forces of nature formed a bridge from the rock. Natural Bridge State Park is in Powell County.

Cumberland Falls

One of the physical features of Kentucky is Cumberland Falls on the Cumberland River in Whitley County. On certain nights, something special happens there. When the water goes over the fall, the light from the full moon creates a moonbow. You probably have seen a rainbow in daylight. The moonbow at Cumberland Falls looks like that in some ways. It is the only moonbow in the western part of the world.

The other natural feature that gives this region a name is coal. It is taken from the earth in two ways. One way to mine coal is through deep underground mines. The other way, called strip mining, is to remove the dirt and take the coal from the surface.

✦ Cultural or Human Regions ✦

Perhaps a better way to understand Kentucky is to divide it into regions in a different way. The regions we just read about are based on natural or physical features of the state. If you ask people from the northern part of the state where they live, though, they will probably not say the geographic region of the Bluegrass. They are likely to say "Northern Kentucky." People who live in the Pennyroyal Region will probably say "West Kentucky." So another way to look at regional differences is to divide the state as people would if you asked them. That might not be very exact, but it shows better how people think of themselves.

Culture is a way of life shared by a group of people. It includes what they believe, what they do, and what they have done over the years. A state may have a certain overall culture. Various parts of a state may have their own special culture.

Kentucky has seven different cultural areas—Appalachia (or Eastern Kentucky), Northern Kentucky, the Bluegrass, South-Central Kentucky, Louisville, West Kentucky, and the Jackson Purchase.

APPALACHIA (EASTERN KENTUCKY)

Because the Appalachian Mountains cover the eastern part of the state, some people call that area Appalachia. Others simply refer to it as Eastern Kentucky. Either way, it is a place of hills and mountains, with few large cities. Only two towns have a population of more than ten thousand—Ashland and Middlesboro. Towns about half that size are London, Corbin, Williamsburg, Pikeville, Hazard, and Morehead.

More than any other region of the state, Eastern Kentucky has been shaped by its past, by its geography, and by writers from outside the area.

Eastern Kentucky was one of the last parts of the state to be settled. It was hard to get there because of the hills. Slowly people began to move in because it had good hunting, good water, and good land in the valleys. These settlers had small farms, just like others in most of Kentucky. Over the years, however, the region became more cut off from the rest of the state and did not grow. Some bitter feuds were started. A **feud** is a fight that continues for a long time between different families or groups. The most famous feud is the Hatfield-McCoy Feud in Pike County. Many others raged for years as well. Hundreds of people were killed in them.

A **stereotype** is saying that the people in a group are all alike. It may not be true at all, or it may be true about only a few people. For example, when you talk to people from outside of Kentucky, they might ask you if you own race horses. Their stereotype of Kentucky is that all Kentuckians own horses. They do not, of course. Suppose someone came to your classroom and heard a student singing poorly. Then if that visitor told people that everyone in your class was a bad singer, the person would have created a stereotype about your class. Is that fair? How do you avoid stereotypes?

Appalachia became stereotyped more than a century ago. People from outside the region

Some national stereotypes of Kentucky grew out of the feuds. This picture shows the Hatfield family, of the Hatfield-McCoy Feud. But the person who made this photograph had the people pose this way to fit the violent "hillbilly" image people had of the feud.

Do you think the little boy on the right side normally carried a gun?

Another stereotype of Kentucky came about when people made illegal whiskey. They did it at night and called it moonshine.

came in and wrote stories and then made films about it. They said it was a place where everyone was poor, talked differently, and fought in feuds. That was not true. Once the "hillbilly" image was formed, though, it was difficult for the region to overcome that unfair stereotype.

At about the same time, the region began to change. People began to mine coal in large amounts. Almost overnight, quiet farmland became coal camps. People left their farms to dig coal in the mines. Many people moved to the region, and its population went up.

Coal mining is not as important now as it once was. Tourists and visitors to the many scenic parts of the region are more important than ever. Still, to many people Appalachia means coal.

Northern Kentucky

The three northern Kentucky counties of Campbell, Kenton, and Boone and the smaller rural counties around them form Northern Kentucky. For the longest time, the people there tended to see themselves as more tied to Cincinnati, Ohio, across the river, than to Kentucky. The Cincinnati and Northern Kentucky International Airport is the largest in the state and is located in Kentucky.

Once, Newport and Covington were the second and third largest cities in the state. The area grew slowly during much of the twentieth century, and first Lexington and then other cities passed them in size.

Recently, however, Northern Kentucky has been one of the growth areas of the state. The cities of Florence, Fort Thomas, Erlanger, Independence, and Burlington have joined Covington and Newport as cities with more than ten thousand people. Now Northern Kentucky is an area that grows more on its own, not just as a part of Cincinnati across the river. Northern Kentucky University and Thomas More College bring students to their halls of learning. The region has become the North American headquarters for Toyota, as well as the national center for Ashland Oil.

A view of the northern Kentucky riverfront in Covington, on the Ohio River. The historic Roebling Bridge, opened in 1867, is in the background.

Northern Kentucky is one part of what has been called the Golden Triangle in Kentucky. If you drew a mark that went down Interstate I-75 to Lexington, then west on Interstate I-64 to Louisville, and then from there on Interstate I-71 to Covington, that would be the Golden Triangle. It is called that because much of the state's recent growth has taken place there.

BLUEGRASS

If you started with Lexington at the center and then drew a circle that stretched forty miles in all directions, the circle would include most of the Bluegrass. Cities with a population of over ten thousand in that area include Richmond, Frankfort, Nicholasville, George-town, Winchester, and Danville.

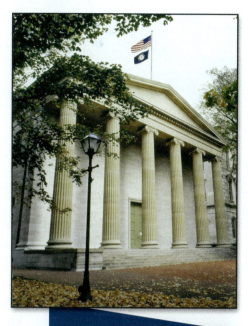

For some 80 years, this beautiful building served as the capitol of Kentucky. It is now called the Old Capitol.

This area of Kentucky was the first to be settled and includes many historic places. Danville was where statehood was talked about and started. At Frankfort, the Old State Capitol stands, and it is there that we can see where people ran the state for eighty years. Rebuilt forts at Harrodsburg and Boonesborough remind us of the frontier. Also near Harrodsburg is Shakertown at Pleasant Hill. It takes us back to the time when a religious group lived and worked in its now-quiet buildings and grounds. Cane Ridge in Bourbon County has the church that was at the center of one of the greatest religious events in American history, the Great Revival in 1801. The full story of such events can be seen at the Kentucky History Center in Frankfort. Many old homes also dot the region. People can walk the same floors and look around them at the same walls that the leaders of long ago walked on and saw daily.

The religious group called the Shakers no longer exists in Kentucky, but their massive and beautiful buildings still remain to remind us of the Shaker presence. Villages were at South Union in Logan County and Pleasant Hill in Mercer County.

From those early times to the present, the Bluegrass has also been known for its horse farms. More than 180 years ago, a person from England wrote: "Their horses are the best in the United States." They continue to be. Racetracks like the historic Keeneland Race Course in Lexington prove that to be true every year. The Kentucky Horse Park near Lexington tells the story of horses.

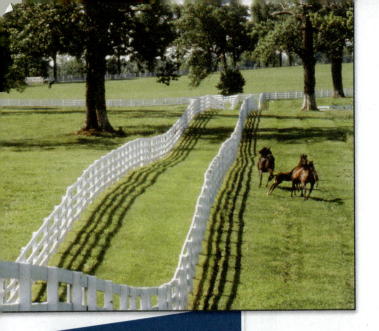

Kentucky is known as the horse capital of the world.

Rock fences were used early on to keep horses on their farms. These fences were built first by Irish workers, then later by skilled black builders. Some say that Kentucky has the largest number of such stone fences in the world. Later, they were replaced by wood plank fences on horse farms and in other places in the region. In addition to horses, tobacco and other crops are important on Bluegrass farms.

Most people who work in the area do not work on horse farms. Many work in what are called service and information industries. Those are businesses that provide a service to people—in hospitals, banks, schools, or government. In Frankfort, the capital of the state, workers help serve all of Kentucky. Many doctors, lawyers, and bankers work in Lexington.

The region also has some of the oldest and best colleges and universities in Kentucky. State-supported schools include the University of Kentucky in Lexington, Kentucky State University in Frankfort, and Eastern Kentucky University in Richmond. Private colleges set up more than 175 years ago include Transylvania University in Lexington, Centre College in Danville, and Georgetown College. Several other colleges were formed later. The professors and the other professionals who work in the area make the region a very highly educated part of Kentucky.

Workers used the rocks from fields to build rock fences. Many of those fences still remain today.

Other people who work in the Bluegrass make things, from computer printers produced by Lexmark in Lexington to cars built by the large Toyota Plant near Georgetown. The region's central location, airport, and good interstate and parkway roads have helped it grow.

The heart of the Bluegrass remains Lexington, the second largest city in the state. In the first thirty years after Kentucky became a state, Lexington was the major city. In fact, it was the largest city west of the mountains for a time. That changed when steamboats on rivers became important. Lexington is not on a major river. (It still is the largest city in the eastern United States that is not on a major body of water.) Lexington went into decline for a time. In the 1950s, however, it began to grow again, doubling in size over the next thirty years.

A popular recreation area in South-Central Kentucky is Lake Cumberland.

Lexington was one of the fastest-growing cities in the nation at that time.

SOUTH-CENTRAL KENTUCKY

Not eastern, nor western, nor the Bluegrass, this part of Kentucky stretches from Somerset in the east past Glasgow and Bowling Green in the west. In between those cities are small farms and major tourist places on Lake Cumberland and Barren River State Parks. Though often not mentioned when people speak of Kentucky, the region is just as important as any other. The largest city is Bowling Green, which is also the fourth largest city in the state. There, Western Kentucky University offers higher education to people of the region. Other schools include Campbellsville University and Lindsey Wilson College in Columbia.

Nearby, Mammoth Cave brings large numbers of visitors, and the tourist trade helps people make a living as well.

Just north of the Mammoth Cave area is a part of Kentucky whose people may view themselves as being part of several regions. The cities of Elizabethtown and Radcliff in Hardin County and Bardstown in Nelson County may be part of the outer Bluegrass, or of the South-Central region, or even tied to Louisville. However they see themselves, they have a rich history and play an important part in Kentucky.

The largest cave system in the wold is Mammoth Cave.

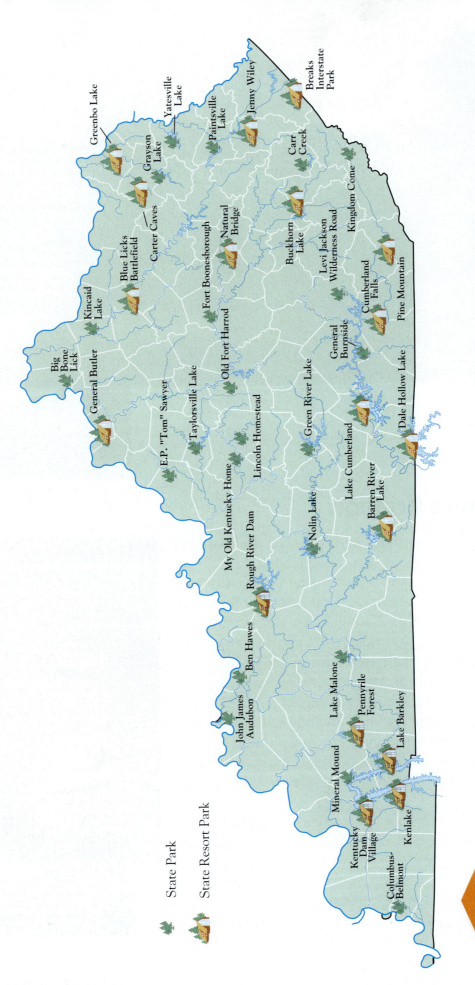

State Park

State Resort Park

Greenbo Lake
Yatesville Lake
Grayson Lake
Carter Caves
Paintsville Lake
Jenny Wiley
Breaks Interstate Park
Carr Creek
Blue Licks Battlefield
Kincaid Lake
Natural Bridge
Fort Boonesborough
Buckhorn Lake
Levi Jackson Wilderness Road
Kingdom Come
Big Bone Lick
Old Fort Harrod
Cumberland Falls
Pine Mountain
General Butler
General Burnside
E.P. "Tom" Sawyer
Taylorsville Lake
Lincoln Homestead
Green River Lake
Dale Hollow Lake
Lake Cumberland
My Old Kentucky Home
Rough River Dam
Nolin Lake
Barren River Lake
Ben Hawes
John James Audubon
Lake Malone
Pennyrile Forest
Mineral Mound
Lake Barkley
Kentucky Dam Village
Kenlake
Columbus-Belmont

Map 3.7 Kentucky state parks and resort areas (2004 data).

Abraham Lincoln was born near Hodgenville, not far from Elizabethtown. Nearby, in Bardstown, is the house called Federal Hill. Some say it was the source for the state song, "My Old Kentucky Home." Near Bardstown, workers produce another product people think of in connection with Kentucky—bourbon whiskey. The state ships bourbon all over the world.

The nation stores many of its gold reserves in Fort Knox.

Near Radcliff is Fort Knox. It is an army base best known as the place where the nation's gold is stored and guarded. Not as well known is the fact that during wartime, some of the nation's greatest treasures were sent there for protection—the Declaration of Independence, the U.S. Constitution, Abraham Lincoln's Gettysburg Address, and more. Those items were taken back to Washington, D.C., when it was safe.

LOUISVILLE

Louisville is by far the largest city in the state (see map 3.9) and has been since 1830. Part of the reason for its size lies in geography. All the way down the Ohio River there is only one place where boats cannot go. That is called the Falls of the Ohio, where the river drops more than twenty feet within two miles. That is where Louisville grew up. It was named for a king of France who helped America during the Revolutionary War. Boats had to stop, unload their cargo, and then re-load it on the other side of the falls. Louisville became the place where all that took place and grew as a result. Later a canal was built so that ships could go around the falls and move down the river faster. Still later, the first bridge (beyond Cincinnati) to cross the Ohio River was built at Louisville. That bridge and railroads brought more people. By 1850, Louisville was the tenth biggest city in the United States. One of every five Kentuckians lives in or near Louisville, and it now ranks as the sixteenth largest U.S. city.

On the first Saturday in May, the world watches Churchill Downs to see which thoroughbred will win the Kentucky Derby.

Louisville is known all over the world for something that takes place there each year on the first Saturday in May. That

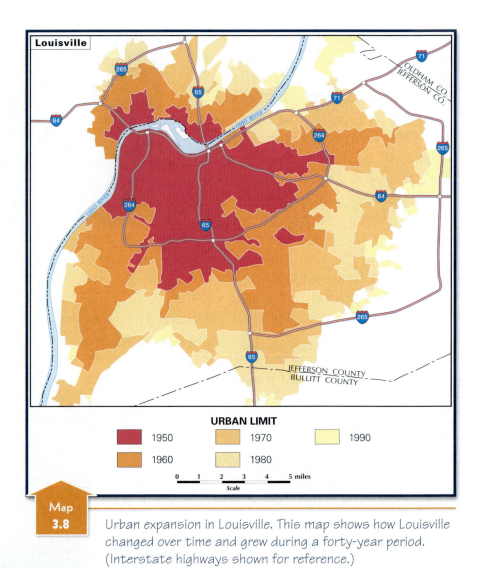

Map 3.8

Urban expansion in Louisville. This map shows how Louisville changed over time and grew during a forty-year period. (Interstate highways shown for reference.)

URBAN LIMIT

1950   1970   1990
1960   1980

0 1 2 3 4 5 miles
Scale

The waterfront of the state's largest city, Louisville.

event has happened in the city ever since 1875. Do you know what it is?

On that day in May, three-year-old racehorses run in the Kentucky Derby. It may be the world's most famous horse race. There are few horse farms in the Louisville area, but the racetrack of Churchill Downs brings fame to the Derby winner every year.

Louisville is also known for other things. Much of the heavy industry of the state is located there, and it produces many of the goods Kentucky makes. (For more on that, see chapter 8.)

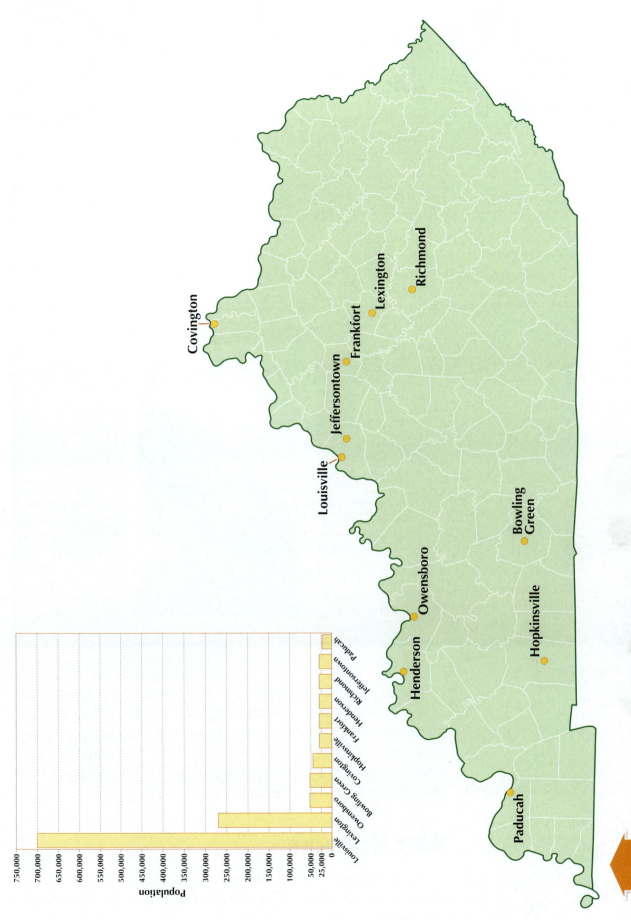

Covington

Richmond

Lexington

Frankfort

Jeffersontown

Louisville

Bowling
Green

Owensboro

Hopkinsville

Henderson

Paducah

Population

750,000
700,000
650,000
600,000
550,000
500,000
450,000
400,000
350,000
300,000
250,000
200,000
150,000
100,000
50,000
25,000
0

Louisville
Lexington
Owensboro
Bowling Green
Covington
Hopkinsville
Frankfort
Henderson
Richmond
Jeffersontown
Paducah

Map
3.9

Kentucky's most populous cities (2003 data).

John James Audubon

The world-famous painter of birds and animal life spent many of his best years in Kentucky. John James Audubon was born in Haiti to French parents and spent much of his early life in France. Later, he came to America, met the woman he would marry, and moved to Louisville to operate a store. Three years later, he went to Henderson, Kentucky.

All four of Audubon's children were born in Kentucky during the eight years he lived in the state. He and his wife, Lucy, felt their years here were the happiest of their lives. Audubon also spent much of his time in the woods. There he painted the fine bird portraits that made him famous.

Audubon was a better artist than he was a businessman. His stores failed, and he was briefly jailed for not paying his bills. After that, the Audubons left Kentucky and went elsewhere. They had little money. Finally, he sailed to England and got his pictures printed in beautiful color in his great work, *The Birds of America*. That won him fame, respect, and wealth.

Audubon died in New York, but his wife moved back to Kentucky to be with a sister-in-law in Shelbyville. She died there. John James Audubon's work lives on through a state park and museum in Henderson and, most of all, in his paintings of birds.

John James Audubon painted many of his famous wildlife pictures while living in Kentucky.

Audubon's portrait of a wild turkey.

Louisville also has the University of Louisville and the private colleges of Bellarmine and Spalding. The people of the city have many cultural events to choose from as well. They can go to museums, to the opera or a ballet, to a play or a concert, or do other things that a large city offers. Many of those events take place in the Kentucky Center.

WEST KENTUCKY

Going west from I-65 all the way to the Jackson Purchase, the western part of Kentucky is the most varied in the state. It has coal mining, yet it also has rich farmland. Crops grown there

Kentucky Faces

Bobbie Ann Mason

Where you are born may influence your life in many ways. Bobbie Ann Mason was born in Mayfield in western Kentucky. She grew up on a farm and became the first person in her family to go to college. After college, she went to New York.

Mason later taught at a college herself but did not like it. What she liked and wanted to do was to write stories about her Kentucky. Success did not come easily. Nineteen times she sent articles to be printed in a magazine, and nineteen times she was turned down. On the twentieth try, the magazine accepted her work and printed it. She was forty years old. Her effort showed that if you really want to do something, you must keep trying. She became an author because she didn't give up.

Mason has since written many books. Some of them have won national prizes. One book, *In Country*, was made into a movie starring Bruce Willis. Almost all of her books come out of her western Kentucky background. They tell about rural, small-town, working-class people.

Bobbie Ann Mason said she left Mayfield because "I wanted to go places and see the world." She did travel a lot, but she never forgot the things that shaped her. She said "We're free to roam, because we've always known where home is."

Finally, she did come home again. She and her husband live in Anderson County, Kentucky. There Mason can read and can write more books that help us understand who we are.

include corn and soybeans, as well as tobacco. The region has a big military base at Ft. Campbell. It also features some of the best places to have outdoor fun in the state.

Between West Kentucky and the Jackson Purchase is the area known as Land Between the Lakes. Dams built on the Tennessee and Cumberland Rivers created the huge lakes named Lake Barkley and Kentucky Lake. People from Kentucky and other states enjoy boating and fishing there. Lakes at Rough River and Nolin River, and at several smaller places, offer water sports to people in other parts of the area. A Shaker Village at South Union and a state park honoring John James Audubon at Henderson represent the region's history.

Owensboro is the largest city in the region and the third largest in the state. It features an art center, museums, good barbecue, and the private colleges of Kentucky Wesleyan and Brescia. Two-year community colleges dot the region also. Other cities larger than ten thousand in population include Hopkinsville, Henderson, Madisonville, and Ft. Campbell.

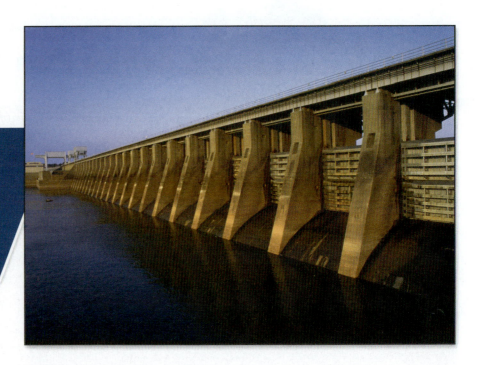

This is Kentucky Dam. Dams on the Cumberland and Tennessee Rivers formed two large lakes. The area in West Kentucky between Lake Barkley and Kentucky Lake is called Land Between the Lakes.

JACKSON PURCHASE

The Purchase came to be a part of Kentucky later and in a different way than other regions of the state. Its land patterns and even its roads were set up differently. Also, the people who settled there came north out of Tennessee. Most of the other parts of the western half of Kentucky were settled by people moving west from other sections of Kentucky.

The three largest cities are Paducah, Murray, and Mayfield. One of the state's regional universities is Murray State University. Resort parks at Kenlake and Kentucky Dam Village bring tourists to the region. Many people go to the small town of Fancy Farm in Graves County every year for a picnic that brings in political leaders from all over the state to talk to voters.

★ Regionalism ★

What does it mean for Kentucky and its people that the state has many counties and several regions?

On the good side, it may help us feel that we belong somewhere, that a place is our home. We may feel a part of the land.

DOCUMENT 3.3

What do these documents tell us about how Kentuckians view themselves? They were written over a period of 150 years. Do you agree or disagree with what they say?

My *dear honeys, heaven is a Kentucky of a place. (The Christian Traveller* [1828])

*Daughter of the East, Mother of West
Link that binds North and South.*

(quoted in Josiah Combs, *All That Is Kentucky* [1915])

No matter how far or how long her children roam, once a Kentuckian, always a Kentuckian. (Lorine L. Butler, My Old Kentucky Home [1929])

Kentuckians are different. (M.B. Morton, *Kentuckians Are Different* [1938])

I live here in Ohio, and I'll die here. But I want my wife to put on my tombstone: Here lies Stanley, but he'd rather be in Kentucky. (1976 statement, cited in Wade Hall, *The Kentucky Book* [1979])

What would you say about Kentucky if someone asked you?

Those counties and regions may have other effects, however. When we talk about Kentucky, we should remember that there are many Kentuckys, not just one. Each county and each region is different.

The distances and those regional divisions may also mean that we in Kentucky have to work very hard to live together.

Covington, in northern Kentucky, is closer to Canada than it is to the most western part of the state. Pikeville, in the east, is nearer to the Atlantic Ocean than it is to the far parts of the Purchase. Students at Murray State University in the west live closer to the University of Mississippi than to the University of Kentucky. Often towns and areas far away from the Golden Triangle feel that they do not get enough attention. Kentucky has to make a special effort to live up to the first part of its motto: "United we stand; Divided we fall."

★ Kentucky Names ★

In counties and regions all across Kentucky, small towns have special names. Sometimes we do not know why they have their names; sometimes we do. Are there towns near you with names that are unusual? Do you know how they got those names?

Some of the unusual names in certain places are:

Monkey's Eyebrow (Ballard County)
Eighty-Eight (Barren County)
Bugtussle (Monroe County)
Mousie (Knott County)
Whoopflarea (Owsley County)

There are also towns in Kentucky named for cities in foreign countries. Can you think of some of those?

Kentucky has a Moscow, a Paris, a London, a Cadiz, an Athens, a Versailles, and a Berlin, for example (although we may not say the names in the same way that people in the foreign countries say them). What would you name a town if you had the chance?

By whatever name and in whatever region, Kentucky places are very special to the people who live in them.

The Federal Hill estate in Bardstown, part of My Old Kentucky Home State Park.

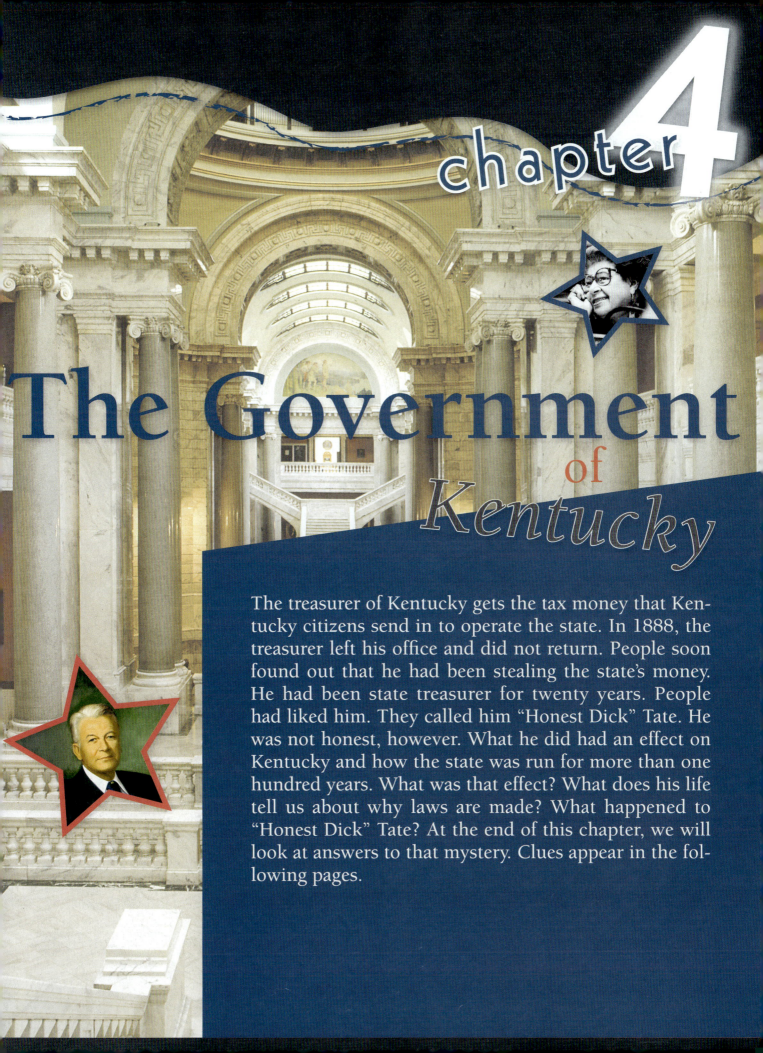

The Government
of
Kentucky

The treasurer of Kentucky gets the tax money that Kentucky citizens send in to operate the state. In 1888, the treasurer left his office and did not return. People soon found out that he had been stealing the state's money. He had been state treasurer for twenty years. People had liked him. They called him "Honest Dick" Tate. He was not honest, however. What he did had an effect on Kentucky and how the state was run for more than one hundred years. What was that effect? What does his life tell us about why laws are made? What happened to "Honest Dick" Tate? At the end of this chapter, we will look at answers to that mystery. Clues appear in the following pages.

★ Government ★

One definition of **government** says that it is a system of laws and rules by which a nation, state, or some other organization is directed or governed. The power behind a democratic government comes from the people. In the end, they are the important ones.

People have formed various kinds of governments for thousands of years. Why do they do that? Part of the reason is that little can happen without some set of rules and people to put those rules into effect. Government gives order to a society. It can protect the safety of people. It can also protect their rights to do certain things. Government also helps promote what is called the common good. It can provide health care, roads, safety, and schools to people who might not have all those things otherwise.

"Honest Dick" Tate stole the state's money when he was treasurer. What happened to him after that?

How is this American flag different from the one we have today? Hint: It is the first one that includes Kentucky's star in the flag.

★ The Kentucky Constitution ★

The nation uses a written document called the **Constitution** to guide its government. When Kentucky became a state in 1792, it wrote its own state constitution. That document started out by saying who was behind the forming of the new state—"We, the people of the commonwealth of Kentucky."

What is a **commonwealth**? Only four states call themselves common-wealths. Why does Kentucky? How is a commonwealth different from a state?

Actually, there is no real legal difference. Virginia had taken that name from some events connected to England. Kentucky was part of Virginia at first. So when Kentucky became a separate state, it simply called itself a commonwealth as well.

So the new commonwealth (or state) started out because the people wanted to form a separate government. They asked the U.S. Congress to make that happen. Congress agreed

DOCUMENT 4.1

The Congress of the United States agreed to Kentucky statehood in a law passed in February 1791, to go into effect in June 1792. It said:

That the Congress doth consent that the said district of Kentucky be formed into a new state, separate from and independent of, the said Commonwealth of Virginia.

And be it further enacted, that the State of Kentucky shall be received and admitted into this Union, as a new and entire member of the United States of America.

and said that the new state would begin on June 1, 1792. (See document 4.1.)

Kentucky needed to set up general rules on how the new state would operate. A group of people met in Danville to create the framework of government. They wrote the first constitution. It made it clear who had the final right to make decisions in Kentucky—"All power is inherent in the people." Kentucky's first constitution was very liberal in some ways. In other states at the time, you had to own land in order to vote. Kentucky became the first state where people could vote whether or not they owned land.

Voting is an important duty. At first only men voted. Slaves could not vote, nor could women. Finally, after much struggle, all citizens, black and white, male and female, won the right. In 1955, Kentucky gave eighteen-year-olds the right to vote. The nation did not allow eighteen-year-olds to vote until sixteen years later. Again, the commonwealth was a leader.

Sadly, many people do not vote even when they become old enough to vote. They do not know the history behind their right to vote. They may not understand that voting is a duty as well as a right. People set up governments. They are the final power in those

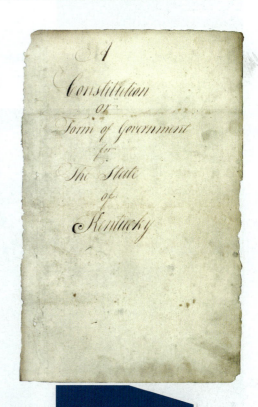

A constitution has guided Kentucky's government since this first one was written in 1792.

Voting is an important right and benefit. But not all groups have always had the right. These women could vote for the first time only in 1920.

governments. If they do not vote and are not active citizens, they are not doing their duty. In a race for mayor in Lexington in 1973, thousands cast their votes. But one man won by only 54 votes. Had just a few more people voted, that election might have turned out in a different way. People who do not vote are not honoring all those who worked so hard to make certain that they could vote.

★ Change ★

In other chapters, we have already read about many ways different things have changed over time. Governments change as well. Sometimes they change in response to some event or problem. At other times people's views change and voters bring in new leaders to create new rules and laws. Perhaps some part of government simply becomes outdated, due to new technology or something else, and must be changed.

Kentucky's government has changed many times and in many ways over the years. For instance, more and different people can vote now than were allowed in the past. How they vote has changed also. For a long time, when it was time to vote, people could vote over a three-day period, rather than on one day, as now. Voters used to stand before officials and tell them out loud how they wanted to vote. Everyone who was nearby would know how you voted. Later voting was done by placing a secret, paper ballot in a box. Now we use electronic voting machines in Kentucky.

In voting machines like this one, voters make decisions about their government.

In a broader way, Kentucky's constitutions have changed as well. That first one lasted only seven years before changing ideas made it necessary to write a second one. A third followed later. Now we are under Kentucky's fourth constitution, which was adopted in 1891. The United States has had only one constitution. It is shorter and much more general than Kentucky's constitution. But they are alike in some places. Look at the two sections on the next page. How are they the same, and how are they different?

All of the constitutions contained certain basic features. A **Bill of Rights** gave citizens rights regarding free elections, religious freedom, freedom of speech, and protections in various criminal justice issues. The body of the constitution told

> *Kentucky Constitution:*
>
> Section 32—No person shall be a Senator who at the time of his election is not a resident of Kentucky, has not attained the age of thirty years, and has not resided in the state six years.

> *United States Constitution:*
>
> Article I, Section 2—No person shall be a Senator who shall not have attained the age of thirty years, and has been nine years a citizen of the United States, and who shall, when elected, be an inhabitant of that State for which he shall be chosen.

how the government operated. A section also explained how voters could change the constitution. That is done by what are called **amendments**. Amendments are passed by those who govern the state and can be either accepted or turned down by vote of the citizens. If approved, they take the place of an older part of the constitution. Over the years, Kentucky has changed its constitution a great deal by passing amendments.

★ Levels of Government ★

Government exists at three different levels—local, state, and national. The first level is local government. Cities and counties provide people's first contacts with government. What services do local governments offer in your area?

Early in the state's history, citizens dealt mostly with local government. A higher level of government usually affected them only when they paid their taxes, went to the post office, or voted. Later, state and national governments began to offer many more services than before. People now deal with those governments a great deal. What are some things that come from state and national government?

★ Branches of Government ★

At each level, government is divided into different parts. In Kentucky at the state level there are three branches of government.

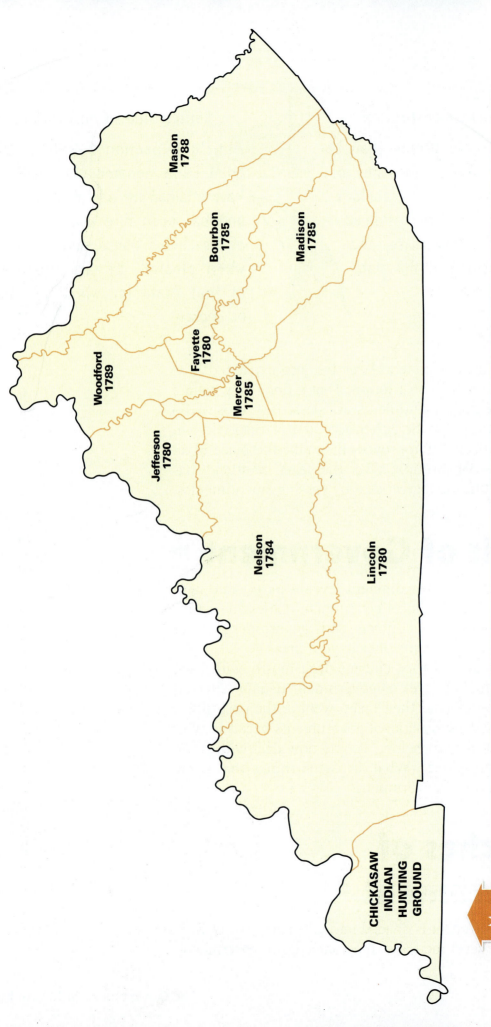

Mason
1788

Bourbon
1785

Madison
1785

Woodford
1789

Fayette
1780

Mercer
1785

Jefferson
1780

Nelson
1784

Lincoln
1780

CHICKASAW
INDIAN
HUNTING
GROUND

Map
4.1

Kentucky counties, 1792. Counties have always been an important part of Kentucky life. At the time of statehood these nine counties covered all of Kentucky. Does your county have the same name it had back then, or was it a part of another county at that time?

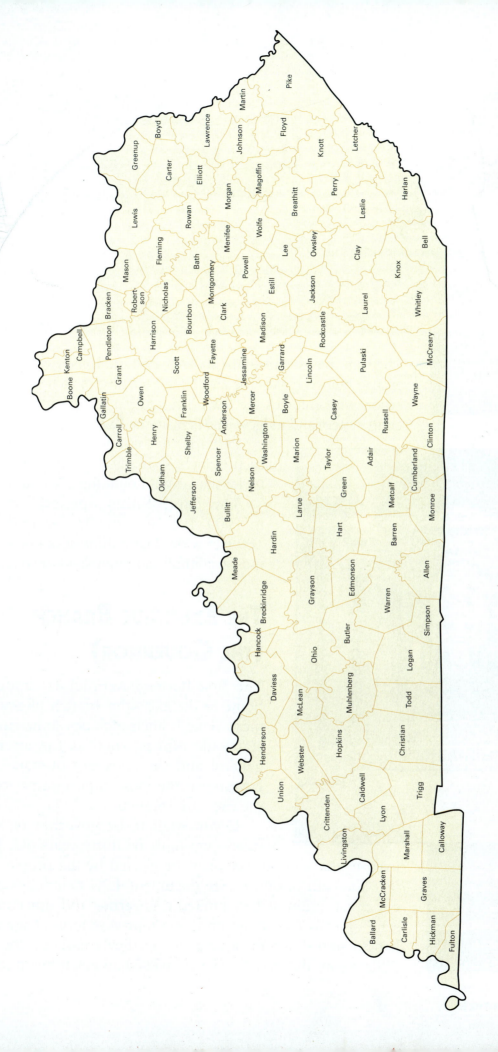

Map
4.2

Kentucky counties, 1912 to present. Kentucky now has 120 counties. Only two other states have more.

The center of Kentucky government is its beautiful capitol building.

They are the executive, the judicial, and the legislative. The legislative branch makes the laws. The executive branch is the governor, who enforces the laws. The judicial branch includes the court system and judges, who explain the law.

Perhaps the best way to understand each branch is simply to go into the Kentucky state capitol building and start there.

The capitol was opened for use in 1909. It is almost 403 feet long and 180 feet wide. Many think it is one of the most beautiful state capitols in the nation.

THE EXECUTIVE BRANCH (THE GOVERNOR)

The first floor of Kentucky's capitol is home to the executive branch of government. That branch includes some elected statewide offices, such as the attorney general and the secretary of state. The governor is the most important person in the executive branch.

If you want to be governor of Kentucky, you must be thirty years old, have lived in the state for six years, be elected by the people, and take the oath of office. (See document 4.2.) Kentucky's present constitution at first limited a governor and other major state officials to serving only one four-year term. They then had to step down for a time before they could run for that office again. But in 1992, voters passed an amendment to the

The inside of the capitol. At one end of the third floor is the House of Representatives Chamber, and the Senate meets at the other end.

DOCUMENT 4.2

The governor takes an oath of office before becoming the executive of the state. Kentucky's oath was written into the 1891 constitution. Do you see a part of it that is now outdated?

I do solemnly swear that I will support the Constitution of the United States and the Constitution of this Commonwealth, and be faithful and true to the Commonwealth of Kentucky as long as I continue to be a citizen thereof, and that I will faithfully execute, to the best of my ability, the office of governor according to law; and I further solemnly swear that since the adoption of the present Constitution, I, being a citizen of this State, have not fought a duel with deadly weapons within this state nor out of it, nor have I sent or accepted a challenge to fight a duel with deadly weapons, nor have I acted as second in carrying a challenge, nor aided or assisted any person thus offending, so help me God.

constitution, allowing officials to serve two full terms in a row. If a governor leaves or is forced out of office or dies during a term, the lieutenant governor becomes governor for the rest of that term.

Governors usually are the most important people in state government. The constitution and history give them a great deal of power to carry out their tasks and duties. A governor sitting in the office on the first floor must be a leader. The governor must ask the lawmakers to approve a budget to run the state. Governors must send the legislative branch ideas for laws to make the state better, and then try to get them passed. Governors also must run state government. That means that all the people who work in the areas of education, roads, health, the law, and other human needs are guided by the governor. The governor must help bring businesses and jobs to the commonwealth, for its future well-being. Governors also usually are expected to be leaders of the political party that helped them get elected.

The Kentucky Governor's Mansion.

Kentucky Faces

Bert Combs

Bert Combs seemed an unlikely person to be elected governor. Yet he was selected and became one of the best governors of the twentieth century. His story tells us much.

Combs was born in Clay County in eastern Kentucky. He first went to a two-room school and then later rode a pony to get to high school. A very bright boy, he skipped some grades and finished high school at age fifteen. Soon after he became a lawyer, Combs moved to Prestonsburg in Floyd County. He served in World War II and returned home to enter new careers in Kentucky.

Lawyer Combs seemed best suited to be a judge, not a political leader. He was quiet and not a very good public speaker. In fact, he served six years as a justice on Kentucky's highest court. Combs had taken a pay cut to go into that job, but he felt his region needed someone to speak for them on the court. So he took the post. Powerful political leaders wanted him to apply his talents to other offices. They got him to run for governor in 1955, but he lost.

Four years later, Combs ran for governor again and won. At the same time he became governor, voters approved a sales tax to pay bonus money for those who served in the armed forces. Part of those funds, though, went to other things the state needed. Governor Combs helped expand schools, human services, roads, and much more. He wanted to try to keep politics out of state government. He set up a merit system, so workers would not have to worry about losing their jobs each time a new governor came to Frankfort.

After Combs left office, he led the legal team that pushed for changes in education. (See document 4.3.) The Kentucky Education Reform Act came about partly because of his work. He died in 1991, when his car was caught in a flash flood near his home in Powell County.

Combs once said: "I think all of us would like to leave a few tracks around to let people know we've been here." Kentucky honored him by naming the Mountain Parkway for him, but he left tracks much wider than that. People knew Bert Combs had been here.

Voters in Kentucky must register, or sign up, to vote. Usually they register either as a Democrat or a Republican, or as an Independent with ties to neither party. Such political ties are not as strong or as crucial as they once were. They are still important, though. Political parties can get groups together to help a candidate become elected. They can work together to get things done. They can speak out on issues they consider important and let people see various viewpoints. They can help people get involved and feel more a part of the whole political process. Parties can help a state move forward, or they can ignore what is good for a state and act only for their

own interests. If they act in a selfish way, they can hold back the state's progress.

THE JUDICIAL BRANCH (THE COURTS)

The executive branch is on the first floor of the capitol. The judicial branch is on the second. Like other branches of government, the courts are on three levels. Courts on the local and state level were set up by an amendment to the state constitution in 1975. District and Circuit Courts hear cases and make decisions at the local level, either by a judge or by a jury. A jury is made up of people from the area. Witnesses to the case swear an oath that what they will say is the truth. Once the jury has heard all the witnesses, they decide what they think happened. They vote guilty or not guilty in criminal cases. If someone is found guilty, the judge then sets a sentence—usually either a fine or a jail term.

People who are found guilty may ask that the decision be changed. They may feel that a judge or jury made a mistake. That is called an **appeal.** At the state level, the Court of Appeals and the state Supreme Court hear appeals.

The most important court in the commonwealth is the Kentucky Supreme Court. The Kentucky Supreme Court

DOCUMENT 4.3

In 1985, some citizens said that Kentucky did not treat all its schools fairly. They said the old education system did not work and asked the court to see if Kentucky was doing what the constitution of the state said it must. A Circuit Court judge ruled that the system of giving funds to schools did not do as the constitution required. He said the state must come up with a more fair system of funding. That ruling was appealed to the Kentucky Supreme Court. In the case of *Rose vs. Council for Better Schools* in 1989, the court went beyond the Circuit Court's ruling and decided that Kentucky's existing school system was unconstitutional. It said that the whole system did not do what it should and that a new one must be created. The court said:

This division applies to the entire sweep of the system—all its parts. Since we have, by this decision, declared the system of common schools in Kentucky to be unconstitutional, Section 183 [of the constitution] places an absolute duty on the General Assembly to re-create, re-establish a new system. We view this decision as an opportunity for the General Assembly to launch the Commonwealth into a new era of educational opportunity which will ensure a strong economic, cultural, and political future.

By its actions, the court caused a new law to be written. In the next session of the General Assembly in 1990, House Bill 940 (H.B. 940) was passed by the General Assembly and then signed into law by the governor. As the court required, it set up a new system of schools. We now call that law the Kentucky Education Reform Act, or KERA.

---

hears most of the key cases on state law. The court is made up of seven people, called **justices.** For almost two hundred years, all the justices were men. The face of the court changed in the 1990s when Sara Walter Combs of Powell County became the first woman on the Supreme Court, and Janet Stumbo of Floyd and Pike Counties became the first female elected to a full term as justice. Each justice is elected from a certain area of the state and serves an eight-year term.

Some cases can be taken on appeal to still another level. At the national or federal level, the U.S. Supreme Court makes the final decision. That court has nine justices, all selected by the president of the United States. They serve as long as they want to. It is a great honor to be selected to that highest of courts. Over the years, eleven people who were either born in Kentucky, or lived here at the time, have been appointed to the U.S. Supreme Court. (For a list of them, see appendix 3.)

The three most important judges from Kentucky on the Supreme Court have been John Marshall Harlan (see "Kentucky Faces," page 88), Louis Brandeis, and Fred Vinson. The president selects one of the judges to guide the court. That person is called the chief justice of the United States. One person from Kentucky, Fred Vinson of Louisa in eastern Kentucky, has been named chief justice.

Judge Vinson liked to say that he was born in jail. At the time of his birth, most women had their children at home, not in a hospital. His parents lived in the jail because his father was the jailer, so the future chief justice really was born in the jail. He later was elected to Congress and became friends with Harry Truman. When Truman became president, he named Vinson as chief justice. Vinson served seven years before he died in 1953 at the age of sixty-three.

The entire judicial or court system is set up on all levels to make sure that people can get justice in the end.

THE LEGISLATIVE BRANCH (THE GENERAL ASSEMBLY)

The third floor of the capitol is the home of Kentucky's legislative branch. In general terms, the place where Kentucky laws are passed is called the legislature. In specific terms for the state, it is called the General Assembly. People elected to serve there are called legislators.

The Legislators. Legislators are elected to one of the two parts of the General Assembly—the House of Representatives or the Senate. To be a member of the House of Representatives, you must be at least twenty-four years old and have lived in Kentucky for two

Sara Combs served as the first woman member of the Kentucky Supreme Court.

Fred Vinson of Louisa became the chief justice of the United States and served on the Supreme Court from 1946 to 1953.

John Marshall Harlan

John Marshall Harlan became a justice of the U.S. Supreme Court when he was forty-four years old. He served as a judge there for almost thirty-four more years before his death in 1911. During that time, he became known as "The Great Dissenter." He got that name because he often disagreed with the court decisions that other judges made. So he wrote his views in what is called a **dissent.**

For instance, when the court ruled that it was legal for a state to have separate schools for black and white students, he said that decision was wrong. In his dissent, Harlan wrote that "Our Constitution is color-blind, and neither knows nor tolerates classes among citizens." At the time, many people did not like what he said. He had the courage to say what he thought, however. He had the will and the skill to be great. Years later, a different group of justices looked at that same issue and decided that Harlan had been right and those other justices wrong. His dissenting views became the rule of law. A change in views had taken place over time.

Harlan was born near Danville, lived in Harrodsburg, and then settled in Frankfort. He ran for Congress once and lost by seventy votes. Twice he lost in races to become governor of Kentucky. Harlan served as attorney general of the state, but most of the time he was not a winner in political races. As a justice he was a winner, though, in the eyes of history. When people selected the dozen greatest Supreme Court justices of all time, they named Kentuckian John Marshall Harlan as one of them.

The legislature of Kentucky is called the General Assembly.

years. There are one hundred members of the House. They each serve a two-year term and then may run for re-election.

State senators are elected to four-year terms, twice as long. They must be a little older (thirty years old) and have lived in the state longer (six years). There are thirty-eight members of the Senate.

Until the year 2000, the legislators from both parts of the General Assembly met only every other year for a sixty-day session starting in January. In 2000 the voters approved an amendment that now allows the legislators to meet every year.

Who are the people who make the laws that set the rules for the state? Some 138 members make up the legislature, 38 senators and 100 representatives. In a recent session, most

Georgia Davis Powers

Georgia Davis Powers was the first black woman to serve in the Senate of Kentucky. She was born in Springfield in Washington County in 1923. Her family had nine children, and she was the only girl.

When she was seventeen months old, a tornado destroyed her family's home. They moved to Louisville. A dozen years later, the flood of 1937 covered their house and they had to leave it for two months. Then they returned. Her family lived very close to where boxer Muhammad Ali grew up.

Georgia Powers attended college and then worked in a factory that made planes during World War II. Later she grew interested in working for equal rights for all races and became a close friend of Dr. Martin Luther King Jr. She was in Memphis the night he was killed.

In 1967, she won election to the Senate of Kentucky and served there for more than twenty years. Her efforts went to many projects. One was to get passage of an Open Housing Law, which gave all people the same rights to buy a house.

When she wrote a book about her life, she said at the end of the book: "I prefer just to be called an American, because that is what I am. I am more interested in how I am treated than in what I am called. I shared the dream that we shall all be free."

Her book and her story are part of history. As Mae Street Kidd, another black member of the General Assembly, said: "I have always loved history. It helps you find out who you are and how you got to be who you are." Kidd and Powers knew who they were.

members were well-educated people. Almost 100 of the 138 had college degrees. Voters had selected mostly men—there were 122 males and 16 females. More and more women are being elected each time, as a rule, however. The average legislator was fifty-one years old, belonged generally to either the Baptist or the Catholic Church, and worked as an attorney, teacher, farmer, home builder or seller, or small business owner. There are many different kinds of people with many different backgrounds who serve in the General Assembly.

In the Kentucky capitol, the legislators go to the third floor. At one end of the building is the Kentucky House of Representatives. At the other stands the Senate. To become law, a proposal must pass in both the Senate and the House. It then goes to the governor, who can approve or disapprove the law. If the governor disapproves it, that is called a **veto.** The law then goes back to the General Assembly. If enough legislators agree, they can re-pass the law and it will become the rule of the state even without the governor's approval. If there are not enough who vote for it, the law fails. Even if a law does pass, the Supreme Court of Kentucky can be asked to decide if the law does what the constitution permits—that is, if it is legal. If the court says it is not, that law cannot go into effect. This whole process is called **checks and balances.** Each branch of the government can check what the other branches do. They each balance the others. The national government works the same way.

Passing a Law. Each member of the Kentucky House or Senate is elected from a certain area or district. The legislators keep in touch with the people they represent. Often, people go to legislators and ask them to try to help them in different ways. They may want to get a law passed. In order to see how the system works, we will follow it step by step.

Let's suppose that your class has been studying Kentucky government, and the class decides that the voting age should not be eighteen. Because you can drive a car at age sixteen, your class thinks you should be able to vote at sixteen as well.

You go to your member of the Kentucky House of Representatives and ask him or her to introduce a bill to lower the voting age in Kentucky to sixteen (a bill is a proposed law). A lot of bills are suggested each time the General Assembly meets. Many do not become law; many do.

When the session of the legislature begins, your representative writes a bill that says the voting age will be lowered to sixteen. It is given a number. We'll say it is House Bill 700 (H.B. 700). It is then read in the House so everyone knows that it has been written. Next, the bill is sent to a committee for action.

Committees are made up of a smaller group of legislators. Those committees are very important. They hear bills on a specific subject. Many bills never get beyond the committee and "die" there. Your H.B. 700 goes to a committee on elections. At some time there will be an open meeting, where your class could tell the committee why you think they should support the bill. Others may speak against it. Usually,

House Bill 700 would look like this.

IN HOUSE

2004 Regular Session

HOUSE BILL NO.

Tuesday, January 6, 2004

people from the different sides also try to talk to legislators in their offices as well, hoping to convince them.

After the committee members have heard what people have to say about a bill, they vote. If your bill does not get a favorable vote, it does not usually go any further. In this case, let's suppose that one member of the committee suggests an amendment to the bill. That person wants to change the voting age in the bill to seventeen, not sixteen. The committee supports the change and sends the bill on, as amended.

Committees like this one play an important role in making laws.

Next, it is given what is called a formal First Reading in the House of Representatives. After a Second Reading on another day, the bill goes to another group, the Rules Committee. They decide whether it should move on. If they decide it should, they place it on the schedule for a vote. On its Third Reading, the bill is up for debate and possible passage. It can be amended again at that time if someone can get enough votes to do so. During the time between the committee hearings and the Third Reading, you have been asking other representatives to support your bill. Now the vote comes. The amended bill passes by a vote of fifty-three to forty-seven. It was close, but it passed.

Now you are still only halfway to getting it made into law. The same process takes place in the state Senate. Let's suppose that most people on the committee it goes to do not favor the bill. They vote against it, and it dies in committee. You are disappointed. There is another session next year, however, and you will talk to more legislators before then, especially those in the Senate. You will try again. One day you might get the law passed. That is how it all works.

★ The Mystery of "Honest Dick" Tate ★

At the beginning of this chapter, we read about how "Honest Dick" Tate stole the state's money. We asked several questions. What effect did his action have on the state? What does his life tell us about how laws are made? What happened to

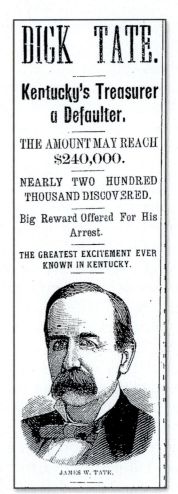

him? Did you find any clues to help you answer the first two questions?

Remember that Tate had served as state treasurer for twenty years. His theft occurred just before Kentucky wrote its fourth constitution. The people who wrote it did not want elected officials to stay in office for very long because of what Tate did. So they set up a one-term rule, which lasted for one hundred years. Times change, and voters in 1992 decided to let officials serve two terms. Laws—and constitutions—often reflect the times around them. As times change, laws may change as well. Tate's actions caused a rule to be made. Time caused that rule to change.

What happened to "Honest Dick" Tate? We do not know. He left behind a wife and child. He wrote to them for a while. His letters came from Canada, Asia, and South America. Then the letters stopped. Did he die, or did someone kill him for his stolen money in one of those places? Did he sneak back into America? No one knows. That is another history mystery.

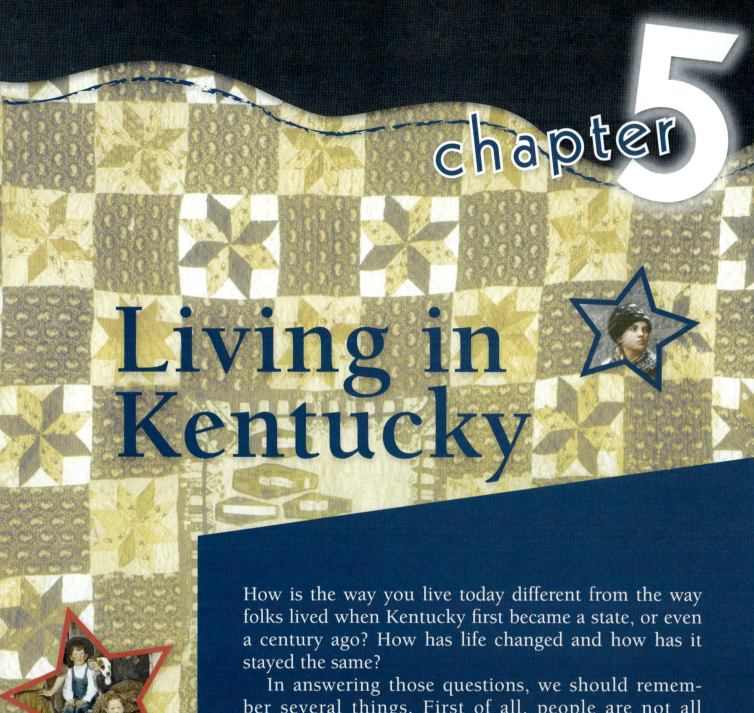

chapter

5

Living in Kentucky

How is the way you live today different from the way folks lived when Kentucky first became a state, or even a century ago? How has life changed and how has it stayed the same?

In answering those questions, we should remember several things. First of all, people are not all alike. The people in your class may live in different places and enjoy doing different things. The same thing was true one hundred or even two hundred years ago. A second thing to think about is that all places in Kentucky are not the same now, and were not the same in earlier times. In some parts of the state, how people lived may not have been very different fifty years ago than it was at the time statehood began, more than two hundred years earlier. People in other parts of the commonwealth may have lived closer to the way we do now. In this chapter we will talk about how the **average** person lived in the past. So you should remember that some lived in worse situations and some in better ones. Some people in certain parts of the state were not like the average at all. The same thing is true now.

Let's look at a day in the life of a person soon after Kentucky became a state and compare it to your life.

★ Daily Life ★

When the first person in your home gets up in the morning, an electric alarm clock is probably what awakes him or her. Was that true on the frontier, or even a century ago?

A century ago, people did not have electricity. In fact, as late as the 1940s almost everyone living on a farm in Kentucky still had no electricity. Think of all the things that you do not have if the electricity goes out now. Those people never had electricity to start with.

They had no electric lights or televisions or radios or DVD players or computers or telephones. When one man finally did see someone talking on the new invention of the telephone for the first time, he said: "Look—That old fool is talking to the wall." Soon after statehood, people also knew nothing about automobiles or airplanes or railroads. A century later—and one

Years ago, in many homes the fireplace served as the center of activities.

What is the person on the right doing? What has this family used for wallpaper?

hundred years ago now—many people used the train, but even then cars and planes had just begun to be invented. Today you can get into a car with others and go twenty miles in just a few minutes. For them to go that far might take all day.

Once the alarm or someone in the house wakes you up, you get out of bed. On cold days, your home is probably warm. On hot days, it may be cooled by air conditioning or an electric fan. Their homes were very different. They had no air-conditioning—most homes did not, until a few years ago. People in those early days usually had no central heat. A fireplace might offer the only warmth. If you slept far away from the fire, it could be very cold. Some people told how a glass of water near their bed might freeze at night.

Until the twentieth century, matches were not common in homes. A boy from the Jackson Purchase area recalled that if the fire in their house went out, he had to walk a mile to the next house to get fire from a neighbor. A century ago, a woman from Owsley County in eastern Kentucky recalled how "it was a common thing for people to go to their neighbors to borrow fire." One of the first things people did in the morning in those days was to start a fire to warm their house.

A frontier child might jump out of bed to a cold—or very hot—house. The bed itself was different from ours today. We sleep on a mattress that usually has a set of springs under it, and sheets and blankets cover us. In frontier times, the mattress might be filled with straw and be placed on either ropes or wood planks for support. Other beds were filled with feathers. You would sink deep into those feather beds, and they helped keep you warm in winter. Each year people would re-fill their mattresses with fresh straw or new feathers. What would those feather beds be like in hot weather?

A young boy or girl of the past might sleep under

What are some of the reasons people made quilts? Perhaps they made them for bedding, for beauty, and to express ideas. The "Graveyard Quilt" pictured here is very famous. If you look around the edges you can see "coffins" sewn to the quilt. When a person died, his or her name was put into one of those "coffins" and moved to the "graveyard" in the middle.

heavy quilts during cold weather. Some of those handmade quilts still exist. They have very interesting patterns on them and histories behind them. Family members needed those quilts to help keep them warm. Hand-built houses might have cracks in the walls that let in the cold. In the twentieth century, one Barren County man in south-central Kentucky said that "in the winter when the snow blew it often came through the cracks and [got] on our beds."

After you get out of bed, what do you do next? You might go to the bathroom. We have indoor plumbing now. They did not. Some homes a century ago might have had a "slop jar" or a bowl they used for a toilet. They would throw the contents out into the yard. Most people used an outdoor toilet in a plank building called a privy or an outhouse. Other people simply went into the woods. Either way, you might expect to go out into the cold or rain as soon as you woke up.

One of the first things we might do when we get up is to turn on a light if it is still dark outside. They had no electric lights. Louisville had the first ones in the state in the 1870s. So

For places that did not have a water system, an outdoor toilet had to do.

people in early times either got up in the dark or rose when the sun did. Their days might go from dawn to sundown and no later. Later, people had lamps that burned whale oil or coal oil to produce a faint light. Those lamps had to be cleaned often because of the soot they made.

Today you might wash or even take a quick shower in the morning. Those children of the past had no running water. They might have a pitcher of water and a washbowl on a stand to use in cleaning up. They probably got the water from a well or even a nearby stream. If they had soap, it was homemade. People took fireplace ashes and ran water over them. Then they boiled that mixture and added hog or even bear fat until soap formed and could be scooped off the bottom. Soap was made that way well into the twentieth century.

Next you might put on your clothes. How are clothes different now?

✦ Clothes and Fashion ✦

How people dress and look at a certain time is called **fashion.** Over the years, fashion changes, sometimes rapidly. What was the usual fashion in one time may not be common at all in another period. For instance, men of Daniel Boone's time wore their hair long. Later, most men cut their hair shorter. Then in the 1960s some men had long hair again. During the time of Abraham Lincoln, men tended to wear beards. A century later, only a few men had beards. Now we have more of a mix of hairstyles and beards.

Women's fashions change as well. A century ago, people thought it was wrong for a woman to show any part of her leg above the ankle in public. Sixty years later, women wore short miniskirts. Shoe styles change from time to time too.

The same thing happened long ago. So when we talk about how people looked or dressed, we should remember that those fashions changed a great deal over time.

This is an 1819 painting of an upper-class Richmond, Kentucky, family: thirty-seven-year-old John Speed Smith, twenty-one-year-old Eliza Clay Smith, and their one-year-old daughter, Sallie Ann Smith.
What else do you notice about the painting?

Entitled "Mountain Family" in the early twentieth century, this photograph was hand-colored by the photographer.
How would you describe the clothes that these family members are wearing?

The dress of the average person who worked on a farm did not change as much over the years as did the dress of people in the city. At first most clothes were homemade. It took a lot of time to make clothes. If people wanted to add any color, they usually had to make their own dye from tree bark. Later people could buy some things at stores to wear. Still later, they could use the mail to order clothes from catalogs and have them sent to them—as people do who shop over the Internet now. The invention of the sewing machine also helped people make better clothes.

Almost all children, and many adults, wore no shoes at certain times of the year. A man born in 1800 wrote, "All the children, both male and female, went barefoot from early spring until late in the fall." A hundred years later, a Danville boy said he had never worn shoes until he was five years old. If people did wear shoes, for a long time they did not worry about whether they had the shoe on the correct foot or not. Not until the middle of the nineteenth century did shoes have a right or left foot. People would buy shoes and wear them to make them fit their right or left foot.

People dressed in simple ways. In warm weather, usually only wealthy people wore any underclothing. In colder weather, both rich and poor people might put on flannel "long johns." When they worked in the fields, men tended to wear overalls or jeans, while women wore loose dresses.

There were some other differences from the fashions of today. Women in the nineteenth century tried to protect their skin from the sun as much as possible. They wore bonnets or hats or carried umbrellas to keep the sun off their faces. They had long sleeves and long dresses as well. That practice changed in the twentieth century, when men and women sought to

The Ashton sisters— well-dressed young women, with their hats, from a century or so ago.

A wealthy man in the late 1800s would have worn a suit similar to the one pictured here.

get a tan from the sun's rays. Well into the twentieth century, people also did not use zippers in their clothes. They used buttons instead.

When people "dressed up"—usually to go to church—they put on very different clothes. Men wore wool suits and vests in both winter and summer. Their shirt collars and cuffs were heavily starched. Sitting in a hot building in such clothes could not be comfortable. Women's formal dresses could be uncomfortable too. Early in the nineteenth century, large "hoop" skirts were heavy and hard to move in. Across that century, women wore tight, laced corsets to make them appear thin. Their long dresses often dragged on the ground. The invention of the bicycle late in that century helped bring about looser clothes for women so that they could ride.

At the end of a day, people remove their dirty clothes. Now we clean our clothes by using a washer, a dryer, and an iron, or by taking them to the dry cleaners. Until the twentieth century, such machines were rare. Women would put the family's clothes in soapy water. Then they used a paddle or a stick to beat on the wet clothes to try to get the dirt out. They usually had several irons. They would heat the irons over the fireplace or on a stove, then iron for a time with one. When that one cooled, they would get another hot one off the stove. That same stove would be used to cook food.

★ Food ★

After you get dressed in the morning, you might have breakfast, either at home or at school. Breakfast and other meals are much easier to prepare today than they were at the time of statehood.

These days, people can go to a grocery and buy most of what they need. The meat has been cut up and is ready to cook. Canned and frozen foods are easy to fix. Fresh fruit and bread and milk are available all year long. For a change, you can eat out or even get a fast-food meal and bring that food home. Things were much different two hundred and even one hundred years ago.

For many farm families, if they wanted meat, they had to kill it.

People often lived in a very limited economic system. It was not easy to get food and supplies from very far away. They usually had to supply their own food. They did that in many ways.

Many farms had gardens where people grew many of the vegetables they used. They might grow corn, green beans, potatoes, peas, peppers, and more. Hunting and fishing could bring some meat to the table. Many farms also had chickens. People used the eggs daily and at times killed the chickens for food. One of the key sources of meat was the hog. In the fall it became cool enough to help keep meat fresh. At that time hog killing took place. People would kill a hog, scrape off all its hair, drain out all the blood, and then cut up the meat. They cut it into bacon, chops, jowls, and other pieces. Part would be ground up and made into sausage. Sometimes they stored the sausage in the hog's intestines, or just in cloth sacks, to "season."

Those people of the past had no electric or gas refrigerators. They still wanted to keep meat, milk, and vegetables longer than just a few days, though. How would you try to do that? How did they?

They did several things to preserve food. They could lower it into a well or a cold spring. Sometimes they would cut winter ice from a frozen pond or river and put it in what they called ice houses. Those were small buildings, mostly under the ground. Such places helped keep the ice cool longer. By the late nineteenth century, people who lived in or near towns could also buy ice from an ice factory that made it. Each day a household would put out a sign saying how much ice they wanted—maybe fifty or sixty pounds. The ice would be brought to their home and placed in an icebox, which served as an early refrigerator.

Another way to preserve food was to salt the meat or smoke it and keep it in a smokehouse. If you have ever eaten salty country ham, that is how it was preserved. One boy recalled that in his family's smokehouse his mother always had hams, deer meat, and possum to eat. People also preserved vegetables by drying them in the sun. Later they used home canning to preserve them in a better method. One eastern Kentucky woman recalled that her family had "dried beans, dried pumpkin, green beans dried with the hull on, and black eyed peas. I have been hungry many times for more nourishing food. All children were." But others ate better. (See document 5.1.)

If you were a Kentuckian of the nineteenth or early twentieth century, your choices of food were mostly limited to what you grew or killed. Some honey or molasses might flavor a meal, but often your food was the same from day to day. In one region of Kentucky, a person said that the daily fare tended to be fat pork, beans, potatoes, cornbread, coffee, and a little honey.

Later, people had more choices when country stores opened near them. One man told how when he was a boy the nearest store and post office were ten miles away. It took him a half day to go there and back. Others lived closer to a country store, which would be the economic and social center for the area. There people might receive their mail, buy groceries, buy things for the farm, buy clothes, and just visit with friends. That one store might have a little of everything.

Most people would either buy or barter for flour, salt, sugar, and coffee at the country store. Other choices were all around them, however. Want material to make a dress? That was there. Want a new pair of shoes? You could buy them. Need a new plow for the farm? It could be bought. Want to try something different to eat? The owner could offer canned oysters or canned sardines. Need some pills for an illness? You could buy them

Country stores provided many of the items people needed, all in one place.

DOCUMENT 5.1

Henry V. Johnson grew up in Scott County, Kentucky, in the middle of the nineteenth century. He came from a wealthy farm family and remembered his life this way:

We got our ice from the creek, and in summer we would go fishing and rowing on the Elkhorn.

We had a large garden. We raised many chickens and turkeys, and always had six or eight fat hogs to make sausage and bacon and smoked hams. We had a beautiful cow [that] would bring in great buckets of rich, foamy milk.

We raised all the fruit and vegetables we needed. We put up all the potatoes, cabbage, beets, turnips, and such things for winter. Wheat and corn we sent to our miller, and [we] had all the flour and meal we needed. With the exception of coffee and tea and fancy groceries, we had all on our little farm that we needed. Those were certainly the good old days!

Were they? When we read over what people remember, we should note that studies have shown that as people get older, they tend to forget the bad things and remember the good.

For example, Johnson said nothing about all the hard work on the farm. He said nothing about the fact that slaves did much of that work. It was not the "good old days" for them.

there. From the time of birth to the time of death—from baby clothes to coffins—the country store kept Kentuckians supplied with what they needed. They were like small versions of the larger stores we have today.

Most farmers did not have a great deal of cash and perhaps only got money once a year when they sold their crops. So the country store also served as a bank. The owner sold items on credit and wrote in a book the buyers' names and how much they owed. Once a year people would pay off their debt—or go into more debt to the owner of the store. Do we do anything like that today?

✦ Work ✦

During part of the year, when you get up in the morning you go to school. We will read about what school was like in early days in chapter 11. Let's continue to compare your life with the lives of people in the past, beginning with summertime, when school was not going on.

Remember that conditions varied from city to farm as well as from one time to another. In the city, people could buy more things. They could also go to a library to read, or could go to a play. Yet special problems existed in cities too. One man remembered how people burned coal to heat their houses: "This resulted in an atmosphere laden with smoke and soot and was the bane of the housewife hanging out her laundry for drying." He noted that when snow fell, it looked like it "had been gone over with a huge pepper-shaker." City and farm life could be different.

Most people in Kentucky in earlier times lived on farms, however, and seldom went to the city. You can see just how many farmed by looking at Whitley County in southeastern Kentucky in 1850. People there worked in these jobs:

For a long time, mules made up an important part of most Kentucky farms.

961 farmers	4 millers	1 boat builder
15 blacksmiths	4 barrel makers	1 carpenter
8 preachers	3 doctors	1 grain dealer
8 merchants	2 stonecutters	1 coalminer
7 schoolteachers	2 lawyers	1 silver miner
5 store clerks	2 hat makers	1 chair maker
5 shoe and boot makers	2 tailors	1 sheriff
4 laborers	2 wagon makers	

In this list, how many people were not farmers? What jobs surprise you? Why are there so many blacksmiths? What did black-smiths do?

In Whitley County, more than nine out of every ten people worked on a farm. The same was true of other counties in Kentucky. In good weather, the men and young boys would usually work in the fields. Some of them liked that work. One boy recalled: "There is a sort of thrill that comes to a barefoot boy when he plows up the ground, turns it over, and steps into the fresh furrow with his bare feet. There is a good feel and a good smell to the earth." Others liked to see things grow.

DOCUMENT 5.2

Below are accounts of daily life by two women in Louisville. One wrote her story in 1837. The other described her life 110 years later, in 1947. How can you decide which one came first?

Account A

[My normal week:] Monday—wash clothes and woodwork—Tuesday iron, finish woodwork, darn socks—Wednesday bake, garden, mend clothes—Thursday catch up—Friday clean house and wax floors—Saturday perhaps bake and Bill's home so working with him washing walls or fixing lawn—Sunday church and _relax_.

Account B

I should like to tell how I spend the day. I rise at 6:00 and start a fire with shavings and cord wood. We drink coffee at half-past six and eat meat and wheat bread with butter.

I dress the children, fix the beds and straighten up the rooms. This takes most of the morning. We eat our main meal. After the dishes are washed, I clean up again. When this is done, I have to sew, patch, or knit until towards evening. I prepare coffee or tea which are taken together with bread, butter, meat, and fried potatoes.

In many ways, the daily life of a woman in 1947 could be like life more than a century earlier. What are clues that help you decide which account was written in 1837 and which one in 1947?

But many people found farming hard work. Walking behind a mule that pulled a plow across dusty ground on a hot day could be hard to do. Someone had to get up early to take care of the farm animals every day of the week. Winter might bring relief from tending crops, but not from tending cows, chickens, goats, sheep, mules, horses, or other animals. Farmers planted a crop, kept the weeds out, and hoped it would rain enough—but not too much. Then they harvested the crop and kept what they needed to feed themselves and the animals. Any left after that was sold to pay off debts.

Women worked just as hard as men on the farm. They also had a rough time because they could be very alone. If there was no nearby house or church, a woman might not see

KENTUCKY FACES   Linda Scott DeRosier

She was born Linda Sue Preston in a feather bed in a log house on Greasy Creek in Johnson County, Kentucky, in 1941. Her father worked in a coal mine, and her mother was a teacher before she got married and quit. The family lived near where singer Loretta Lynn grew up in eastern Kentucky.

Linda's book *Creeker* tells her story. In her young days, she never thought about being anything other than a wife and mother living on that creek. "We saw the same folks day after day," she writes. She recalls that she saw no strangers until she was about twelve years old. She might go to church or listen to the Grand Ole Opry and the U.K. Wildcats on the radio, but that was all. It was hard, she writes, "for us to find heroes; God and the Wildcats had to do." That was her small world.

She tells of a typical day for her in the 1950s: "My typical morning involved getting out of bed; hauling the slop jar to the toilet; cleaning myself up [by] taking a sponge bath; going across the road [to get] two buckets of fresh water; eating a breakfast of sausage, eggs, biscuit, and sawmill gravy; and walking to the store to wait for the school bus." As it turned out, school changed her, bit by bit. She went on to college. She married at age nineteen, had a child, then later divorced. She never grew lonely, though: "If there is a book at hand, I am never alone."

Slowly she began to see that she could do more than she had thought: "Education changes the inside of our heads so that we do not see the same world we previously saw. I read those books and truly fell in love. I fell in love with ideas."

Linda went on to get as much education as she could—a Ph.D. She taught college herself and later married a college president. Now as Dr. DeRosier, she still teaches. She has never forgotten her Appalachian and Kentucky roots.

anyone but her husband and children for months at a time. The men often went on hunting and fishing trips with other men or rode to town or to the country store. So they had more variety in their lives.

A woman spent her days doing a lot of different things. She helped on the farm by tending the garden, milking the cows, and gathering the eggs. In her home, she cooked three times a day and cleaned the dishes. She washed and ironed clothes. She swept the floors and dusted. When time allowed, she might sew new clothes, make a quilt, or mend old clothes. She might churn and make butter, or peel apples, or can food. The mother also had to take care of the children, and people usually had big families. Often younger children would help out with some of those chores.

Often men worked on the farm, while women worked in the house.

Young boys and girls often had to work at an early age. This painting shows a boy selling the Louisville Courier-Journal on a winter day.

Something that made a woman's job even harder was the dust. Even in towns and cities, most roads were not paved and were made only of dirt. As people and horses traveled the roads, clouds of dust arose. With no air conditioning, people left their windows open to let in air. Since few homes had window screens until the twentieth century, it was almost impossible to keep the dust off of everything in the house, even for the hardest-working housewife. The open windows also let flies and other insects in.

Yet, many adults remembered the fun they had as children growing up on the farm. They could roam and explore in the woods all around. That was their huge playground. Their parents taught them how to do the work they might do as adults. Young boys looked forward to learning to shoot and hunt and fish. Young girls learned to sew and cook at an early age. They did not expect to have many choices about what they would do when they grew up. Years later that would change. New choices now exist.

★ Health ★

Those open windows and flies and those barefoot walks by children had an effect on the health of people. So did a lot of other things. All of it meant that people of the past lived much shorter lives than we do now. A century ago, the average American lived to be forty-seven years old. People lived even shorter lives than that in frontier times. Many young children died. In many Kentucky counties, one of every three newborn babies never reached their first birthday.

Some of the diseases that struck so hard do not even bother us today. Smallpox, cholera, tuberculosis, polio, and deadly flu epidemics killed thousands of men, women, and children of all ages and races. When cholera swept across Kentucky in the nineteenth century, it left whole towns almost deserted. People either had fled or had died. The great Spanish flu epidemic of 1918 came at the end of World War I. More Kentucky people died of that disease than had been killed in the war. In Louisville alone, the Spanish flu killed some twenty-four hundred people. Overall, fourteen thousand died in Kentucky. That is more than the whole population of some counties.

Many things added to your chance of getting a disease. In schools and public places, everyone drank from the same dipper at the well. That practice spread disease easily. The many outhouses and the waste that horses and other animals left on the streets all brought flies. They too spread disease. In many towns and cities that had water lines, the river water was not filtered. One person in Louisville recalled that the water from the river was yellow and muddy. But people drank it. It too probably carried diseases. In 1909 the city began to filter its water.

The flu killed many people in 1918. Here people at Camp Taylor in Louisville try to protect themselves from disease.

Walking barefoot could result in a health problem also. One study in 1913 showed that over four of every ten people in Kentucky likely had hookworms. Those people had a growing worm inside them that took away their strength.

Also, when people needed to go to a hospital, they might not be able to reach one in time. A woman who grew up in Burnside, in Pulaski County, said that the nearest hospital to her was ninety miles away. In an era of horses and wagons, that was a very long way.

Doctors did make house calls. They would get on their horses in all kinds of weather and go to sick people. Many of the doctors were excellent, caring people. There were no tests or rules for a long time, however, so anyone could be a doctor. Some doctors were so poorly trained that you might be better off not going to them. One Gallatin man recalled of his youth: "For fever, the first thing, the doctor would bleed the patient. Women would get bled for a headache. My left arm has today many scars left by the lancet." Loss of blood would hurt the person, not help. No laws limited drug use until the twentieth century. As a result, many people took drugs that are illegal now. They did not know the dangers and became drug addicts. The drug problem is not new.

Today, many of the health problems of the past have ended. We still find new viruses or epidemics that cause sickness. However, new medicines and shots to prevent disease have helped a great deal. Research and better-informed doctors

Ephraim McDowell performed a pathbreaking operation. It would save many lives. Here he prepares to operate on Jane Todd Crawford, who had a large tumor.

have also aided in making Kentucky much healthier. These days, people live to an average age of over seventy-seven—thirty years longer than a century ago. That has been one of the greatest changes in life in Kentucky over the past century. People now live almost another lifetime longer than before.

Many Kentucky people have helped make a longer life possible. If you walk into the hall in the center of Kentucky's capitol building, you see statues of five nationally known people from the state. One of the five is a doctor. Dr. Ephraim McDowell lived and worked in a house that still stands in Danville. He first came to Kentucky over the Wilderness Road when he was twelve years old. McDowell later went back across the mountains and crossed the Atlantic Ocean to study medicine in Europe. He returned and became known as a skilled doctor. Future president James K. Polk came all the way from Tennessee to be treated by him.

In 1809, Dr. McDowell faced a hard choice. Forty-seven-year-old Jane Todd Crawford had been told she was going to have twins. McDowell, however, correctly stated that she had a deadly tumor that would kill her. Other doctors at the time said to operate meant quick death for the patient. Dr. McDowell and Mrs. Crawford decided to risk it. They had no way to put her to sleep during the operation, so she sang and held on tight to the operating table. It went well. For the first time, Dr. McDowell had done one of the most important operations in medicine. He showed that a person's body could be opened up and they could still live. Five days after the operation, Jane Todd Crawford was on her feet. Less than a month later, she rode home to Green County, where she lived to be seventy-eight years old. Dr. McDowell did the operation other times, too, when people needed it. He became a leader in the field of medicine.

Another national leader in health care was Mary Breckinridge. She had seen her two children both die young.

Breckinridge wanted to make certain that other mothers did not suffer like that. Eastern Kentucky had few doctors. In 1925, she went to live near Hyden in Leslie County and set up the Frontier Nursing Service. A midwife is someone who is not a doctor, but who helps bring babies into the world. For a long time most births took place with a midwife's help. With that fact in mind, Breckinridge began to ask trained nurses to become nurse-midwives. She set up a school to train new people as well. Over the years, her idea worked. Deaths of mothers and babies in childbirth fell to almost zero. People from all over the world came to see what she had done.

Many other Kentuckians improved health care in the state as well. Linda Neville of Lexington started a group to help prevent trachoma, an eye disease that can cause blindness. In one study, it was found that out of about four thousand people in one part of the state, almost five hundred of them—one in eight—had the disease. She helped do away with trachoma. Dr. Joseph N. McCormack and his son Dr. Arthur McCormack, who lived in Bowling Green and other places, together set up county health departments. That did much to help control disease. In more recent times, doctors in Kentucky have also taken a leading role in such things as hand and heart transplants.

Mary Breckinridge and her nurses rode horseback to help mothers and children in the Kentucky mountains.

★ Fun and Games ★

People worked hard and often played hard when the state was new. Once your school day ends, or during vacation times, what do you do for fun? Do you play outdoors with friends? You might watch television or listen to music. Perhaps you read a book or just shop in stores. Playing a video game or watching a movie on a DVD player or in a theater might appeal to you. In the summer you might swim or fish or go boating on a lake. If you like sports, you may go to a soccer or baseball game. In other seasons, there are football and basketball games. Some towns offer museums or concerts or even a zoo or aquarium. Adults might do other things in addition to those just mentioned. They may go to a

Youth soccer has become a popular sport in recent years.

People often worked together on a project. This group is building a barn.

dance at night, or play golf, or go to a race track, or visit with friends, for example.

How many of the things you do for fun did people do two hundred years ago or one hundred years ago?

In frontier times, the division between work and play was not clear. People might come together to help build a house or to take the "shucks" off the corn. When they did that, they often made it like a game with one side trying to do better than the other. Prizes might go to the winner. At the end, they often had a party.

For a long time, people worked this way. A century ago, an eastern Kentucky man recalled how they still worked in groups: "Most of the time we did our work as a family unit, but sometimes the neighbors were called in to help out at clearings, brush-burnings, bean-stringings, and apple-peelings, hay-making, hog-killing, and such." He said the other things they did for fun included square dancing, card playing (Rook), and folk singing.

Across Kentucky, people did simple things for fun. At the end of a workday, they might simply sit on the porch and tell stories. They would talk of the past or share ghost stories. Other times, the family might sit around a flickering fire and sing folk songs. Often these old tunes had been brought from Europe or elsewhere. Hunting and fishing helped supply food for the table, but they also could be fun for those who took part. Every now and then, in later times, something special might happen. A fair or a traveling circus could come through the area and bring some excitement.

In towns and cities, there were always more choices. From almost the earliest days, Lexington had a library, a place to play billiards (pool), and taverns where people came together. One 1814 visitor wrote that "Society is polished and the dresses at the parties are tasty and elegant." A boy of a century ago remembered that in Louisville his family and friends went to watch a live play at a theater—the way we go to a movie now—and enjoyed picnics in the good park system. Girls played cards together while boys went to ball games.

In frontier times, the things people did for fun were usually with the family (singing, for example) or were work related, such as corn-shucking. About the only organized sport was horse racing. That sport has been part of Kentucky culture from the early settlement period. William Whitley of Lincoln County built a track near his home, but with a difference. He did not like the British because they were the enemy in the Revolutionary War. So he had horses run in the other direction than they do on British tracks. That now is the American way.

Racing took place at Oakland Race Course in Louisville before the Civil War. Well-dressed men and women went to watch the horses run.

Isaac Murphy

Many people said Isaac Murphy was the greatest American jockey of the nineteenth century. He rode in 1,412 races and won 628 of them. That is a greater winning margin than any jockey since has had. Three times he won the greatest of horse races, the Kentucky Derby. Murphy was the first to win it two years in a row. Yet his success did not come easily.

"Ike" Murphy was born the same year the Civil War started. His African American father died while in the army, when Murphy was young. The boy and his mother lived in Lexington. There he began racing horses when he was fourteen. At that time most jockeys were black. In fact, fifteen of the first twenty-eight Derbys had African American jockeys on the winning horse.

Just five feet tall, he weighed about 110 pounds. That was about right for a jockey. He had a hard time keeping his weight down as he got older. But Murphy still won race after race. He earned a great deal of money, and he and his wife became leaders in black society.

In 1896, Murphy died. He was only thirty-four years old. Over the years his grave became covered with weeds. No one knew where it was. Murphy seemed forgotten. Finally, someone found it years later. One of the greatest jockeys born in Kentucky now lies with one of the greatest horses—Man o' War—at the Kentucky Horse Park. A sporting pioneer has found his home.

Kentucky had racing all over the state. A year after statehood, Lexington passed a law against "jockeys racing their horses through the streets." By 1800, Kentucky had more horses per person than any other state. The commonwealth became known for its race horses. The Kentucky Derby in Louisville started in 1875 and added to that fame. In the twentieth century, such great horses as Man o' War and Secretariat increased interest in the sport. Racing is the oldest major organized sport in the state.

Another sport that a lot of people watched in early years was boxing. It was done at first without gloves and then later had stronger rules. Boxing did not grow as other sports did. Kentucky did provide three major champions in boxing, though. The best known of those boxers was Muhammad Ali. People all around the globe knew Ali. He may be the best-known Kentuckian worldwide.

Of the sports we think of as major sports today, baseball was the first to flourish. It was played even before the Civil War.

DOCUMENT 5.3

Sports that we may think have not changed much over the years really have. The rules below show how baseball was played in the 1860s. To understand the rules, you need to know the different names they used. The "hurler" or "thrower" is what we call the pitcher today. The "behind" is the catcher, and the "striker" is the batter. A "foul tick" is a foul ball, and to be "dead" is an out. Got all those names? If so, here are some of the nineteenth-century rules (in modern language):

1. The thrower must attempt to throw the ball where the striker wishes it thrown.

2. The thrower must throw the ball underhanded.

3. The striker is obligated to hit well-thrown balls. The umpire may call strikes or even declare a striker dead if the umpire believes the striker fails to swing at well-thrown balls.

4. Foul ticks do not count as strikes. Foul ticks caught in flight or on their first bounce cause the striker to be dead.

5. Runners may not slide into base.

6. Fielders must stand in the middle of their areas until the ball is hit. [That means the second baseman must stand on second, etc.]

7. Runners may not lead off bases.

8. Stealing bases is prohibited. [It was considered a gentleman's game, and gentlemen do not steal.]

9. Fly balls caught in flight or on the first bounce cause the striker to be dead.

10. All handling of the ball should be done with bare hands.

11. The behind may play at any point up to 45 feet behind home base.

12. The shortstop may play anywhere on the field.

13. The four bases are at the corners of a square 30 yards apart.

14. Use of foul language and gambling is prohibited.

What are the major differences between baseball then and now?

After the Civil War, teams formed and paid people to play on them. Those professional teams created leagues. Louisville had teams in the major leagues through most of the last part of the nineteenth century. One boy recalled watching newspaper offices post the scores outside for people to see. He said that

the city "was really a baseball-mad place." Those teams were usually called the Louisville Grays or the Louisville Colonels. By 1900, however, Kentucky teams only played minor league ball. Many people from the state still played at the major league level, though. Four were named to baseball's Hall of Fame—players Earle Combs of Owsley County, Pee Wee Reese of Elkton and Louisville, and Jim Bunning of Ft. Thomas,

and baseball commissioner Happy Chandler of Corydon and Versailles. Most of these players had used Louisville Slugger brand bats. The Slugger Museum in Louisville now tells the story of its bats. All across Kentucky, however, people played baseball. Different towns had their own semiprofessional teams. In most sports, blacks and whites were not allowed to play together until about fifty years ago, so African Americans formed their own teams and cheered for them.

The next major sport that Kentuckians became interested in was football. The first football game in the state was played as early as 1880. For a long time after that, football was the chief sport at colleges. Probably the high point for Kentucky college football came when a Kentucky school pulled off what was called the greatest upset in the first seventy years of twentieth-century football. In 1921 Harvard University was unbeaten and had not lost a game in five years. Tiny Centre College played Harvard and won by a score of six to zero. Since that time, various teams have won some national titles at different levels—Eastern Kentucky University twice, Georgetown College three times. But none of them ever got as much notice as that little Centre College team called "The Praying Colonels" did.

★ Basketball ★

The last of the major sports to be formed is the one that is first in the hearts of many Kentuckians today. Basketball was invented in the 1890s to give people an indoor sport to play in the winter. At first it was viewed more as a game for women than for men. The University of Kentucky had a women's team in 1902, a year before it had one for men.

For thirty years, women's basketball was played in the state. Then in 1932, the last high school women's tournament took place. Women were not allowed to have another basketball tournament until 1975. Soon after that, other sports started their own women's state tournaments—softball in 1983 and soccer in 1992.

During the time that women were not allowed to play basketball, the men's sport grew. At the college level, that growth came about chiefly because of the success of one man. Adolph Rupp grew up in Kansas speaking German and only later learned English. He went to college and learned to play basketball, first from the man who invented the sport and later from the first real coach of the game. When Rupp was twenty-nine, the University of Kentucky (U.K.) hired him as its head coach. Called "The Baron of Basketball," he served there for the next forty-two years. During that time he won more games than anyone else had before him.

Rupp hated to lose. Few of his players liked him very much because he was so hard on them. They did like to win, though. Four times between 1948 and 1958 Rupp's team won the national title. He was not modest. When someone asked him the secret to winning those titles, he said: "That's easy. It's good coaching." Three others who followed Rupp as

In many places, women played basketball before men did. These young women played for the Barrett Manual Training School in Henderson, Kentucky, in 1921.
What do you notice about their uniforms?

Compare the women playing basketball at Northern Kentucky University with those in the previous picture.

Coach Adolph Rupp (center) won four national basketball championships while coaching at the University of Kentucky. Here he is with members for the undefeated 1953–54 team and his assistant coach Harry Lancaster.

coaches at the University of Kentucky also won titles—Joe Hall, Rick Pitino, and Tubby Smith. Those seven national titles ranked U.K. second of all time in major college titles won. By 2004, U.K. had also won more games than any other college team. Rupp and the other coaches had given Kentuckians a reason to feel good about themselves.

Over time, that interest in basketball brought success to other schools in the state. The University of Louisville under Coach Denny Crum won two national titles in the 1980s. At the small-college level, Kentucky Wesleyan in Owensboro has won eight titles, Kentucky State University three, and Georgetown College one. One of the most successful major programs may not have brought home a national title, but Western Kentucky University has won many games over the years. It ranks high in overall victories. Its colorful coach, Ed Diddle of Adair County, gave the Hilltoppers national attention. In his forty-two years at the school, Diddle won his league's title thirty-two times. He, Rupp, and Crum would join many, many players from Kentucky in the national Basketball Hall of Fame.

Western Kentucky University's Coach E. A. Diddle (right) won many games while at the school.

Center Wes Unseld won titles while in high school and in the professional ranks. He is in the National basketball Hall of fame.

In some ways, however, the real heart of basketball in Kentucky is at the high school level. Interest in the sport in towns big and small sparked the growth of basketball. Sadly, not until 1957 was there a true state tournament for high schools. Before then, black and white players had to have separate tournaments. Only after 1957 could players of all races compete together to see who had the best team. Black players like Wes Unseld

could gain statewide respect for their play, as had such white players as "King" Kelly Coleman before them. Only later would both males and females have a tournament.

Kentucky's state high school basketball tournament is called the "Sweet 16." The sixteen teams are from both large and small schools, from all areas of the state. Kentucky is one of the last states where all teams play together. Interest in the tournament really grew because of one championship game in 1928. In it big-school Ashland played Carr Creek, from the mountains. Carr Creek had only eight male students in the school. They had no uniforms or gym. Their basketball goal had a hill behind it. If you made a bad pass or missed a shot, the ball would roll away down the hill. Those two schools played each other into four overtime periods before Ashland won the game. Carr Creek had won the support of Kentucky, although its team lost. Since then, people cheer the underdog small-school teams that come from places like Brewers in Marshall County in the Purchase, which won the 1948 title. Brewers was the last undefeated team in Kentucky high school basketball history.

Kentuckians have played and been interested in many sports other than the major ones for a long time. A century ago, tennis and croquet were popular. People also joined bicycle clubs to enjoy that new invention. Now they might play golf. (One of the first golf courses in the nation was built at Middlesboro more than a century ago.) Fans watch automobile races, where several Kentuckians have been successful. In recent years, more people have begun to play soccer. Many people from Kentucky like to play different sports, and even more enjoy watching them. That is one of the ways life is different now than it was a century or two ago.

A very popular sport is car racing. These drivers are competing at the Kentucky Speedway in Gallatin County.

★ Religion ★

Religion is important to many people today. It was an even more central part of some people's lives in the past.

Religion came to Kentucky early. Of course, the Indians had had their own religious services and beliefs for thousands of years. In the first year of English settlement of the land, the settlers brought their religion to Kentucky. Public worship first

Churches like St. Joseph Cathedral made Bardstown an early center of the Catholic Church in America.

took place at Boonesborough when an Anglican minister offered a prayer. Because Kentucky was still part of England at the time, he asked for the king's blessing as well.

Soon people from specific churches made their way to the new land. In 1781 the "Traveling Church" came to Kentucky from Virginia. Some six hundred Baptists moved as a group. An enslaved man called "Uncle Peter" preached to the slaves with them. That same year, the first Baptist church started in Kentucky at Severns Valley near Elizabethtown. It is said that as many as one-fourth of all the Baptists in Virginia came to Kentucky. They wanted more freedom to worship and found it here. Other Protestant groups came also. Bishop Francis Asbury helped start many Methodist churches, for example.

Four years after the "Traveling Church" arrived, a large number of Catholics moved from Maryland. They journeyed down the river to Maysville, then overland to Nelson County and places around there. As a result, those areas had a very large Catholic population. The first Catholic church was set up in the year of statehood. The first Catholic priest ordained in the United States was Stephen T. Badin. He came to Kentucky to help other Catholics. Soon Bardstown became one of the first four centers for Catholics in the nation and the first one west of the mountains.

Other religious groups came later. Those of the Jewish faith, for example, set up their first place of worship fifty years after statehood. They seemed to be well accepted. Somerset's first mayor was Jewish, as was an early mayor of Paducah and a later mayor of Louisville.

The central event of religion in early Kentucky was what became known as the Great Revival. On the frontier, few churches existed. Long distances between settlements kept people apart. Soon after statehood, a strong spirit of religious feeling started to sweep the commonwealth. It began in Logan County in western Kentucky at the Gaspar River, Red River, Muddy River, and other places. One person wrote of people at the services: "Many fell to the ground, lay powerless, groaning, praying, and crying for mercy."

The movement spread, and the biggest meeting took place in 1801 at Cane Ridge in Bourbon County. The church at the center of the outdoor revival still stands. Later writers have called Cane Ridge the "most important religious gathering in American history." Perhaps some twenty thousand people went to the camp meeting. That was almost one of every ten people in Kentucky at the time.

The Cane Ridge meeting became like a temporary city. A man said that "for more than a half mile, I could see people on their knees in humble prayer." Another told how you could hear the camp meeting before you could see it: "The noise was like the roar of Niagara." He wrote about "the vast sea of human beings" he found there—young and old, black and white, male and female.

People who had not seen many others on the frontier now saw thousands. They lived in a time of great change around them, with life short and dangers all around. At Cane Ridge they could escape from everyday cares. They could also be a part of something that seemed bigger than themselves.

A lot of things happened after the Great Revival. New churches sprang up. In older churches, membership increased. People had a greater sense of order in their lives after the frontier period. Churches seemed more open to new people. In Kentucky the Disciples of Christ or Christian Church started and spread over America. Small religious groups found a friendly home in the state as well. The best known of those was called the Shakers.

Shakers got their name from the fact that they danced and shook in their worship services. They never had many members, but they got a lot of attention because of their beliefs. They said people could have a perfect and sinless society on earth. People could break free of the greed of the world. The Shakers set up villages at Pleasant Hill in central Kentucky and at South Union in the more western part of the state. There they tried to live their beliefs. No member could own property. Men and women had to stay apart.

On a typical day, the Shakers got up at four in the morning, worked for an hour and a half, then ate breakfast. Men and women sat at separate tables. No one spoke. More work, lunch, work again, supper at six, prayers, and then to bed—that was their day. The last Kentucky Shaker died in 1923, but the beautiful Shaker villages still remind us of their ideal.

Black churches, like the Farristown Baptist Church near Berea, have long been a center of African American life.

At the same time the Shakers were gaining members, black churches also developed. The oldest may have been the First African Baptist Church in Lexington. It was started by a slave named Peter, known as "Old Captain." He was perhaps the first black preacher in the state. London Ferrill, a freed slave, followed him as church leader. By the time of Ferrill's death before the Civil War, that church had more than eighteen hundred members. It was the largest church in Kentucky. The Reverend George Dupee set up many other African American churches across the state, especially in western Kentucky. Religion became important to African Americans. Churches helped form leaders who would guide the black community once freedom came and slavery ended. They also were one of the few places enslaved people could come together to talk and hope. The churches offered the promise of a better life in the future.

In the services of many white churches at the time, women sat on one side of the church, and men on the other. Most buildings had little or no heat. In winter, people warmed bricks in the fire, then wrapped the bricks in cloth and brought them to church. They put the bricks on their feet to provide some warmth. A service usually lasted from two to three hours. Some churches had music, but others thought it sinful. After the preaching, people might have a meal on the church grounds, if the weather allowed. That gave people a chance to talk to their neighbors. Young boys and girls often met their future spouses that way as well. Going to church was both a religious and a social event.

Churches had different views on varied matters. Less than a century ago, a group of churches said that dancing was "indecent, immoral, and immodest." They called movies "the devil's work shop." That same group also attacked card playing, Sunday baseball games, and horse racing. Other churches thought these practices were all right. Such differences still exist among religions.

Today in Kentucky, half of all church members in the state belong to the Baptist Church. The next largest religious groups are Catholics, then Methodists. One church organization has its national headquarters in Kentucky. The Presbyterians lead

Thomas Merton

Thomas Merton was born in France to a New Zealand father and an American mother. Both his parents had died by the time he was fifteen. After college, he joined a Catholic religious group of monks in Trappist, Kentucky, near Bardstown. He became a U.S. citizen and lived in Kentucky the rest of his life.

The monks wanted to worship in as simple a way as possible. Their clothes, life of prayer, and hard work did not differ much from those of people living centuries earlier. First of all, they almost never spoke. Instead they used sign language. So they had a place of silence. In a typical day, Merton and other monks would wake at two o'clock in the early morning. They went to prayers and read the rest of the night. With dawn came breakfast. They did not eat meat, eggs, or cheese, and in fact ate as little food as they could. At seven o'clock in the evening, they went to bed. The monks slept fully clothed on a straw mattress with a wood frame. They had little heat, and water sometimes froze in the rooms where they slept. They felt that the hard life helped make their spirits strong.

Merton stood out in that group because he was a writer. The rules said he could not write for more than two hours a day at first. That was enough time. His book *The Seven Storey Mountain* told of his life to that point and became an international best-seller. That and other religious writings made him world famous. At the same time, he grew critical of wealth while there were still poor people. He wrote against war when there could be peace. He opposed waste when there could be plenty.

Merton finally got to travel to other nations to study and learn from their religions. He went to Thailand for a Buddhist-Christian meeting. As Merton stepped from his hotel shower, he touched an electric fan, which electrocuted him. He died in 1968 at the age of fifty-three, exactly twenty-seven years to the day after he became a monk. Thomas Merton remains the best-known Kentucky religious figure.

their churches from their Louisville base. As in the past, religion is important in the lives of many Kentucky citizens.

In this chapter we have looked at how people did things in the past and how they lived. Some things are very different now. Houses and health care have changed a lot, for example. Other things are only a little different. People in the past got credit in a country store. Today we get it through a credit card. There are also things that have not changed much at all. For instance, you might read or swim, or listen to music or talk to friends, just as children did in earlier times.

Although there are many differences between the way people live now and the way they lived in the past, the people of each time period share some very basic things. All of us go through the same cycle—birth, life, death. In all ages, people fall in love. Children are born. All have the same fears and same hopes for a better future. They know happiness; they know sorrow. They have victories; they have defeats.

The important point is that no matter what the time period, people share common emotions. We are bonded to people of earlier times as humans. We all are part of Kentucky's continuing story.

When a death took place in a family, the women would wear long black dresses for a period of time. This is a mourning dress.

DOCUMENT 5.4

When people died in the past, an inventory was made of what they left behind. Below is the inventory for two people who died in Metcalfe County in south-central Kentucky in 1901.

As you look at these documents, think of these questions:

- How did each person live?
- What did they have in their houses?
- What surprises you?

- Compare the two. How did they differ?
- Now look at what they owned. What did they own that most of us do not have today?
- Make an inventory of what you have in one room of your home. How many of those things of today are found in these 1901 inventories?

ESTATE OF DAVID WADE

1 tea kettle	$.25	8 tumblers	$.25
1 muffin pan	$.15	1 molasses jug	$.10
1 bureau	$1.50	3 dishes	$.30
1 sugar chest	$1.00	4 pitchers	$.30
1 book case	$.50	2 mirrors	$.30
1 dresser	$.25	2 lamps	$.50
1 cross cut saw	$.10	16 books	$1.05
1 blanket	$.50	2 chests	$1.75
1 mowing blade	$.25	2 bedsteads	$3.00
1 posthole digger	$.60	2 sugar bowls	$.10
1 family bible	$1.00	12 plates	$.60
1 fruit dish	$.25	2 water buckets	$.10
7 oz. yarn	$.35	1 bushel salt	$.25
11 quilts	$6.35	6 chairs	$.75
3 table clothes	$1.00	3 feather beds	$12.00
1 kettle	$.75	1 set knives and forks	$.50
6 curtains	$.40	1 candle stand	$.65
1 clock	$.50	2 watches	$.85

TOTAL VALUE: $59.45

ESTATE OF **C.C. SMITH**

1 mule	$65.00	25 barrels corn	$75.00
1 mare	$60.00	100 pounds bacon	$12.50
1 cow	$20.00	64 pounds lard	$8.00
1 cow	$20.00	10 barrels corn	$30.00
1 plow	$2.00	1,500 pounds millet	$6.00
1 plow harness	$1.00	47 "shoots" [pigs]	$38.50
1 hoe, 1 ax	$.25	25 shocks fodder	$1.50
1 wagon	$25.00	1/2 bushel salt	$.75
2 beds	$30.00	4 irons	$.40
1 table	$.50	1 churn	$.10
1 cooking stove	$3.00	1 fly brush	$.05
1 set knives and forks	$.50	1 mirror	$.40
1 set, cups, saucers	$.30	1 bedstead	$1.50
1 set chairs	$5.00	1 clock	$.50
1 sewing machine	$3.00	1 surrey [wagon]	$15.00
2 beds	$6.00	1 cultivator	$8.00
1 bedstead	$3.50	1 posthole digger	$.25
1 lamp	$.40	1 washing machine	$3.50
1 dresser	$3.50	1 spade	$.60
1 wardrobe	$4.00	1 pair scales	$.10
1 washstand	$1.50	1 grindstone	$.50
1 dresser	$3.00	1 wash kettle	$1.25
1 cupboard	$2.00	1 roller	$.25
stoneware	$2.00		

TOTAL VALUE: $534.65

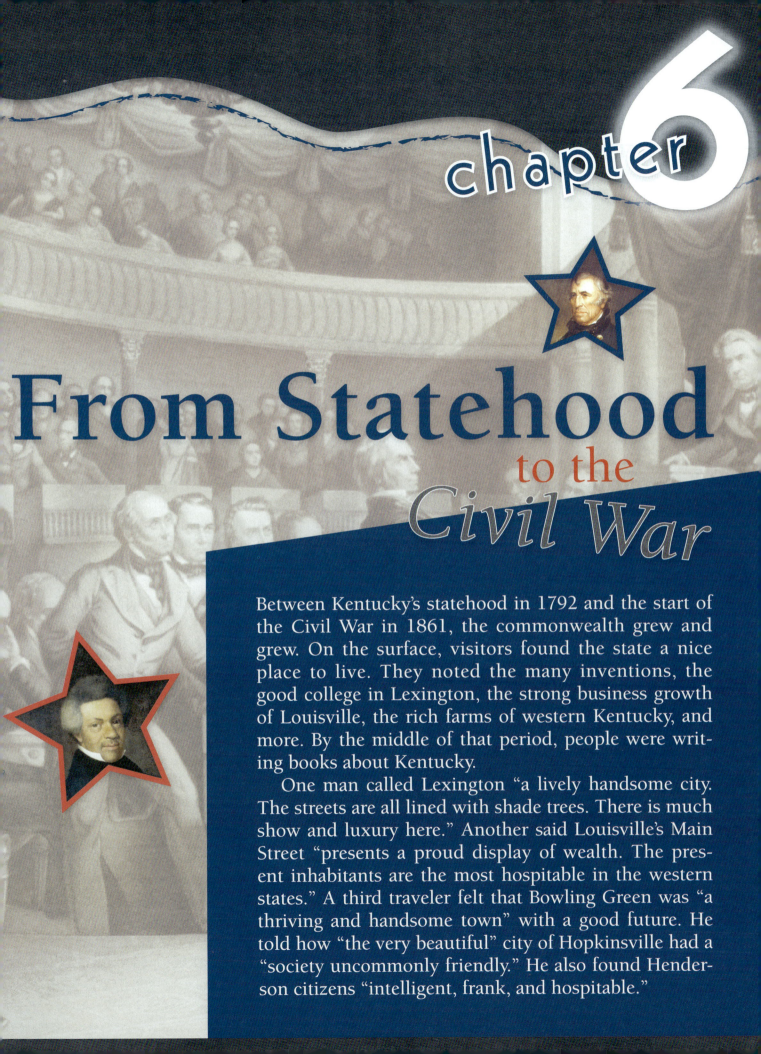

chapter 6

From Statehood

to the

Civil War

Between Kentucky's statehood in 1792 and the start of the Civil War in 1861, the commonwealth grew and grew. On the surface, visitors found the state a nice place to live. They noted the many inventions, the good college in Lexington, the strong business growth of Louisville, the rich farms of western Kentucky, and more. By the middle of that period, people were writing books about Kentucky.

One man called Lexington "a lively handsome city. The streets are all lined with shade trees. There is much show and luxury here." Another said Louisville's Main Street "presents a proud display of wealth. The present inhabitants are the most hospitable in the western states." A third traveler felt that Bowling Green was "a thriving and handsome town" with a good future. He told how "the very beautiful" city of Hopkinsville had a "society uncommonly friendly." He also found Henderson citizens "intelligent, frank, and hospitable."

One of those visitors wrote that in Kentucky "every man stands on his own individual merits." That was not true. Behind the nice towns and friendly people that the visitors described was another Kentucky—the one that refused to let a large number of people in the state go forward on their own merits and ability. These people were kept down because they were enslaved. The visitors said little or nothing about the slaves, even though much of Kentucky's wealth came from slave labor. Slaves' lives were part of the hidden story of the state.

★ Slavery ★

It took the most terrible war in our nation's history to end slavery. Today we may find it hard to understand why people would hold other people as slaves. Why did Kentucky allow slavery to go on? Why was a bloody war necessary to end it? Answers to these questions are not simple.

Slavery is a system in which one group of people controls another group. It comes about when the group in control thinks they are better than the other. They do not feel it is wrong to keep the other group as slaves. They even decide that slavery is good for the slaves. They do not ask the slaves what they want or think.

The group in control forgot that we are all humans. Each person is different and should be judged by his or her actions, not by skin color or beliefs. It is very dangerous to look at a group of people and think that you are better than they are just because they are different from you. Such beliefs caused slavery and have cost the nation much grief over the years.

Long before the English began to settle in Kentucky, there was slavery in America. The enslaved people had been brought from Africa across the ocean to the New World. Many slaves died during that trip. Once the survivors arrived in North America, they had to learn a new language and a new religion. They had to find out about new crops and new ways of doing things. That was hard to do, but they did it. They kept some of the old ways. They sang some of the African songs and used some African words—and some of those words are now part of the English language. The culture that the slaves developed was not

Clara Brown was born as a slave in Virginia. In 1809 her owner brought her to Kentucky. She married and had four children. But her children were sold. After she became free, she searched for them.

African, and it was not European. It was a mix, for each group changed the other. It was American.

Once something has been in place for a long time, it can be hard to change. Slavery had been in America for more than 150 years when Kentucky was settled. We can be glad that some people in the new state tried to end that awful system. Most, unfortunately, did not.

Settlers from Virginia and other places brought slaves with them into Kentucky. The very early explorer Christopher Gist had only his black slave with him when he came to the area. Daniel Boone turned back after his first trip to settle Kentucky, but there were slaves with his group then. On the next try, a slave and a white man were killed in an Indian attack. The two men were buried side by side. The survivors considered them equal in death, even if they did not treat them as equal in life. A slave later died defending Boonesborough; one of every ten people in early Fort Harrod was a slave. Blacks and whites fought together, and both shaped Kentucky.

Kentuckians met to write a constitution just before statehood in 1792. They voted on whether to keep slavery or end it. They kept it by a vote of 26 to 16. Those twenty-six seemed to forget how blacks and whites had fought as equals against their shared enemy. They did not remember enough about how both groups had worked to build a state out of a wilderness. They could not throw off the old ways totally, even on this new frontier. As they planned for their freedom as a new state, they left the slaves out of that freedom. Slavery continued.

A visitor soon after wrote about what he found in Kentucky: "The fertility of the lands generally vastly exceed any thing I ever saw before. But, O Alas! Here, as in Virginia, the slavery of the human race is unfortunately tolerated. Here the cries of the oppressed are heard." Those cries would go on for a long time.

At the time of statehood, about one in every four white families in the new state owned at least one slave. The average number of slaves per family was 4.3. About a half century later, more families had slaves, and the average number had gone up to 5.4 slaves per family. How did that compare to other states? (See document 6.1.)

Although well over half of the white families in Kentucky did not own slaves,

This very old photograph shows slaves being sold at auction at Cheapside in Lexington.

DOCUMENT 6.1

The table below shows how many people out of one hundred Kentuckians were slaves in the years before the Civil War. As you can see, one in every four or five people in Kentucky was an African American slave during that time.

Year	Non-slaves	Slaves	Total
1790	84	16	100
1800	82	18	100
1810	80	20	100
1820	78	22	100
1830	76	24	100
1840	77	23	100
1850	79	21	100
1860	80	20	100

Here are some more numbers from 1850. The second column shows the number of people who held slaves in the states that allowed slavery. The third column shows how many slaves each owner had, on the average. How did Kentucky rank?

State	Number of Slaveholders	Average Number of Slaves per Family
Alabama	29,295	11.7
Arkansas	5,999	7.8
Delaware	809	2.8
Florida	3,520	11.2
Georgia	38,456	9.9
Kentucky	38,385	5.5
Louisiana	20,670	11.8
Maryland	16,040	5.6
Mississippi	23,116	13.4
Missouri	19,185	4.6
North Carolina	28,303	10.2
South Carolina	25,596	15.0
Tennessee	33,864	7.1
Texas	7,747	7.5
Virginia	55,063	8.6

many of them still supported the slave system. Those who owned slaves may not have owned very many compared to other states, but a few did. One man in Henderson owned 214 other human beings. Slavery was not about to end on its own in Kentucky. Slaves had to continue their lives under a slave system.

This rare drawing shows slaves working in hemp fields. In the background are the owner's home and slave dwellings around it.

★ Slave Life ★

Many people have tried to compare slavery to some situation in modern life. Some have said it was like being a private in the army. You had to obey orders and do what people said, but you had some free time to yourself. Others have said it was more like being in jail. You might have some time when you could do what you wanted, but you were limited by the walls around you and the guards watching you. Of course, the main difference is that a prison term can end, and you can leave the army after a time. Slavery was for life.

Other people have tried to study slavery in Kentucky. Many black and white people who saw slavery with their own eyes said slavery was milder here than in other slave states. Whether that is true or not really does not matter. Slavery was still slavery. It was a system in which another person controlled you. If someone had given slaves the choice of being well fed and warm in prison, or being hungry and cold as free people, almost all would have picked freedom. One wrote: "Better liberty with poverty, than plenty with slavery." But freedom remained a distant dream for most of the slaves.

How people treated slaves could be very different from one place to another. Some masters might treat slaves as well as could be expected under the system. Others treated them very badly. Some owners might provide food and clothes that were like those of free workers of the time. Others might give slaves very little. In such ways, slavery was not the same everywhere.

Slaves who were being sold in the South were often chained together as they traveled.

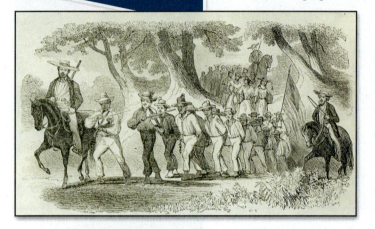

One thing, however, showed that the differences in treating slaves really did not matter. The slave trade in human beings showed how harsh the system really was. People would read newspaper ads like this 1809 one from Bardstown: "For sale a negro man and woman, each about twenty-four years of age, both are excellent plantation hands, together with two children. They will be sold separately or together."

At slave markets, people bought and sold other humans. Some of those they sold stayed in the state. Others were taken farther south. Perhaps eighty thousand Kentucky slaves never saw their old Kentucky home again after they were sold. Even if an owner of slaves did not want to sell them, they could be sold after his or her death to pay off the owner's debts. Under the law, slaves were property, just like a horse or a house.

Young slave Isaac Johnson was eleven years old when his family went up for sale. He was sold first. His four-year-old brother Ambrose went next, to someone else. Johnson's mother came before the crowd. She had her baby Eddie in her arms. Someone said to sell them apart. They took the baby from her and sold him, and then sold her to another person. Isaac Johnson, age eleven, never saw any of his family again. Slavery harmed all it touched, black and white.

Those who were not sold and taken south still made the best living they could under slavery. With hope for a better day, they married. Preachers usually did not ask them to say they would be married "till death do us part." They said the marriage would go on until ended by "death or distance"—that is, a slave sale. Strong black families grew, despite their problems.

In Louisville, black preacher Henry Adams of Fifth Street Baptist Church started one of the first schools for African Americans in Kentucky. All across the state, black churches sprang up. At least seventeen of those churches existed before the Civil War. There the music of spirituals gave slaves a sense of worth and hope for a better life in the future. That enslaved people were able to build such a strong life while under slavery shows the strength of the human spirit. Some also worked to become free at once. They did not want to wait for freedom in the future.

★ Freedom ★

A few—very few—slaves got their freedom either by being freed by their master or by buying it. The best known were the slaves York and Frank.

The famous Lewis and Clark trip to the Pacific Ocean and back could be said to have started in Louisville. That is where the two leaders first came together. About half of the people on that trip to explore new land had some tie to Kentucky. One of them was a slave owned by William Clark, one of the leaders of the expedition. His name was York.

Dennis Doram

Diademia Taylor Doram

These are the only known nineteenth-century portraits of an African American couple in Kentucky. Dennis Doram and his wife Diademia Taylor Doram were free blacks who lived in Danville. Very wealthy for the time, they owned 300 acres of land, four lots in town, eight horses, thirty cattle, and thirty hogs.

York was born in Virginia and came to Kentucky before statehood. By joining Lewis and Clark's group, he would become the first African American to cross what is now the United States. He became an important member of the team. Many Indians had never seen a black man and thought York had great powers. That helped the group. He also hunted for food and aided in other ways. The men gave him full voting rights when they had to make a decision. What they found on their trip set the stage for the next wave of settlers moving west.

When that most famous exploring trip in American history ended, York was still a slave, however. Later his master finally freed him for his help on the trip. York then disappears from the record of history. Some say he died of disease in another state. Others say he went back to Indian lands and became a chief. Either way, he died a free man. Most who had been born slaves could not say that.

The man who became known as Free Frank got his freedom another way. A few owners allowed their slaves to earn money, once they had done their work for the day. Frank spent almost all his time working to earn money to buy his freedom.

He was born a slave in South Carolina, then came with his owner to Pulaski County, Kentucky. Frank met his wife there, and they started a family. Frank hired himself out to work. After seven years, he had enough money to buy his wife's freedom. Why do you think he got her out of slavery before himself? The law said that children became free or slave depending on the

DOCUMENT 6.2

In 1840, slave-owner John Young of Laurel County in eastern Kentucky wrote his will. Seven years later, after his death, it went into effect. In it he tells what he wants done with his slaves:

I make the following disposition from a principle of humanity. I give to my daughter Polly Parker my boy slave Wiley until he arrives at the age of 25 years at which time he is to be free. I give my boy slave Green to my grandson Hiram upon the same conditions. And to my daughter Theny Johnson I give my boy slave Duke upon the same conditions as above. And to my daughter Susan Johnson I give my girl slave Polly until she shall be 21 years of age when she is also to be free. As to my slave Sally it is my desire that she shall be free at my death. As to Juliann I will that she remain a slave, and I give her to my son Pleasant but the child she is now pregnant with I give to my little granddaughter Theney. All of the children of Juliann shall be free at 25 years of age.

At the time of Young's death in 1847, Wiley was seventeen years old, Green fifteen, Duke fourteen, and Polly about seven. How many more years would each be a slave, by the terms of his will?

mother's status. Frank bought her freedom first so that their children would be born free. Two years later, he had funds to buy his own freedom. He kept working and used the money to buy freedom for others.

In 1830, those of his family who were free moved to Illinois. Frank set up a town there. He died in 1854 at the age of seventy-seven. Frank had said in his will that some of his land should be sold to buy freedom for even more members of the family. That money freed seven of his grandchildren and great-grandchildren. Overall, he bought the freedom of sixteen people. Not many slaves were given the chance to do that. He was, and he did everything he could to make sure that his family would not be slaves.

What happened to York and Free Frank was unusual. Most slaves were not freed, and very few slaves had the right to purchase their freedom. Slaves who wanted to be free had few choices. To end their life of slavery, they would have to escape.

Josiah Henson

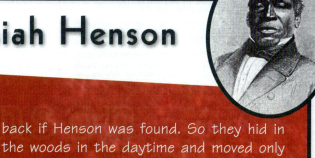

President Abraham Lincoln said that the book *Uncle Tom's Cabin* helped to lead the United States into the Civil War. He told how it caused people to see slavery as the evil it was. The author of that book, Harriet Beecher Stowe, based part of what she wrote on her visits to Kentucky slaves. Different slaves may have been the model for Uncle Tom. One model may have been Josiah Henson of Daviess County in western Kentucky.

Henson was born into slavery in the state of Maryland. His owner sent him to Owensboro to work with slaves near there. In Kentucky he heard white and black preachers and became a Methodist minister. Still a slave, he tried to raise money to buy his freedom. His master cheated him, though, and Henson found out that he and his family might be sold to the Deep South.

In the middle of September 1830, on a dark, moonless night, Henson, his wife, and their four children got in a boat and fled across the Ohio River into a free state. By law, though, his owner could still take him back if Henson was found. So they hid in the woods in the daytime and moved only at night. They had little to eat. The children cried. It took them two weeks to reach Cincinnati, where the hungry Hensons got food. They then headed north. Sharp briars tore their clothes. The howls of wild animals scared them. Finally they got almost to Canada. A friendly white boat captain took them to where no slave catcher could get them. After a six-week trip, they were in Canada.

There Henson preached and started a school. Twice he came back to Kentucky to lead other slaves to freedom. Whether Stowe used him as her model for Uncle Tom is uncertain.

We do know that our state song, written by Stephen Collins Foster, was first called "Poor Uncle Tom, Good Night." Now, of course, its title is "My Old Kentucky Home." Look at the words. (See appendix 4.) Read them as if they were the words of slaves who had been sold away from their old Kentucky home, which was "far away."

Only a few slaves made that dangerous choice. It was hard for a whole family to escape, and if you were caught, you might be taken from your family and sold down the Ohio River out of Kentucky. Other owners whipped slaves who tried to run away. Most slaves struck back at slavery not through escape but in other ways. They might work very slowly to protest slavery. They might also break some work tools and say it was an accident. They resisted slavery in many different ways.

For years people said that runaway slaves found freedom with the aid of the **Underground Railroad.** That name came about when someone asked a Kentucky master how his slaves had escaped, and he said they must have taken an underground road to safety. Of course, the Underground Railroad

$2,500 REWARD!

RANAWAY, from the Subscriber, residing in Mississippi county, Mo., on Monday the 5th inst., my **Negro Man named GEORGE.**

Said negro is five feet ten inches high, of dark complexion, he plays well on the Violin and several other instruments. He is a shrewd, smart fellow and of a very affable countenance, and is twenty-five years of age. If said negro is taken and confined in St. Louis Jail, or brought to this county so that I get him, the above reward of $1,000 will be promptly paid.

JOHN MEANS.

Also, from Radford E. Stanley,

A NEGRO MAN SLAVE, NAMED NOAH,

Full 6 feet high; black complexion; full eyes; free spoken and intelligent; will weigh about 180 pounds; 32 years old; had with him 2 or 3 suits of clothes, white hat, short blue blanket coat, a pair of saddle bags, a pocket compass, and supposed to have $350 or $400 with him.

ALSO---A NEGRO MAN NAMED HAMP,

Of dark copper color, big cheek bones, about 6 feet high, weighs about 175 pounds, 36 years old, with a scar in the forehead from the kick of a horse; had a lump on one of his wrists and is left-handed. Had with him two suits of clothes, one a casinet or cloth coat and grey pants.

Also, Negro Man Slave named BOB,

Copper color, high cheek bones, 5 feet 11 inches high, weighs about 150 pounds, 22 years old, very white teeth and a space between the centre of the upper teeth Had a blue blanket sack coat with red striped linsey lining. Supposed to have two suits of clothes with him; is a little lame in one ancle.

$1,000 will be given for George---$600 for Noah---$450 for Hamp---$450 for Bob, if caught in a free State, or a reasonable compensation if caught in a Slave State, if delivered to the Subscribers in Miss. Co., Mo., or confined in Jail in St. Louis, so that we get them   Refer to

**JOHN MEANS &
R. E. STANLEY.**

ST. LOUIS, August 23, 1852.   (PLEASE STICK UP.)

Runaway slaves sought freedom in the North and in Canada. Many came through Kentucky in their search for freedom. This advertisement offers a reward if the four Missouri slaves are captured.

Delia Webster (bottom of picture, left) helped slaves to escape, but she was put in prison for her efforts.

was a name for a system of escape that was neither underground nor a railroad. According to the stories, a well-planned system helped slaves. They would be taken or would go from one "safe" house to another. Whites and a few free blacks helped move them to safety.

Actually, in Kentucky and in most of the South, runaway slaves usually escaped to free states with little aid. It was too dangerous to trust people in slave states. But once slaves reached one of the free states north of the Ohio River, they might get help there from people who disliked slavery. Josiah Henson and most other African American slaves took no "railroad." They escaped on their own.

In a few cases, slaves had help from other sources, mostly from the few free blacks in Kentucky. The most famous white people to help runaways were Delia Webster and Calvin Fairbank. Delia Webster came from Vermont to Lexington to teach. She and Preacher Fairbank hated slavery. They helped the slave Lewis Hayden and his family escape. Afterward, someone found out what they had done, and both went to jail as "slave stealers."

Webster was given her freedom after only a little while. She moved to Trimble County and helped more slaves escape from there. Finally, people forced her to leave the state. Fairbank had a harder time. He served five years in prison. Soon after he was freed from prison, he started helping runaways once more. Again he went to jail and had to stay twelve more years. During those years, he counted the times he was whipped for having helped slaves. He said that he had been given 35,105 lashes from a whip. When he finally got out of prison, his weight had dropped from 180 pounds to 117 pounds. Fairbank's friends did not know him when they first saw him. He had lived by what he believed and suffered for it.

In one case near Danville, a college student gathered some slaves together and they fled as a group—some forty to seventy of them. They made it to Bracken County, within fifteen miles of the Ohio River and freedom. There they were caught. The student was sent to prison. He died there.

The story of those who gained freedom by running away is mostly a story of one person or one family doing it alone. William Wells Brown, for example, was born in Kentucky and later was taken to Missouri. He worked on a steamboat.

When it landed on free soil, he got off and fled. Brown then helped others escape. He wrote about his efforts in a book. Threats on his life forced him to go to Europe for five years. He wrote a novel. It was the first novel written by an African American in the United States.

Henry Bibb was born into slavery in Shelby County, Kentucky. After he married, his wife's owner bought him and took him to Trimble County. There he escaped when he was twenty-two. Bibb came back to try to free his wife and child, but "slave-catchers" seized him. He escaped again. Bibb tried another time to get his wife but was caught once more. He and his family were sold down the river to the Deep South. Bibb escaped and followed the North Star to freedom in Canada. He also wrote his story to tell others. Bibb later wrote to his former owner, telling him why he left: "To be compelled to stand by and see you whip and slash my wife without mercy was more than I felt it to be the duty of a slave husband to endure. My infant child was also flogged until its skin was bruised literally purple."

Henry Bibb, William Wells Brown, Josiah Henson, and Lewis Hayden—who escaped with the aid of Webster and Fairbank—all became successful in freedom. Their lives showed what slaves could do once they were free. But very few slaves had that chance.

Henry Bibb escaped from slavery several times before he finally was freed.

★ Antislavery ★

Some white Kentuckians did not try to help slaves escape directly. Instead, they wanted to end the whole system of slavery. They did not agree on how that should happen, but they did want to make slavery stop.

At first, a few said that slaves should be freed and then sent back to Africa. That did not work. Only 661 former slaves from Kentucky went to Africa. Why? By that time, the parents and grandparents of most slaves had been born in North America. They saw the United States as their home. They were Americans, not Africans, so the movement failed.

Others spoke out in stronger terms, saying that slavery itself should end. Some said it should end over a period of time, while others believed it should end overnight.

Some in Kentucky boldly spoke out against slavery. One such man was Cassius M. Clay of Madison County.

The most colorful person in that group was Cassius M. Clay of White Hall in Madison County. He once said, "I believe slavery to be an evil—an evil morally, economically, physically, intellectually, socially, religiously, politically, an unmixed evil." When he spoke such words in public, people who owned slaves grew angry. He got in many fights. In one fight, a man shot Clay, but Clay kept coming toward him. Clay pulled out a big knife that he carried and used it to hurt the man who had shot him. Later, Clay found that the bullet from the man's gun had hit Clay's knife case and had not harmed him.

Clay said he spoke against slavery because it hurt the state's growth. He did not stress how it hurt the people held under slavery. Another antislavery leader, John G. Fee, believed that all men were created equal. Born in Bracken County to slaveholding parents, he went against their beliefs. Fee became a preacher and called for an end to slavery at once. He set up a school in Berea to allow both races to attend classes together. Fee and sixty of his followers were forced to leave the state because the things he said and did stirred up anger in those who supported slavery. His words were among the last in the slave South calling for freedom. Soon the issue would be solved not by words but by war.

★ Key Political Leaders ★

Many issues divided the citizens of Kentucky before the Civil War, but slavery brought forth the strongest words. Various political leaders tried to keep the sections of the nation together. They all found that hard to do. Across the United States, people saw Kentucky as an important state in that debate. After all, it had a large number of people for that time. It also was a rich farming state when the United States was mostly a farming nation. A New York paper said of Kentucky: "The followers of Boone have become breeders of fine stock and cattle that have given them a fame everywhere." The state had more key leaders in national political jobs than at any other time, before or since.

Two of those leaders served as vice president. The first was Richard M. Johnson of Scott County. He gained a lot of national attention during the War of 1812 because it was said that he had killed the great

Vice President
Richard Mentor
Johnson

Indian chief Tecumseh in a battle. Later when he ran for office, people cried out:

Rumsey Dumpsey
Rumsey Dumpsey
Colonel Johnson killed Tecumseh.

The wartime hero was elected as vice president of the United States in 1836.

The other person from Kentucky who was a vice president during this time period was John C. Breckinridge of Lexington. His grandfather had been attorney general under President Thomas Jefferson. From the time he was a young boy, Breckinridge knew that people expected him to be great. He did not disappoint them. By the time he was forty years old, the tall and handsome Breckinridge had been a member of the U.S. House of Representatives, had been vice president of the United States, and had run for president. He is the youngest man ever elected vice president. Breckinridge's only political defeat came in 1860, when he lost the race for president to another man born in Kentucky—Abraham Lincoln.

People wanted a person from Kentucky running for either president or vice president because the state had a lot of votes and because it was an important state. In fact, in the last ten races for president before the Civil War, someone from Kentucky ran for either president or vice president in seven of the ten elections.

Three times the person from Kentucky running for president was Henry Clay. (See "Kentucky Faces," page 138.) He lost each time. Yet he is the greatest Kentucky political figure of all time. Clay showed that you do not always have to win to be great. He was a leader.

Many other Kentucky leaders won national attention during this period. Linn Boyd lived in the Purchase area of the state for most of his life and became the leader of the U.S. House of Representatives just before the Civil War. John J. Crittenden lived in Russellville and Frankfort. He had an important and varied career, serving as Kentucky governor, as U.S. senator, and twice as attorney general of the United States. Crittenden suggested a way to keep the nation together as the Civil War grew near, but his plan was not accepted. As a result, two Kentucky-born men became leaders of the two sides when the war did start.

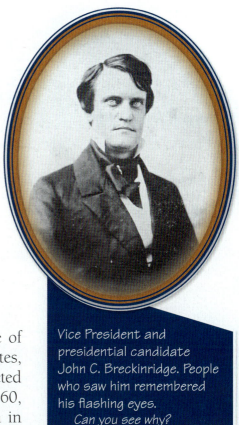

Vice President and presidential candidate John C. Breckinridge. People who saw him remembered his flashing eyes. *Can you see why?*

Henry Clay

Henry Clay was born in Virginia in 1777 and came to Lexington, Kentucky, twenty years later as a lawyer. He married Lucretia Hart, and they had eleven children. However, sadness filled that part of their lives. They had six daughters, and all died before their father did. One of their five sons was killed in the Mexican War, and another spent most of his life in an insane asylum. Clay called his home "Ashland" and enjoyed the time he spent there. The memories of his dead children hurt deeply, though.

A great speaker, Clay became a leader of the nation. On the first day that he stepped onto the floor of the House of Representatives as a member, he was named to the highest job there, Speaker of the House. During the War of 1812, he pushed for the war and then helped make the peace that ended it. Later he became a senator.

Clay gained much fame for trying to keep North and South from breaking the nation apart. He often suggested compromises to settle disputes between the two groups. They called Clay "the Great Compromiser." He spoke for America, not just for one section. Clay said: "I know no South, no North, no East, no West, to which I owe my allegiance. The Union, sir, is my country." During his lifetime, he kept America united.

Three times he ran for president; three times he lost. The last time, a few more votes for him would have made him president. Later, when Clay took an unpopular stand, someone said it might hurt him if he ran for president. Clay said, "I would rather be right than be president." He knew there are times when compromise is the best course. He also knew that on some matters you must not go against what you think is best. You must do what you know is right.

Because of what he did, Clay was more important than many of the presidents of that time. When people not long ago picked the five greatest U.S. senators ever, they named Henry Clay of Kentucky as one of them.

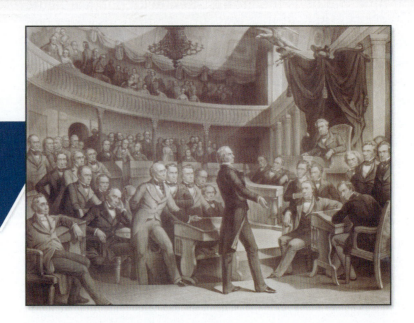

The most important Kentucky political figure of all time was Henry Clay. Here, Clay is speaking in Congress.

★ Three Kentucky Presidents ★

No one has ever been elected president who was living in Kentucky at the time of the election. Kentucky can claim close ties to three people who served as a president, however. Can you name them? Abraham Lincoln is an easy guess, for he was born near Hodgenville, Kentucky. Who else? You could also name Jefferson Davis, for he served as president of the Confederacy during the Civil War. He and Lincoln had been born less than a year apart and within one hundred miles of each other. Who was the third person? A hint: he is the only one of the three buried in Kentucky, and he lived in the state much longer than Lincoln or Davis. He was Zachary Taylor.

Taylor came to Kentucky from Virginia when he was only eight months old. He grew up and married here. Five of his six children were born in the Bluegrass State. His home still stands in Louisville. By the time he was about forty-six years old, he had sold most of his land in Kentucky and moved south. Taylor later became famous as a general in the Mexican War. His troops called him "Old Rough and Ready" and loved him. After that war ended, people asked him to run for the nation's highest office. Taylor had never even voted before. His first vote was for himself for president in 1848. He was an open, frank man of good common sense. Taylor sometimes stuttered when he spoke, but in those days—before radio or TV—few people ever saw a president in person and few knew that he stuttered. He died while still in office, five days after the fourth of July in 1850. Taylor is buried in Louisville.

Taylor also played an important role in Jefferson Davis's life, which is one of the great romance stories of Kentucky history. Davis was born in Fairview in Todd County, Kentucky. His family moved south when Davis was young, but he came back briefly to attend school in Washington County and then spent part of his college years at Transylvania University in Lexington. Later he went into the U.S. Army. There he found himself under the command of Zachary Taylor.

Taylor had a pretty young daughter named Sarah Knox Taylor. She and Jefferson Davis fell in love. When Davis asked her father for permission to marry her, Taylor refused. We are not sure why, but he did. Zachary Taylor got Davis moved to

Mexican War hero General Zachary Taylor became president in 1949. He had lived much of his life in Kentucky, but he did not live in Kentucky at the time of his election.

Kentucky-born Jefferson Davis served as president of the Confederacy.

another army fort, far from Sarah Knox Taylor. The two sweethearts wrote to each other and agreed to marry when she reached the age of twenty-one. When that time arrived, Davis left the army, and they married at her aunt's house in Louisville.

Seldom were two people so happy. They went to the South on their honeymoon. There both of them got malaria, a sometimes deadly fever. Davis heard his young wife singing and thought she was better. He got up from his sickbed to be with his bride. She died in his arms. They had been married exactly three months. For eight years, the heartbroken Davis kept to himself, usually seeing no one other than his family and the slaves on his farm in Mississippi. Finally, he got back into public life and later married a second time. During the Mexican War, Davis rejoined the army. He fought under General Zachary Taylor and was badly wounded in a heroic fight. Taylor visited Davis and said to him, "My daughter was a better judge of men than I was." They became friends at last, but Taylor died only a few years later. Davis lived on and held several important political jobs. By the time the Civil War loomed, people spoke of him as a good leader for the southern cause. If he took that post, he

Lincoln visited his friend Joshua Speed at Farmington in Louisville.

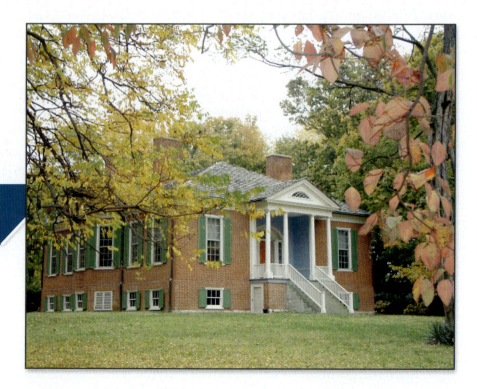

would have to oppose another Kentucky president—Abraham Lincoln.

Lincoln would lead the Union or Northern side when the Civil War started; Davis would lead the Confederate or Southern side. The lives of these two men who were presidents of the two opposing sides were alike in many ways.

Both Lincoln and Davis were born in Kentucky at nearly the same time. Both men married women from Kentucky. Both of them kept their ties to the state after they left it. Davis did so by going to two Kentucky schools. Lincoln's three law partners were from Kentucky. His best friend was Joshua Speed, and he visited him in Louisville. Speed's family home of Farmington can still be visited there.

Both Jefferson Davis and Abraham Lincoln left the state when they were young. One went north and the other south. Did you ever wonder what the nation's history might have been if each had gone the other way? Both of them would suffer several political defeats. Yet they worked on. Both found out that learning does not end in a classroom. They continued to read and learn after their formal schooling ended. Both men also had great family losses. Davis had six children; five died before their mother did. Of Lincoln's four sons, three died before their mother. Both men would seek peace. Lincoln wanted peace for a united nation. Davis sought peace for what he hoped would be a new nation.

Lincoln in wartime with his son Thomas ("Tad").

Abraham Lincoln was born in 1809. His grandfather, who had the same name, had been killed by Indians. Lincoln's mother may have been able to read but could not write. His father was not poor, as many stories claim. His father did have trouble with the land he bought in Kentucky, though. That is probably why he left the state when his son was only seven. Before that, Abe Lincoln had almost drowned near their Knob

Kentucky Faces — Julia Ann H. Tevis

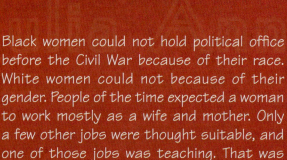

Black women could not hold political office before the Civil War because of their race. White women could not because of their gender. People of the time expected a woman to work mostly as a wife and mother. Only a few other jobs were thought suitable, and one of those jobs was teaching. That was what Julia Tevis did.

Born in Clark County, Kentucky, she moved with her family to Virginia, then to Washington, D.C. Julia met Methodist preacher John Tevis, and they soon married. Husband and wife came back to Kentucky, and in 1825 she set up a school in Shelby County. Tevis called it Science Hill Female Academy.

Very soon, it gained national notice as a fine school for young women. Unlike most other people of that time, Julia Tevis thought that women should not be trained just to be wives. Her school offered classes in such subjects as math and science. She hired teachers who could speak foreign languages and who knew many different things. As a result, a large number of students came to her school. Just before the Civil War, Science Hill had 230 young women in its classes, most of them from the South. When the Civil War came, however, Tevis supported the North. It was simple, she said: "The Negroes must be freed."

Julia Tevis wrote her story in the book *Sixty Years in a Schoolroom*, which was published in 1878. Two years later she died. She had been a leader in women's education. Her school building still stands in Shelbyville as a reminder of her belief. She said, "Woman's mind is limitless. Help it to grow."

Creek farm. A young boy saved him. We barely know the boy's name, but that one action would have a big effect on the nation's history.

Lincoln moved to Indiana. His mother died there when he was ten. His father remarried another Kentucky woman, and Lincoln loved her deeply. He and his father did not get along, however. Later, Abe Lincoln moved to Illinois and made that state his home. He was a clerk in a store, ran a grocery, and served as postman. Then he became a lawyer and entered politics. His ideal leader was Henry Clay.

In Illinois, Lincoln met his future wife. She too was from Kentucky and was visiting relatives there. Mary Todd and Lincoln did not seem much alike. He was tall—six feet and four inches, a giant for his day. She was short. Lincoln had had only about one year of schooling. Mary Todd was one

of the best-educated women in America at that time. He was quiet and humble. She was brash and open in her words. Abe Lincoln came from a family without wealth. Mary Todd came from one with great wealth. He made friends easily. She made enemies easily.

They married. Mary became very important to Lincoln's success. She could help him meet people from her wealthy class. That aided Lincoln in politics. Mary Todd Lincoln could also see great things in her husband's future. She helped push him to greatness.

Lincoln began to attract attention. This man with black hair and gray eyes was not a great speaker. He was also a very poorly educated man as far as school went. However, Lincoln could express himself in the written word perhaps better than any other president. He did not always react the same way to

DOCUMENT 6.3

Here is Lincoln's favorite poem. You may have to look up some of the words in a dictionary. What is the point the poem makes? Why do you think Lincoln thought so much of this poem?

'Tis the wink of an eye, 'tis the draught of a breath—
From the blossom of health, to the paleness of death,
From the gilded saloon to the bier and the shroud;
Oh! Why should the spirit of mortal be proud?

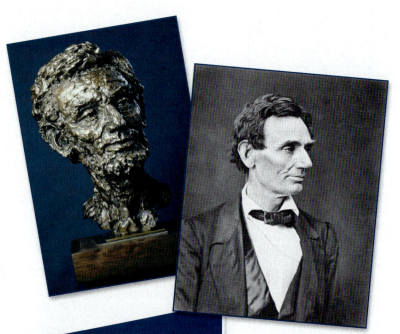

Sculptors are artists who use their skills to create images as seen through their own eyes.

Compare this sculpture of Lincoln to a photograph of him before he grew a beard.

things. Lincoln tried to be flexible and look at each problem separately. When he spoke on the issue of slavery before the Civil War, he saw that it was tearing the nation apart. Lincoln told his views clearly: "A house divided against itself cannot stand. I believe this government cannot endure, permanently, half slave and half free. I do not expect the house to fall—but I do expect it will cease to be divided." Years later his leadership kept the house—the nation—together.

All these Kentucky politicians were major national leaders—Lincoln, Davis, Taylor, Clay, Breckinridge, and Johnson, among others. They could not prevent the coming of the Civil War, however. Once more Kentucky would become a "dark and bloody ground."

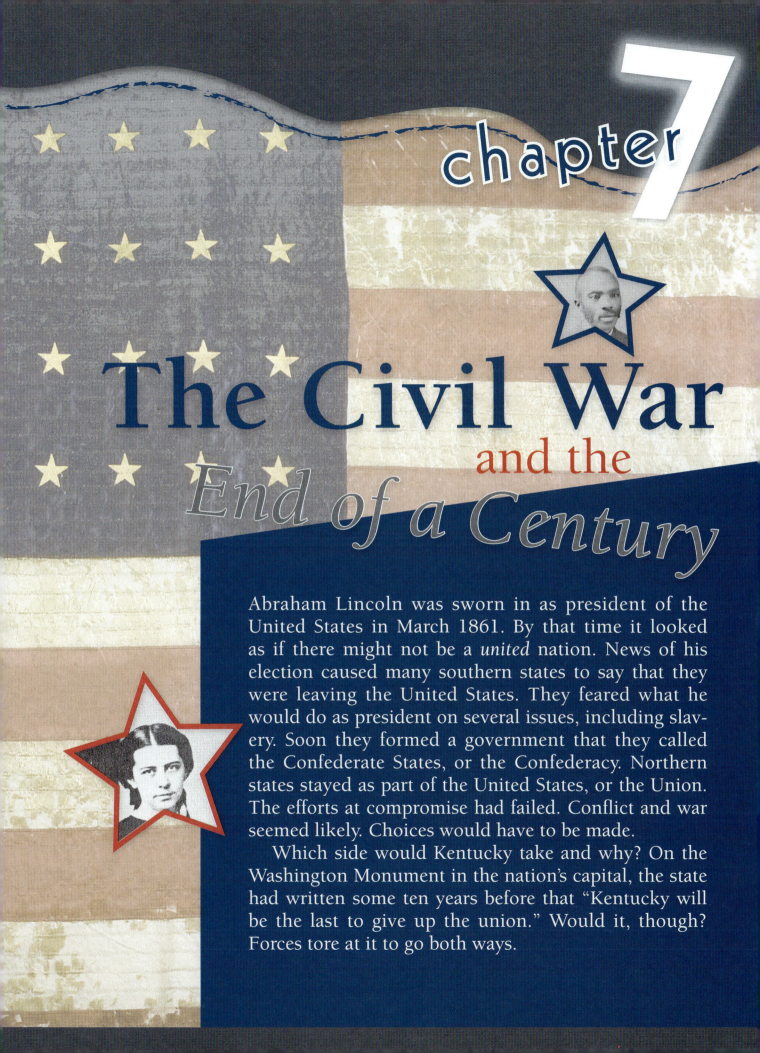

chapter 7

The Civil War
and the
End of a Century

Abraham Lincoln was sworn in as president of the United States in March 1861. By that time it looked as if there might not be a *united* nation. News of his election caused many southern states to say that they were leaving the United States. They feared what he would do as president on several issues, including slavery. Soon they formed a government that they called the Confederate States, or the Confederacy. Northern states stayed as part of the United States, or the Union. The efforts at compromise had failed. Conflict and war seemed likely. Choices would have to be made.

Which side would Kentucky take and why? On the Washington Monument in the nation's capital, the state had written some ten years before that "Kentucky will be the last to give up the union." Would it, though? Forces tore at it to go both ways.

Kentucky first tried to be neutral in the Civil War. Officially, the state would eventually stay with the Union (the North). But those who supported the Confederacy (the South) set up their own government. So Kentucky had a star in both flags. These flags listed the battles where they had been carried.

Do you see one battle where soldiers carrying these flags fought against each other?

Kentucky had ties to both North and South. Some people had left the state to go and live in other states. A decade before the war, some 160,000 natives of the state were living in the North, and about 108,000 in the South. The commonwealth was a slave state, like the South. It also had strong business ties to the North, as well as to the South. The Ohio River flowed through states free of slavery, into the Mississippi River, which went south into slave states. The choices were hard.

Those choices grew even more difficult. The Confederates began shooting at Fort Sumter in South Carolina, and the war had started. Union soldiers there were led by a man from Kentucky, Robert Anderson of Louisville. People at the time gave the war different names—the War of the Rebellion, the War between the States, and others. Most people today call it the Civil War.

Kentucky knew the cost of fighting. It had lost citizens in the frontier period, during the War of 1812, and in the Mexican War. The state of great compromisers like Henry Clay and John J. Crittenden did not see the need to fight as much as some others did. So the state first took an unusual action. Kentucky declared itself neutral. That meant it was not on either side. You had the Confederate States, the United States, and Kentucky—almost like three nations.

Lincoln as U.S. president and Jefferson Davis as Confederate president each knew how important Kentucky was to his cause. Each wanted his native state to join his side. Lincoln said, "I think to lose Kentucky is nearly the same as to lose the whole game"—the war. Why did they think Kentucky was so important? What do you think?

Part of the reason for Kentucky's importance was geography. If Kentucky supported the South, the Ohio River would be a great defense line. Remember that no bridges went across the river then. It would be hard for Union armies to go into the South, if Kentucky became Confederate. The state also had a lot of people. It was the third largest slave state. If it supported one side or the other, it could supply many men for one army or the other. Kentucky was also a very rich

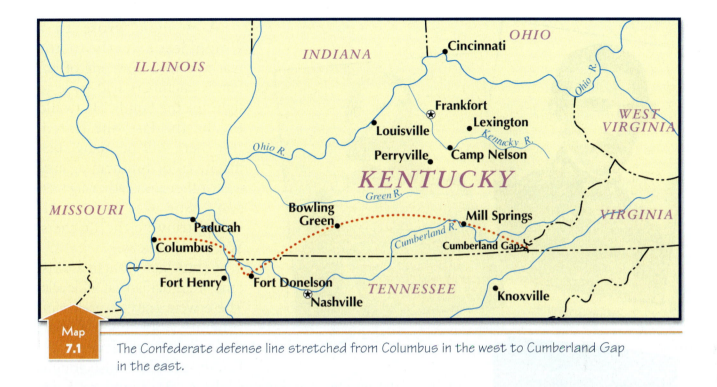

The Confederate defense line stretched from Columbus in the west to Cumberland Gap in the east.

farm state. Its horses could be used by the army, and its crops could feed soldiers. Both sides wanted Kentucky.

For four months the state stayed neutral. Slowly it was moving closer to the Union cause, though. Finally in September 1861, Kentucky decided to remain in the Union. Now people in Kentucky at last had to answer the question, "Who am I, Yankee or Rebel?" How did your ancestors answer?

★ The Brothers' War ★

The people who supported the southern cause at that time did not agree with Kentucky's decision to remain in the Union. They met at Russellville and set up what they called the Confederate State of Kentucky. They made its capital at Bowling Green. That group asked the Confederacy to let them join it. At the end of the year, Kentucky became the thirteenth star in the Confederate flag. Since Kentucky officially never left the Union, it also had a star in the United States flag. That Kentucky had a star in both flags showed the divisions within the state. Kentucky people, more than those of any other state, fought each other. That meant heartbreak.

George Bibb Crittenden

Thomas Leonidas Crittenden

Kentucky brothers often fought on different sides of the war. That was true of the Crittenden family. George Bibb Crittenden became a Confederate general and Thomas Leonidas Crittenden became a Union general.

A woman wrote to a Union leader early in the war and told how one of her family members had gone to fight for the South. He would not be the last, she feared, "for there will be many such instances of brothers against each other and father against son." She was correct. It would truly be the Brothers' War for Kentucky.

Kentuckians fought against other Kentuckians at all levels. There were sixty-seven Union generals from the state and thirty-eight Confederate ones. Family members also fought others in the family. U.S. Senator John C. Breckinridge left his Senate post and became a Confederate general. His uncle, a strong supporter of the Union, saw two of his sons ride south, two north. Crittenden had one son as a northern general, another as a southern one. Even the nation's highest office was not spared those hurts. Mary Todd Lincoln was the wife of the leader of the Union, yet her brother, three half-brothers, and three brothers-in-law fought for the South.

It was not just the famous families that were divided, of course. In an early battle just outside Kentucky, a Confederate brought in a wounded Union soldier. Another Confederate soldier saw the man and knew it was his brother, who was fighting on the other side. He tried to help him, but the Union brother died that night. The Confederate brother fought on.

Harrison County in central Kentucky was like a lot of counties in the state. It had about 2,400 men over twenty-one years old—of fighting age. Some 1,400 people from that county joined one army or the other. About 800 fought for the South, 600 for the North. In a battle in the county, U.S. colonel George W. Berry was shot. On the other side that day was his son. The son had asked not to fight, so he would not be shooting at his father's Union unit. When the son learned of his father's wounds, he went to him and they were reunited amid tears. The father died six days later. His was only one of many, many deaths.

Before the Civil War ended, about 100,000 people from the state fought for the North and about 40,000 for the South. Everyone knew that many would not return. They just hoped it would not be their husband, son, or brother who died. A woman wrote when she saw her brother leave: "I felt as if I would never see him again. I put my face down on the gate and cried with all my heart." Many would shed tears before the war ended.

★ On the Battlefield ★

Some four hundred battles and small fights took place in Civil War Kentucky. Few of them were major battles. After the January 1862 Battle of Mill Springs in south-central Kentucky, Confederates left the state for a time. Then they came back in an attempt to capture Kentucky. In August 1862, at the Battle of Richmond, the South won a major victory and those troops got as far as Frankfort. There they placed a Confederate flag over the capitol. It was the only time in the Civil War that a Union state capitol was taken by the South. U.S. forces made them leave only a few hours later, however.

The major battle in the state was also one of the most important in the war. If the Confederates had won, they could have possibly gone on into the North. Geography played a role. In the hot, dry fall of 1862, the two armies needed water to drink. Both found it near Perryville. Soon the two forces

The faces of young men who fought in the Civil War.

A drawing of the Battle of Mill Springs in Wayne County. Which side do you think the artist who drew this supported?

Julia Marcum

In the first year of the Civil War, Julia Marcum was sixteen years old. She lived in Tennessee. Her family supported the Union cause in a Confederate state. One day, Confederate soldiers came to her family home looking for her Unionist father. They did not find him, and all left except one soldier. He stayed behind, and a fight broke out. In the fight, he hit Julia in the eye with the sharp bayonet on his rifle. She struck back and hit him with an ax. He fired and shot off her finger. At that moment her father rushed in and killed the Confederate. Julia never saw out of her injured eye again. The family soon fled from Tennessee and came to Casey County, then moved to Pulaski County, Kentucky. Her father was later killed in the war.

After the Civil War ended, Julia Marcum went back to Tennessee and taught school for a while. Her wounds grew worse. At that time, a soldier hurt in the war could apply to the U.S. government for aid. Julia applied for that support, and she got it. She is probably the only woman recognized by the U.S. government to have fought in the Civil War—not as a member of an army but as a defender of her home.

Later, Julia Marcum moved to Williamsburg, in Whitley County, Kentucky. She died there in 1936, at the age of ninety-one.

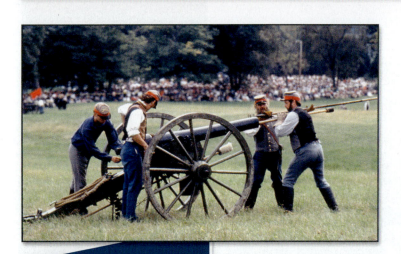

A modern-day view of the Perryville battlefield as people re-create the fighting.

started fighting there. In one day the Union lost about forty-two hundred men who were either dead or hurt. The Confederates lost some thirty-four hundred. One person recalled, "The ground was slippery with blood." (See document 7.1.)

Neither side had won. The next day, though, the Confederates started to move out of the state. The last major invasion by the South had ended. After that, only smaller raids took place, led by men on horseback like General John Hunt Morgan of Lexington.

Whether the fighting was in Kentucky or outside the state, soldier life was hard. First of all, many people got sick. At the beginning of the war, most of the soldiers had never been in large groups of people. They had lived on farms far away from one another. When they came together in big armies, they got many diseases they had never been exposed to before. Many died. Union soldier John Tuttle of Wayne County wrote about

DOCUMENT 7.1

Twelve-year-old William McChord walked over the Perryville battlefield the day after the fighting ended. He went to a hospital. At that time, doctors did not know very much about what caused diseases or infections. Often if a soldier was shot in the arm or leg, the doctors would cut off the wounded area. If they did not, the infection from the wound might kill the person. Nowadays we can easily treat such wounds. Civil War doctors could not. Young McChord later wrote of the horror he saw at one of those hospitals:

The house, tents, and yard were full of wounded Federal and Confederate soldiers. I can never forget the groans, wails, and moans of the hundreds of men as they lay side by side, some in the agony of death, some undergoing operations in the corner of the yard. Near the table was a pile of legs and arms, some with shoes on, others with socks, four or five feet high. The dead were in a row 300 feet long, every one with eyes wide open with a vacant stare.

his feelings: "We buried 11 of our regiment there. It looked a little hard to see the body of a friend of happier times now simply rolled in a blanket, dropped into a shallow hole, and covered with earth." Later, troops marched and slept outside in all kinds of weather, which hurt their health as well. They also did not know much about germs and often drank impure water that made them sick. In fact, more people died from disease during the Civil War than died from bullets.

Being a soldier could be boring. Most of the time, the men marched or stayed in a tent in a camp waiting for a battle. They might practice for the fight, or play cards, or go to a religious service, or play baseball, or read letters from home, or do other things. Then came the battle. Perhaps the best way to understand what they felt is to listen to the soldiers telling about it.

Many had gone to war filled with excitement. They wanted to fight and be a part of the war. The reality of war soon caused them to change their minds. Union soldier Terah Sampson wrote to his Shelby County mother. He had to tell

Confederate General John Hunt Morgan and his wife Mattie.

DOCUMENT 7.2

One of the important things we can learn from history is **perspective.**

Often when we see something or do something, we act or think only from our own perspective. That is, we react only from what we have personally seen or done. History tells us how others acted, or how others viewed things. By seeing their perspective, looking at an issue through their eyes, we can make better decisions. We can balance different views and then decide. We need to have a broad perspective in our life.

Look at these two examples. Both tell about the same soldiers—Confederate John Hunt Morgan's men. In the first account, a nineteen-year-old girl tells what she saw. She supported the Union.

A sketch by Union supporter Frances Dallam Peters, possibly a portrait of herself.

Frances Dallam Peters of Lexington wrote of Morgan's soldiers: "A nasty, dirty looking set they were; wore no uniforms but were dressed in grey. They looked like the tag, rag, and bobtail of the earth and as if they hadn't been near water [for over a year]."

Lizzie Hardin, a supporter of the Confederacy.

Now compare that to the reaction of another young girl. Lizzie Hardin of Harrodsburg was a strong supporter of the Confederates. In fact, she refused to go to her usual church because the preacher supported the Union. She told of meeting Morgan and his men: "At last I saw John Morgan. He was exactly my ideal of a dashing cavalryman. Tall and well formed with a very handsome face. His whole dress was clean and neat."

Two girls from the same time and area wrote about the same group. Each viewed the soldiers from her own perspective. The two gave very different views. What we have to try to do is to look at both perspectives and then form our decisions. That is true in things we do today, also. For example, we may think food in the cafeteria is either good or bad. That is our limited perspective. If we go to other schools and eat there, we get other perspectives. When we come back, we can make a fairer decision about our food. That is because we are looking at it from a broad perspective.

her of his brother's death in battle. Said Sampson: "I have always wanted to see one battlefield and now I have seen it and now I never want to see another." Later he wrote that "There is no fun in war. It took 4 days to bury the dead." A Confederate soldier from Owen County later recalled his days of service. James H. Dorman said, "I was in 42 engagements in all. But I went through them all without a wound. My advice is to keep out of war, if you can do so without a sacrifice of principle and honor."

Despite all the hardship and the deaths and dying, most soldiers fought on to the end. Men were willing to die and give their last full measure of devotion to their cause, North or South.

One of the most detailed stories told by a soldier is that of Confederate Edward O. Guerrant of Sharpsburg in Bath County. He kept a daily record of what took place. Guerrant was a teacher before the war. At age twenty-three, he entered the army. He wrote about his feelings in his first battle. Guerrant thought to himself: "They were men like we that know each other. Never had harmed each other. Personally had nothing against each other. Why [were] *they marching up to kill us*? Strange. No one can fully appreciate this war until he has seen a battle."

Less than a year after he entered the army, Guerrant said, "I want to see no more battle fields. Horses shot dead and the dead and wounded men lying there *alone—alone—alone*." Later, Guerrant's own brother was killed. He was twenty-four. On Christmas Day one year, Guerrant wrote, "We washed our faces in snow, eat our breakfast off a piece of cold cornbread and beef and waited for the war to close. That's all we have to hope for in this country." Finally, on the last day of April 1865, he and his men marched into Mt. Sterling and gave up to the Union troops. They came, wrote Guerrant, "to bury hopes that had been cherished for years, and baptized in the best of blood." Guerrant was one of the lucky ones. He lived. He went on after the war to become a doctor, to heal the hurts of the living, and then a preacher, to heal their souls. Guerrant never forgot the war and became a different man because of it.

★ Guerrillas ★

During wartime, a **guerrilla** is someone who fights outside of a regular army unit. Sometimes small groups of guerrillas would go on raids and attack the enemy as part of one side

Cartoonists often draw things different than they really are, to make a point. Famous cartoonist Thomas Nast supported the Union. Here he drew a scene to make Confederate general John Hunt Morgan look bad.

What kinds of things did Nast include to do that?

or the other. All too often in Kentucky, however, such groups became lawless bands. Some took revenge on their enemies. Others became almost like outlaws. They were a nightmare for Kentucky.

In wartime, many of the men were gone from their families and their farms because they were fighting in the war. Kentucky really did not have a state police force at the time. As a result, many people in small towns and on farms had little or no protection from the lawless guerrillas. They would ride into towns and take what they wanted. Some robbed banks and stores. Some killed people who tried to stop them. Some burned courthouses—twenty-two were burned during the war. A preacher in Logan County in western Kentucky wrote after a year of the war had passed: "My heart is sad over the evils that threaten us. I fear Kentucky will again be the dark and bloody ground. Guerrilla bands are hovering over the state."

In Wayne County in south-central Kentucky, lawyer John W. Tuttle recalled how bad things had been there: "Lawless bands were continually prowling about through this region of country, stealing, robbing, burning. The people knew if they shipped one gang out, another larger one would come and destroy the town." A captured Union soldier worried about his sister's safety back in Kentucky. "Guerrilla bands are said to be roaming at will through many parts of the state," he wrote.

Those guerrilla actions left very bitter feelings. Some people struck back in lawless actions of their own. No law was enforced. Personal actions ruled. The lawlessness did not stop when the war ended, either. People had become used to taking personal revenge, and it went on for years. It was one of the bad results of the war.

★ Results of the War ★

Many changes resulted from the Civil War.

First of all, a very good result was that it ended slavery. During the war, Lincoln had said that African Americans who fought for the North would become free. About half of all male slaves in Kentucky who could fight, did fight. Many of them joined the army at Camp Nelson in Jessamine County. Only one other state had more black soldiers than Kentucky. African Americans fought for their freedom. They earned it.

Just before the war ended, the Union also said that any wives and children of black soldiers would be free. Still, some African Americans remained enslaved at the end of the Civil War. It was the Thirteenth Amendment to the U.S. Constitution that officially ended slavery for all people. Kentucky was one of the two last states where slavery officially existed. It had finally ended, though.

A second result of the war was that Kentucky and its citizens' views had changed during the war. At the beginning, many people had supported the Union. But as the war went on, the Union army made mistakes. They made people angry by their actions in the state. At the same time, the North began to push for an end to slavery. Kentucky wanted both the Union and slavery—an unusual stand. When the Union began to free slaves, some people in Kentucky grew angry. By the end of the war, Kentucky had begun to favor the South more. The state became more southern after the Civil War.

A third result of the war was the effect it had on the state's farms and businesses. A Harrison County man came home from the war: "I found the farm stripped of all livestock. The farm was in very bad condition after four years' neglect." The same thing happened all over Kentucky. The state now had 90,000 fewer horses, 170,000 fewer cattle, and half the

African American soldiers in the Civil War paved the way for others to follow. Charles Young, born at Mayslick, would become the third African American to graduate from the U.S. Military Academy at West Point. By the time of World War I, he was the highest ranking black officer in the army.

and a half later at the age of thirty-seven. Her four children would never forget the effect of the war on their parents.

Another result of the war had to do with the living. More than other states, Kentucky had been divided. As a result, the living had much anger toward people around them. Some forgot the war, made friends with old enemies, and went on with life. But some could never forget. They might walk down a street and see someone who had killed their friend. Those feelings made it hard for Kentucky to follow the first part of its motto: "United we stand; divided we fall." After the war, the state found it hard to be united.

★ From the End of the Civil War to the Start of a New Century ★

Many changes took place in Kentucky over the years between the end of the Civil War and the start of the twentieth century. The greatest change came for those who had been slaves and now were free. The state of Kentucky and many people in it did little to help African Americans make that change. Slowly, however, they began to make a new life. Private schools started to educate the former slaves' children, and then later there were state schools for them. In most cases, blacks and whites went to different schools. That would not change for almost one hundred years. African American males got the right to vote soon after the war. Many southern states kept them from voting, but Kentucky did not. That would be important.

Most of all, leaders of the African American community came forth to help blacks move into the twentieth century. Nathaniel Harper of Louisville became the first African American lawyer, and Henry Fitzbutler was the first black doctor. Dr. Fitzbutler could not use white hospitals and fought such rules all his life. Albert E. Meyzeek of Louisville led several black schools and also showed how unfair it was to keep the races apart.

Over time, many African Americans left the state because of the rules that kept the races apart. They

Nathaniel Harper, the first African American lawyer in Kentucky.

Elijah Marrs

Marrs was born in Shelby County to a free black father and a slave mother. He therefore was a slave. While in slavery he learned to read and write, at night and in Sunday School. Later, when the Civil War started, he read the newspapers to other slaves so they could find out what was going on.

When he was twenty-four years old, in 1864, he led twenty-seven other slaves away from their owners and into the Union Army. Marrs "felt freedom" for the first time. He wrote later of his thoughts on that first day in the army: "This is better than slavery." Once while in the army, he met the son of his former owner. "We talked freely of old slave times," said Marrs. They parted friends, and the son gave Marrs a box of cigars.

His army unit moved all around central and south-central Kentucky. They won a few small battles but once were captured by the Confederates. They were worried that as former slaves they might not be treated well, but they were. After their release, Marrs helped take 750 Bowling Green blacks to the safety of Camp Nelson. There they could get protection.

With war's end, Marrs used three hundred dollars that he had saved to start a new life as a free man. In Shelby County, some men once tried to scare him away, but he drove them off. Later Marrs taught school in Simpsonville, New Castle, and LaGrange. Usually he was the only teacher for 100 to 125 students. He went to college briefly and then decided to start a new college in Kentucky. Marrs and his brother started in 1879 what soon became known as State University, in Louisville. It was the first African American–led college in the state.

Marrs became a Baptist preacher in Louisville and still spoke out for black rights. Freedom had been won, but not equal rights. He died in 1910, still fighting for that goal.

hoped to find better jobs or more freedom in the North or West. Some did. Some did not. At the same time, many immigrants began coming to America once more after the Civil War ended. Before the war, many of the German and Irish immigrants had come to Kentucky. But not many of the new group of immigrants after the war settled in the state. With few immigrants coming in and many blacks leaving, Kentucky did not grow in population as much as other states did.

The story of what happened in Kentucky in those years after the war's end is not a very happy one. Farmers faced hard times and grew unhappy over low prices for their crops. The lawless times filled prisons, which became overcrowded. Railroads crossed the state, bringing both new growth and also more control of some areas by the railroads. Another war—the brief Spanish-American War—took place. A new constitution was written. Near the beginning of the twentieth century, some good writers and artists began to have success. Overall, however, those were not good years for Kentucky. The chief thing that marked them was widespread violence.

★ Feuds and Murders ★

Killing went on in Kentucky long after the war ended. At first it was aimed mostly at the newly freed slaves as they sought their rights. Soon, however, a different kind of killing was seen. It would become known nationally, and it would hurt the state's image and its growth.

Hatfield–McCoy feudists.

A feud is usually said to be a fight between two groups or families. It drags on over a long period of time. After the Civil War, there were many feuds in eastern Kentucky. Major feuds took place in Garrard, Clay, Bell, Perry, Breathitt, Pike, and Rowan Counties. (See document 7.3.)

In all of the feuds, one family or group felt that it could not get justice from the law. They felt that the other group had control of the legal process. So they took revenge outside the law. People killed other people. In some feuds, well over one hundred people died.

The Hatfield–McCoy feud became better known than the rest. Today people across the world still refer to it when they talk about one group feuding with another.

The McCoys lived in Pike County, Kentucky, and the Hatfields had their home just across the river in West Virginia. Why the feud started is not clear. Some say they had an argument over a hog. Others point to a love affair between a Hatfield and a McCoy, one that did not work out. Most say it happened when people from each side got into a fight. One of the Hatfields was killed. His family took three McCoys, the youngest of them a teenager, and tied them to bushes and killed them. The feud grew from there.

DOCUMENT 7.3

A feud in Rowan County had the Tol-livers on one side and the Martin and Logan families on the other. Several times the governor had sent in troops to try to bring about peace. Nothing worked. In 1887, several more people were killed in a shoot-out on the streets of Morehead. The General Assembly decided to try to find out what happened. Below is part of what they learned:

From August 1884 to June 1887, there were 20 murders in the county and 16 persons wounded, and all this in a county whose voting population did not exceed 1100; and during this period there was not a single conviction for murder.

The failure to convict seemed to be that the people were unduly tolerant of crime.

Your committee find that the county officials were not only wholly ineffi-cient, but most of them in the warmest sympathy with crime and criminals. Nor did we find while at Morehead a healthy public sentiment to uphold the law.

Your committee find—

First. That the county officials are totally corrupt.

Second. The want of a healthy moral public sentiment.

Third. The portion of the community attached to law and order has been domi-neered over by the criminal element.

Fourth. The only cure for all the evils that have afflicted Rowan County is the abolition of the county.

By the time the report came out, the feud had pretty much ended. The General Assembly did not do away with the county. Some years later, what is now Morehead State University was set up in the former feud town.

That feud was not the one in which the most people died, nor was it the longest-lasting feud. But it did get a lot of newspaper coverage. Out of that attention grew the stereotype of the feuding Kentuckian. Such feuds also hurt the growth of Kentucky. People did not want to come to the state or start a business here if they could not be safe.

By the twentieth century, most feuds had ended, but the stereotype lives on.

Feuds were not the only kind of killing taking place in Kentucky. In 1900, a Kentucky governor was killed. It is the

Kentucky Faces

William Goebel

In looking at William Goebel as a young boy, few people would have thought he would one day be governor. Goebel's parents had come to America from Germany, and he spoke only German until he was five years old. The family moved to Covington in northern Kentucky.

Goebel grew up poor. He sold newspapers to help provide food for his family. A smart person, he had a strong will to succeed. Goebel became a lawyer and took a lot of cases for poor people. He also started to oppose big businesses that he said hurt the poor by their actions. However, Goebel was not a good speaker at a time when a person running for office needed to give good speeches. He wanted to be governor someday. So when he ran for state senator, he would do other things to get support. Goebel might promise someone a job, if he got elected, if that man's family would vote for Goebel. Some people did not like his approach. Others liked the fact that Goebel spoke for them. People seemed either to love or hate him.

In his hometown, he made one person very unhappy. Goebel wrote some very harsh words about that man in a newspaper. One day the two men met. Only a few feet apart, they both took out their pistols. No one knows who drew first. Goebel's enemy fell dead with a bullet to the head. Goebel had a bullet hole in his coat, but was not hurt. The court ruled it self-defense. Goebel's other enemies called him a murderer.

Four years later, Goebel's party made him their choice for governor. When the election took place, it seemed very close. His opponent from the other party was sworn in as governor, but the General Assembly had the last word on the matter. Most believed the legislature would rule in favor of Goebel, because his party had the most votes there.

While they were talking about the matter in the Old Capitol in January 1900, Goebel walked toward the building. Shots rang out, and he was shot. Four days later he died. Before he died, the General Assembly said he was the rightful governor. Several people were arrested for the shooting, but it remains unclear who shot him. His death added to the bad image of Kentucky.

only time in the nation's history that a governor was killed in office. That event just added to the state's violent image.

To understand why it happened, we must first recall "Honest Dick" Tate. Remember him? He is the one who stole the state's money. After his crime came to light, many people felt that Kentucky needed new leaders. One of those who wanted to lead was William Goebel. (See "Kentucky Faces.")

As the new century dawned, people hoped the twentieth century would be better than the last part of the nineteenth century.

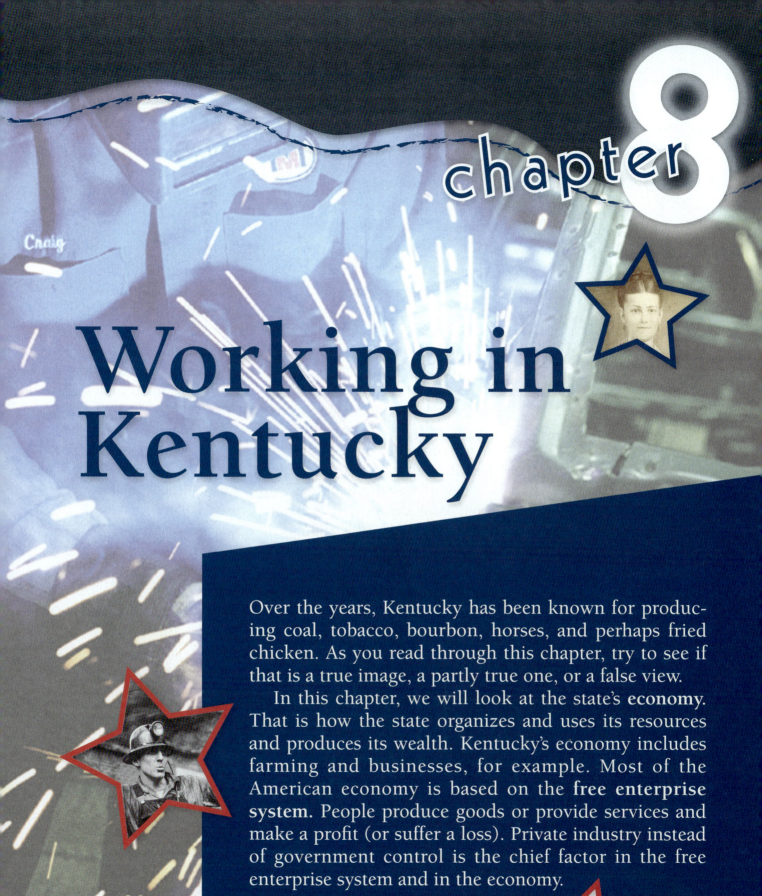

chapter 8

Working in Kentucky

Over the years, Kentucky has been known for producing coal, tobacco, bourbon, horses, and perhaps fried chicken. As you read through this chapter, try to see if that is a true image, a partly true one, or a false view.

In this chapter, we will look at the state's **economy**. That is how the state organizes and uses its resources and produces its wealth. Kentucky's economy includes farming and businesses, for example. Most of the American economy is based on the **free enterprise system**. People produce goods or provide services and make a profit (or suffer a loss). Private industry instead of government control is the chief factor in the free enterprise system and in the economy.

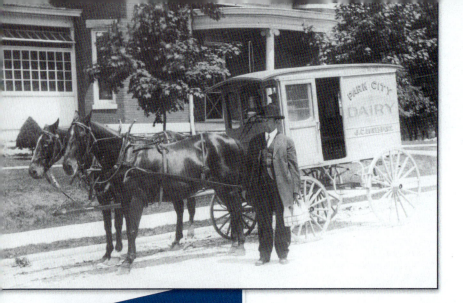

In earlier times, wagons took many Kentucky goods and products to the people.
    What services did this wagon provide?

★ Farming ★

In the early days, most people in Kentucky made their living on a farm. On the frontier, almost everyone planted corn, for instance. It provided food for people and animals. It also grew tall, and its height kept the ears of corn out of the reach of small animals seeking to eat it. Later, farmers grew other crops on their farms.

In the years before the Civil War, Kentucky planted many different crops and became one of the richest farming states. In 1840, for example, it ranked first in the United States in the production of wheat and hemp. It stood second in growing corn and tobacco, and fourth in growing rye. Of all the states, only one had more hogs or mules. Kentucky had a very healthy and varied farming economy.

Hemp was the main cash crop for Kentucky before the Civil War. But now it is barely grown legally in America. Before the Civil War, though, it was a major crop. Do you know what it was used for? At that time, people used the plant to make rough clothing. They used hemp bags to ship cotton in, while hemp rope found heavy use on sailing ships. Kentucky grew more than half of the hemp in America. After the Civil War, people began to use metal wire for cotton bales, and steamboats replaced sailing ships. Kentucky still held onto the crop and grew almost all of it by the end of the century. But it was a dying crop. In the twentieth century, it disappeared from Kentucky farms. Change had taken place over time.

A major part of Kentucky's economy for much of its early history was hemp. Workers used a hemp brake to crush the stalk open and get to the fiber inside.

Instead of the tall, waving stalks of hemp, another crop became the main cash crop on Kentucky farms. After the Civil War, people had to make choices. When you do that, you have to balance what you are giving up with what you are getting in return. Prices are usually set by supply and demand. Scarcity occurs when many people want to buy a product and only a small amount of the product exists. When this happens, the price will go up. If many items are produced, but few people want to buy, or demand, them, then the price will fall.

Tobacco replaced hemp as the main cash crop. It is used less now than it used to be.

After the Civil War, there was little demand for hemp, and it fell from favor. Tobacco prices were fairly high. Kentucky farmers made the choice not to produce as much hemp as before. Instead they grew more and more tobacco. At the time, tobacco seemed to bring them more money. From 1865 to 1929, Kentucky grew more tobacco than any other state. It now ranks second to North Carolina in tobacco production.

People used tobacco in the nineteenth century mostly for cigars and for chewing tobacco. Only in the twentieth century did machine-made cigarettes become more common. As the demand for tobacco grew, so did the supply. Soon more tobacco was being planted than buyers needed. Prices fell, then rose, then fell again. When farmers grew many different crops, a change in the price of one crop did not hurt them so much. Not all of their crops would have low prices at once. Now with one crop, farmers had either good or bad years, depending on the price of tobacco. Finally the government stepped in and helped bring about steady prices.

Later, in the 1960s, some studies showed how tobacco might harm a person's health. The government soon required that a health warning be placed on cigarettes. Many states charged high taxes on tobacco to try to keep people from buying cigarettes. By the early twenty-first century, tobacco's future had become more uncertain. Fewer people grow it than ever before. It plays a smaller and smaller role in Kentucky's economy.

Tobacco, like hemp, was a part of Kentucky farming from a very early time. On the frontier, people could even use tobacco to pay their taxes. Another key part of Kentucky agriculture was present almost from the start of statehood as well. That was the horse industry of the commonwealth.

Kentucky farms had on them many fine cattle, hogs, and mules. Horses, however, ruled. Before the Civil War, several

In the paddock area, horses at Keeneland get ready before the race.

DOCUMENT 8.1

Marmaduke B. Morton, a reporter for a newspaper, wrote the book *Kentuckians Are Different* in 1938. In it he told what it was like when he worked on a tobacco farm in western Kentucky in the nineteenth century:

None of the modern methods of handling tobacco had been discovered 75 years ago. In the winter the plant beds were burned. The seeds were sown by hand and patted in by dancing over the seed bed so that not one would be left exposed. The plants were generally drawn for [re-]planting in June.

We had no planting machines in those days. Plants were drawn from the bed by hand, dropped in the prepared ground by hand, and planted by hand. The planting was a back-breaking job.

The little plants were hoed by hand. When they grew larger they were wormed by hand. When a boy got careless and left a big fat worm, he was sometimes required to bite off the worm's head. Now the use of poison to destroy the worms has lightened his job. Late in the summer or early in the fall, the tobacco was cut and then hung in the barn, where it was either air cured or fired [fire-cured]. When it was dried out, it was stripped [from the stalk]—some mean job.

Then it was sent to market. By that time you had to begin on the plant beds for the next crop, for tobacco was and is almost an all-year crop.

visitors noted that Kentucky had "the best horses in the United States." Beautiful farms with white fences and horse barns that were better than many houses soon covered the central Bluegrass area. Great horses, great jockeys, and great races—like the Derby—added to the image.

While other states have tried to take Kentucky's place in the horse world, no state has done so. Over a ten-year period ending in the 1990s, for every nine major horse races, horses that came from Kentucky would win three. The next closest state would win one. About the same figures are true regarding where thoroughbred horses (or foals) are born. Kentucky leads there as well. The image of Kentucky as a source of fine horses has long been a true one and still is true.

What are Kentucky farms like today? As tobacco has declined in importance, the state has begun to grow more varied crops. In the year 2004, Kentucky crops sold for about $1.58 billion, with tobacco bringing in over one-fourth of that. Other main crops now are hay, corn, and soybeans. Overall, the state ranked twenty-first of all the states in the value of its crops. Kentucky is not nearly as important a farming state as it once was.

The leading producer of corn in Kentucky in 2004 was Union County, followed by Christian and Henderson counties, all in West Kentucky. The state's chief tobacco county was Bourbon County, with Fayette second and Shelby third. Soybeans are chiefly grown in Henderson County, Daviess County, and Union County.

There are two important facts about Kentucky farms. One is that the state has a lot of farms. In 2003 it had more than 85,000 farms, which tied it for the fourth highest number in the nation. The average farm size was 162 acres. The second thing is that more and more people who live on those farms make their main living some other way. About half of the farmers work their farms only part-time and go to another job full-time. Small family farms are becoming fewer and fewer.

★ Early Business and King Coal ★

In the nineteenth century, several businesses grew up in Kentucky. Some supplied only a local demand for goods. Others had a much wider market. Ads for Kentucky bourbon came out as early as 1821, for example, and the state soon became nationally known for that product. Many of the other industries developed along waterways when boats were the chief way to take products to markets.

One of Kentucky's first products was bourbon. Places like this business in Loretto continue to make the state well known in that area.

Clay County in eastern Kentucky, for example, was a major salt-production area. That area shipped barrels of salt down the Kentucky River for sale in states touching Kentucky. On the Ohio River, major businesses formed. Owensboro was one of the largest wagon-making areas in the South, and

KENTUCKY FACES   Caroline Burnam Taylor

In the nineteenth century, some women succeeded in small businesses. They ran a school, or opened a dress store, or something like that. Others might run a large farm if their husbands had died or were gone.

Caroline "Carrie" Burnam Taylor started a dressmaking business in her home in Bowling Green. It grew and grew. Soon she was shipping clothes all over America. Her name came to mean fine clothes. At its peak, her business hired two hundred to three hundred women to make clothes. More women were working there than at any other place in the state.

Taylor often went overseas to buy material for her dresses and get ideas for new styles. On one trip, she delayed her plans to come back so she could see one more dress show in France. Because of the delay, she missed her ship. It was the *Titanic*.

When Taylor died in 1917, she left an estate worth $250,000. That would be like $4 million or $5 million today. Her business declined without her, though. Ten years after her death, it closed its doors.

One of Taylor's dress designs.

One early industry in Kentucky was making wagons. Owensboro wagons were sold across the nation.

Louisville had the biggest plow factory in the world. The Falls City also had major tobacco and whiskey factories.

Railroads and later interstate highways became important matters for business people to think about when they decided where to locate. An iron industry developed early, mostly in eastern Kentucky. On the eve of the Civil War, the state was the third leading producer of iron in the nation. That industry did not last long after the war, however. About the time it died out, the timber industry grew up. All over Kentucky, but especially in eastern Kentucky, people cut trees. They then tied the logs together in huge rafts and floated them downriver to sawmills. The timber business also declined by the early twentieth century, but it came back by the century's end.

Eastern Kentucky had never been so isolated from other places as people would say later. Through the time of the Civil War, it was much like the rest of rural Kentucky. After the war, however, the iron industry died out, then the timber was all cut, and farming also went into decline. Just then, a new industry grew up. It would change the face of the land. King Coal began to rule.

Coal had been mined as early as the time of statehood, but only for local use or in very small amounts. The first major coal fields of Kentucky were in the western part of the state. It was easier to get to that coal, for the area had good waterways, better roads, and earlier railroads. More coal came from the western Kentucky coal fields than from eastern Kentucky until 1914 and the start of World War I.

Slowly, railroads inched into the eastern mountains, and when they did, a coal boom followed. People came in to work the mines, and great increases in population took place. Harlan County tripled in size from ten thousand to thirty-one thousand in the space of only ten years. Those early years were the most dangerous ones. In that same time period of the 1920s, more than 1,614 people of Kentucky died in the mines, from cave-ins or explosions. One blast in a Webster County mine killed 62 people. In 1970, an explosion in a Leslie County mine killed 38 miners, and twenty years later, 10 died in a West Kentucky blast.

Many Kentuckians made money by cutting trees. They then tied them together in rafts and floated them down a river. They lived in little shacks, like the one in the picture.

Coal has gone through periods of boom times and of bust. Demands for coal have brought high prices. The last boom time was when overseas oil production was halted for a time and coal came into higher demand. As time went on, the coal industry began to use machines to dig the coal. That has meant fewer jobs. A lot of the people who moved into Appalachia, or the children of those people, later

An early coal mine.

Sam Hawkins

Harry Caudill, in his book *The Mountains, the Miner, and the Lord*, tells the story of Sam Hawkins. Hawkins was an African American miner who dug coal out of the hills near Fleming in Letcher County, Kentucky.

The year 1932 was a bad one for Sam Hawkins. On the job, hard times across the nation meant less work and smaller paychecks. At home that year, his beloved wife Sadie died. Sam was forty-eight. The remaining love of his life was his only child, Margaret, then nineteen years old. Margaret had gone to college at what is now Kentucky State University. Sam could not read, but he had great hopes that her future would be better.

Then one day things got worse. A man read Sam a letter from Margaret. In it she told her father how she liked school and that she was doing well. Then she wrote: "It looks like I will have to quit school, though, in a few days. My money is all gone. Unless you can manage to send me ten dollars I will have to come back home."

At that time, ten dollars seemed like a fortune. He could not borrow it, because no one had any money to lend him. Sam Hawkins went to his boss. His boss said there was a section of one mine that was too dangerous to mine. It might cave in at any time. But if Sam wanted to try it, he would let him. The pay was thirty-one cents for every two thousand pounds of coal he dug.

Sam dug coal, alone and under the earth, for almost five hours, then ate a meal. Then he dug more coal the rest of the night. The walls groaned but held. He worked on. Twenty hours later he came outside, to rest for just a moment. The roof of the mine fell with a roar. Sam had mined his coal and survived.

For his work, Sam got eleven dollars. He sent the money to Margaret. Soon she got her college degree, and a proud father saw her come back home to teach. Then tragedy struck again. Margaret died of disease the next year. Sam never got over his grief.

Harry Caudill wrote at the end of his story these words: "Sam had put little white markers at the graves of his wife and daughter but no one ever got around to marking his own. Perhaps a coal shovel thrust into the earth like a bayoneted rifle over the bones of a fallen hero would be appropriate for such a man."

Heroes do not have to be famous. They are all around us.

left. They went north to find jobs. At one time more than sixty thousand people worked the mines. In the year 2000, only seventeen thousand did. Mining is still important, but not nearly as important as it was earlier.

Other changes in mining have taken place as well. Early mines were deep shafts into the ground. After World War II, people began to mine the coal a different way. Rather than digging underground to get to the coal, they used large machines to take off a whole hillside. That method is called strip mining.

In the first years, few laws limited strip mining. Large scars on mountains resulted. In some areas, the practice polluted the water as well. As late as thirty years ago, more than half of eastern Kentucky's coal came from strip mining. More recently, the percentage has been smaller.

Kentucky led the nation in coal production until 1983. Now it ranks third among the states in coal mining. The chief coal counties in 2002 were Pike, Knott, and Harlan.

A worker in an early coal mine.

★ Modern Industries ★

The old image of the state should change. In the past, people thought of Kentucky as a state whose economy depended a lot on farming and coal mining. Some still think of it the same way. Now, however, Kentucky is really much more a manufacturing state. That is, it depends on factory products for its wealth, more than on farming or mining. In fact, by the 1990s, manufacturing brought over three and a half times as much money to Kentucky as did farming and mining together.

The change in the economy took place slowly at first. Ashland Oil under Paul Blazer became a major Kentucky industry by the mid-twentieth century. Steel-rolling mills at Newport and Ashland helped the company to grow. Dollar General Stores started in Scottsville and grew from there. The real symbol of the change came in the 1950s when General Electric built a factory in Louisville. That factory became the biggest producer of home appliances in the world. Soon after that, IBM built a large factory in Lexington. Manufacturing then began to grow rapidly.

Kentucky now has a varied economy, as you can see by looking at the biggest companies in the state. The many large businesses in Louisville include Humana, which is involved in health care; Brown-Forman, which started as a producer of whiskey; Louisville Gas and Electric (LG&E), which produces energy; and Yum!Brands, which is in the fast-food business. In Lexington, printers are made by Lexmark; and in northern

One of the larger companies in Kentucky is Humana. This is the company's main office in Louisville.

DOCUMENT 8.2

Paul Blazer led Ashland Oil as it expanded and grew. He believed it was important for the people working with him to have the facts they needed to make decisions. He did not want to tell them what to do all the time. The reason for his view is that

The average person does not understand and fully appreciate the importance of accurate information and details. Most people, not all of them, have pretty good judgment based on facts as they have them, but they often make wrong decisions because they didn't have enough facts. Many decisions have pros and cons in them and you can find many reasons for handling them this way or that way. But the final decision rests upon where is [most] of the information.

Remember what we learned earlier about perspective? Learning the facts—on all sides—can help give perspective. That helps us make a better decision.

People sometimes say you make decisions with your heart and your mind. They mean if you follow the facts, you are using your mind. But people also make decisions based on what they feel—from their heart—sometimes. Should you always follow what you think the facts say? Should you always follow your heart? What do you think? One of the hard things is to learn how to balance the two in making a decision.

Kentucky, Ashland Oil has its national headquarters. Those are all among America's biggest companies.

Yum!Brands in Louisville combines five food chains under it—KFC (Kentucky Fried Chicken), Pizza Hut, Long John Silver's, A&W, and Taco Bell. Papa John's Pizza, Fazoli's, Long John Silver's, and KFC are four of the top one hundred food chains in the United States. These and several others started in Kentucky and still have their homes here. If you have ever eaten at a Rally's, Tumbleweed, Rafferty's, Dippin' Dots Ice Cream, or Giovanni's Pizza, you were eating at a Kentucky-based business as well.

In fact, Kentucky has a long history of making a strong impact on the food industry. The Hot Brown sandwich was started at the Brown Hotel in Louisville. Bibb lettuce was first grown in Frankfort. Duncan Hines of Bowling Green became nationally known in the food field. And Derby Pie is made only by one firm in Kentucky.

Kentucky also became known for four other kinds of businesses—motor vehicles, air transportation, energy, and tourism.

One of the biggest surprises about Kentucky's economy for most people is that the state is the third largest maker of motor vehicles in the United States. In fact, by the late 1990s, four of the top ten best-selling vehicles were made in the Bluegrass state. The Ford plants in Louisville made the F-series pickup truck, the Ford Explorer, and the Ford Ranger. The large Toyota factory near Georgetown in Scott County built the Toyota Camry and other vehicles. Bowling Green had the nation's only factory that makes the Corvette sports car. Have you ever ridden in any of those cars or trucks? Did you know they were made in Kentucky?

Kentucky also plays a key role in air transportation. The Cincinnati–Northern Kentucky International Airport serves as a hub for Delta Airlines. Many flights come and go there as a result. Major airports in Lexington and Louisville are

Which of these fast-food eating places have their headquarters in Kentucky? (Answers can be found in the text.)

The assembly line at the Toyota plant near Georgetown.

Harland Sanders

Colonel Sanders. His picture is known all over the world. Wherever people eat Kentucky Fried Chicken, the Colonel's white-coated image looks down on them.

The man so connected to that successful company was a failure most of his life. He was not even born in Kentucky but grew up instead in Indiana. His father died when he was six years old. He and his stepfather did not get along, and his stepfather threw him out of the house. Sanders quit school after the sixth grade.

Sanders worked at a lot of little jobs, without much success. When he was forty years old, he moved to Corbin, Kentucky. There he ran a gas station, which burned down after a few years. Sanders rebuilt it and added a motel and a place to eat. That is where Kentucky Fried Chicken was born. The good food earned him some local fame.

Made a Kentucky colonel by one governor, Colonel Sanders decided to sell his success to others. For a fee, he would let them use his method and his name. Sanders was sixty-six years old when he started what became his great success. Soon he had sold rights to produce his chicken to six hundred stores across the United States. After eight years, Colonel Sanders sold his business for $2 million plus a sizable salary for himself every year.

The business grew and grew. Twenty years later, Kentucky Fried Chicken was sold again, for $840 million. During those years, the Colonel gave a lot of money to worthy causes and traveled around the world. He became an image of Kentucky.

Sanders died in 1980, at the age of ninety. His picture and his business live on.

A view of the Toyota factory from the air.

busy at times as well. The busiest work at the Louisville airport is done where most people never see it. Day and night, flight after flight arrives there, from all over the world. The planes go to the United Parcel Service (UPS) hub at the airport. UPS not only takes packages all over the United States, but also delivers more packages in Europe than any other company. It works in nearly two hundred countries. Over the twenty years since UPS started using Louisville as its hub, the business has grown and grown. Louisville now has the tenth busiest air cargo airport in the world. State government hires the most people in Kentucky, but UPS is second. It plays a major role in Kentucky life.

A third area where Kentucky has had an impact is in producing energy, especially electricity. In addition to LG&E in Louisville, there are power plants near Land Between the Lakes. In the Paducah area, an atomic energy plant operates. Because of its production of electricity, Kentucky in the year 2003 had the lowest electricity costs in the nation.

Tourism also gives the Kentucky economy a major boost. Over the past half century, the state has made a great effort to let people know just how beautiful Kentucky is and how much it has to offer to visitors. State parks with comfortable hotels and many things to do bring people to Kentucky for vacations. Lakes and rivers provide fishing and boating for both out-of-state visitors and those who live in Kentucky. Many historic buildings and museums draw tourists as well. National forests, a national park at Mammoth Cave, a national historic site at Abraham Lincoln's birthplace, the Big South Fork National River and Recreation Area, and a national historical park at Cumberland Gap all bring people to the state. Kentucky is known as a place tourists want to visit.

Corvettes are made only at the factory in Bowling Green.

★ Global Kentucky ★

When you had more crops than you and your family needed in frontier times, your market was likely people who lived nearby. Later you might ship things across the state or nation to sell. Now Kentucky's markets are all over the world. The state is part of a global economy.

More and more, people who work in Kentucky need to know what happens overseas. Let's look at just one example. Suppose oil prices go down in the Middle East, and thus gasoline prices fall in the United States. How does that matter to Kentucky's economy?

First of all, lower oil prices might mean there will be less demand for coal to be used instead of oil. That means fewer jobs and less money for Kentucky miners. If oil prices go down, it also means less money for oil producers in countries such as Saudi Arabia. Does that have any effect

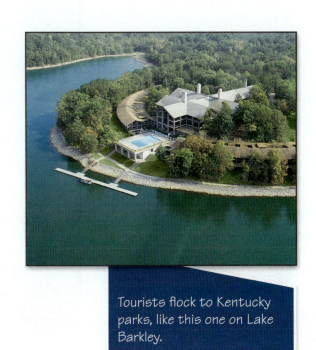

Tourists flock to Kentucky parks, like this one on Lake Barkley.

on Kentucky? Well, the people in Saudi Arabia often buy Kentucky race horses. One-fourth of all horses are sold overseas. If oil producers have less money to spend, they will not bid as high. Lower demand will mean lower prices to the owners.

But lower oil prices also mean lower gasoline prices at the gas station. That fact could help another group that is important to Kentucky's economy. If it costs less to travel, more tourists might come to Kentucky and spend their money here. That would aid some workers in the state. Also, if prices for gas are lower, then more vehicles that use more gasoline might be bought. Kentucky makes some of those vehicles. If demand for them goes up as gas prices go down, then more would be made. Kentucky workers would earn more money.

Map 8.1

Kentucky's place in the United Sates and in North America.

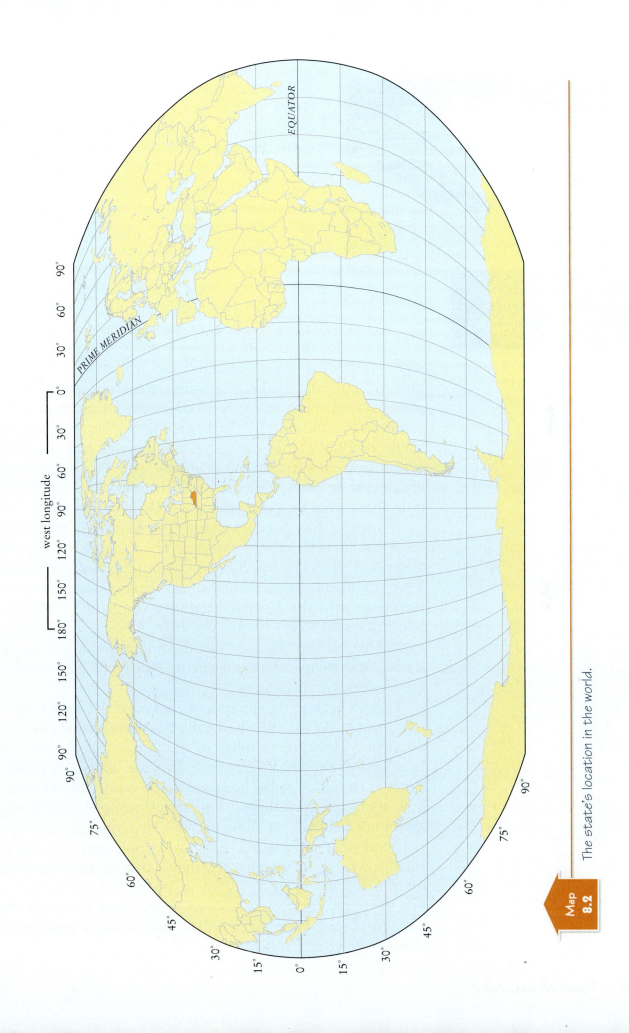

PRIME MERIDIAN

EQUATOR

west longitude

Map 8.2

The state's location in the world.

Day and night, planes fly in and out of Louisville to deliver UPS packages.

Other groups of people in Kentucky could either gain or lose from such a change in prices. Lower prices at the gas station may mean that owners of the stations in Kentucky make smaller profits. Any group that earns less will probably buy fewer items from stores and other businesses in towns across Kentucky. Those businesses might earn less. The groups that gain could spend more, however. Lower gasoline prices might mean that it costs less to ship goods from one place to another by truck. The fast-food businesses in Kentucky might save money that way and thus earn more and have more to spend themselves. Lower gas prices would involve airplanes too. The UPS hub in Louisville could ship things more cheaply. If other prices stayed the same, they would make more money. We could go on and on. The effects are many. That was just one single product in our economy. You can see how overseas events have an effect on our economy. The days when farmers grew their crops, used the products themselves, and cared little about what happened in the world are mostly gone.

Kentucky has been exporting, or sending, more and more products to other countries. The state's main exports are motor vehicles, machinery, computers, and chemicals. These products chiefly go to Canada, Japan, Mexico, France, Germany, and the United Kingdom (England). In 2002, Kentucky sold $10.9 billion worth of goods to other countries. That ranked the state twentieth in exports among the states. Most people think that figure will grow. The world is now Kentucky's marketplace.

Let's go back to the question we asked at the beginning of this chapter. We said that Kentucky has been known as a producer of coal, bourbon, tobacco, and horses. All of those still form part of Kentucky's economy. They are not nearly as vital a part as they used to be, however. If you wanted to be correct now about the main items in the state's economy, you would say motor vehicles, air hubs, health care, computer printers, fast food, tourism, and more. While people may still live in small towns or in the country, they work in manufacturing or in a service industry. A lot of people do not know it, but Kentucky's economy has changed a great deal over the past fifty years. How much will it change—and how will it change—in your lifetime?

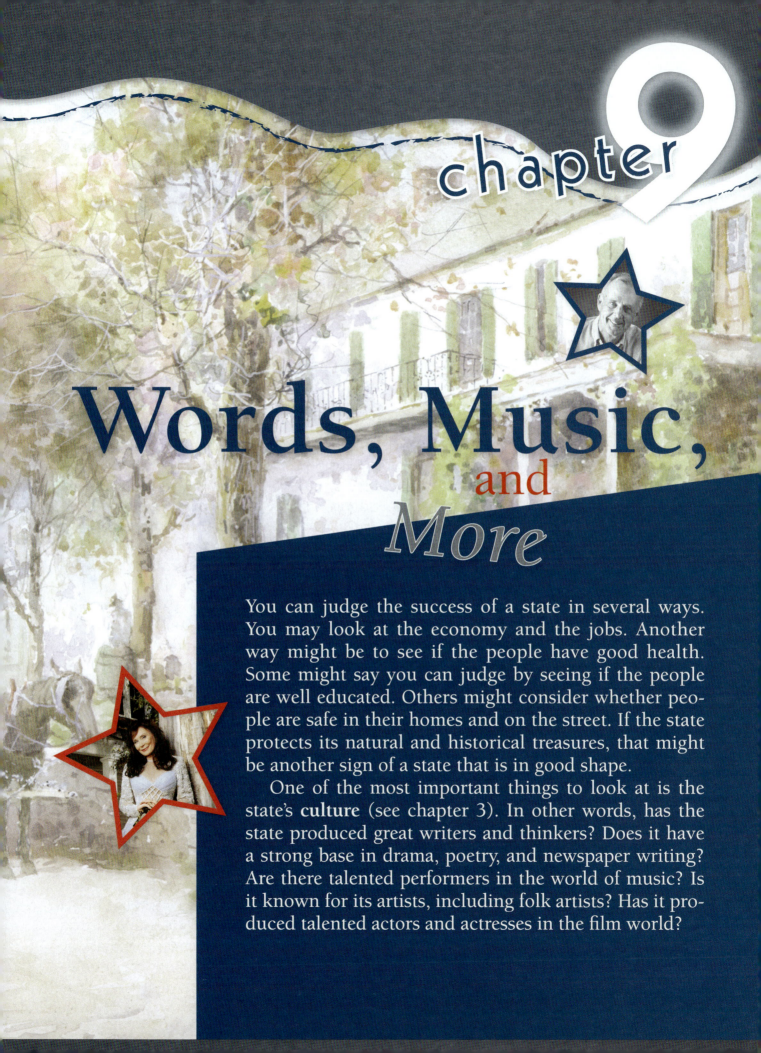

chapter 9

Words, Music, and *More*

You can judge the success of a state in several ways. You may look at the economy and the jobs. Another way might be to see if the people have good health. Some might say you can judge by seeing if the people are well educated. Others might consider whether people are safe in their homes and on the street. If the state protects its natural and historical treasures, that might be another sign of a state that is in good shape.

One of the most important things to look at is the state's **culture** (see chapter 3). In other words, has the state produced great writers and thinkers? Does it have a strong base in drama, poetry, and newspaper writing? Are there talented performers in the world of music? Is it known for its artists, including folk artists? Has it produced talented actors and actresses in the film world?

Kentucky has done very well in many of these areas. People inside and outside the state may not know as much as they should about Kentucky's writers, artists, musicians, and actors and actresses. In fact, in such fields as writing and music, Kentucky has outdone many other states. Those parts of Kentucky's culture have been one of the state's strengths.

Why has Kentucky shone in those areas? What causes a person to be a great writer or singer? That is a hard question to answer. As you read this chapter, though, see if you notice anything Kentucky writers and singers all have in common.

★ Early Writing ★

Early Native Americans did not have a written language, so they left no books telling of their history and hopes. Almost from the time of the first English settlement in Kentucky, however, people like John Filson began to write books in Kentucky and about Kentucky. But it was after the Civil War that most of the strong Kentucky writing was done.

The first two great Kentucky writers started their writing careers in the last part of the nineteenth and the first part of the twentieth century. They were James Lane Allen of Lexington and John Fox Jr. of Bourbon County.

Allen was a teenager when the Civil War raged. After the war, he looked around him and saw that the old ways of doing things had ended. He liked the ideals of earlier times. So he wrote about the frontier, or he wrote about people in his own period who held those earlier views. Sometimes his books do not have a totally happy ending, but they do show people doing the right thing because of their sense of duty.

Allen was a hard person to like. He was strict and formal. When he finished college, he even gave his graduation speech in Latin instead of English. Allen was forty-two years old when his first book went into print. His best-selling book was *The Choir Invisible*, which came out in 1897. It was a story of a schoolteacher on the frontier and his search for love. In it Allen had a woman say what the ideal person should be: "'I mean,' she said, 'that first of all things in this world, a man must be a man. Then he must be a gentleman—with all the grace, the vigor, the good taste of the mind. And then he must

Kentucky author James Lane Allen of Lexington.

try to live a beautiful life of the spirit.'" Allen tried to live his ideal.

John Fox Jr. was very different from Allen. Fox was friendly and well liked, while Allen was not. Fox wrote of the Kentucky mountains, and Allen of the central Bluegrass. Fox liked to live in Kentucky; Allen lived outside it after he became a success. Both wrote best-selling books.

Fox was born during the Civil War, in Bourbon County. His father's family supported the South, and his mother's were on the side of the North. After his graduation from Harvard, he wrote about the hills where he had spent much time visiting. Fox followed an odd schedule in his writing. He could not sleep much at night, so he wrote then. During the day, he would eat breakfast at ten o'clock, write letters, have lunch, play golf or cards, visit with girls and dance, then have a late dinner before going to work.

John Fox Jr. of Bourbon County.

His two major books became very popular. His first best seller was *The Little Shepherd of Kingdom Come,* published in 1903. Later, it would be made into movies several different times. It is a story of a mountain boy who comes to the Bluegrass. He struggles with the love of two girls and fights in the Civil War. The book features much good writing. For example, here is how Fox told of the start of the Civil War in divided Kentucky: "So, on a gentle April day, when the great news came, it came like a sword that, with one stroke, slashed the state in twain, shearing through the strongest bonds that link one man to another.

"As the nation was [torn] apart, so was the commonwealth; as the state, so was the county; as the county, the neighborhood; as the neighborhood, the family; and as the family, so brother and brother, father and son."

Fox followed his first success with another popular book five years later. *The Trail of the Lonesome Pine* (1908) was also made into a movie several times. It was about a mountain girl, a man from the Bluegrass, their love, feuds, and more.

At almost the same time, a woman writing in Pewee Valley in Oldham County also sold huge numbers of books. Annie Fellows Johnston wrote *The Little Colonel* (1905) for younger readers. It too was later made into a motion picture. She told about the time after the war. In her book, the old Colonel's son was killed fighting for the South in the Civil War. The Colonel's daughter has married a Yankee, and therefore the

Colonel refuses to talk to her. He happens to meet his grand-daughter, "the Little Colonel." She helps the family come back together—just as the nation was trying to do at that time.

In 1903, of the ten books on the national best-seller list, five were written by people from Kentucky. A list was made of the best-selling American books in the first forty years of the twentieth century, showing which states the writers came from. Kentucky stood fifth highest among the fifty states on that list. The next group of Kentucky writers would give the state even greater national fame.

★ Twentieth-century Writers ★

Those early writers had all grown up in or near large cities. The next group of great Kentucky writers mostly came from rural or small-town Kentucky. Most of them were born around the first decade of the twentieth century. All of them helped make Kentucky writing known around the world.

The first of those writers, Elizabeth Madox Roberts, is now almost unknown. In her time, however, she was called one of the greatest American writers. Her first and second books were named the best books published in the United States in the years they came out. In fact, her first novel has been called by some the greatest Kentucky novel ever.

Roberts spent her childhood and most of her life in Springfield, Kentucky. Often in ill health, she was in a wheelchair part of the time. She tried to teach, then finally turned to writing. Roberts did not go to college until late in life. Once she did, she got the courage to write. Her first book was *The Time of Man* (1926), and it came out when she was forty-five years old.

In most of the earlier Kentucky books a man was the hero, but Roberts's book had a heroine—a poor woman. The story of Ellen Chesser in *The Time of Man* shows how strong people can be, even in bad times.

Roberts looks at "that proud ghost, the human spirit." Her heroine understands that she has raised a son who wants more than the life she has known. He says: "I want books to know and read over and over. I aim to have some of the wisdom of the world, or as much as ever I can get a hold on.

Author Elizabeth Madox Roberts of Springfield.

Kentucky Faces

Irvin S. Cobb

The stories written by Irvin S. Cobb may have been read by more Americans in his lifetime than those of any other U.S. writer. Later, he became an actor for a time. He was not a great writer or a great actor, but he was very good at both writing and acting. Cobb also was one of the most popular Kentuckians and Americans of his time. To many people, Cobb was Kentucky.

Cobb was born in 1876 in Paducah in the Jackson Purchase. Because of an unhappy family life, he started to work on a newspaper when he was nineteen years old. He wrote in his home city, in Louisville, and in New York City. Cobb did not wait for a thought to inspire him to write. He said: "I have had only three sets of rules: (1) I have never waited for inspiration. (2) I go to my desk at a certain hour. (3) I stay there for a given number of hours."

Whatever he did, it worked. Cobb was a warm, witty man with good common sense, and people just liked to be around him. He seemed to know all the important people in New York. They liked his funny stories and his sharp comments. His best-selling book was *Speaking of Operations*. In it he told of going to a hospital. Cobb said he could not sleep because nurses and doctors kept waking him up, though he was sick—"I was not allowed to get lonely." He also said, "I was not having any more privacy in that hospital than a goldfish." Cobb wrote more than forty other books. His best ones told about a judge he knew back in Paducah. He called him "Judge Priest."

Cobb could not throw off all the views he had grown up with, but in his books he supported rights for African Americans and for women. He also grew very opposed to war, after he saw the horror in World War I.

After that war, he went to California and acted in a half dozen movies. Cobb died during another war—World War II. At his funeral, a friend noted how Cobb could touch everyone's feelings by his writings and his wit. Cobb's tombstone reads: "Back Home." He never left his Kentucky home in what he wrote or who he was.

There's a heap of wisdom in books, it's said, and that's what I want to have, or as much as ever I can." To the mother, the son's "want startled her with its determination," but it makes her happy as well. She knew that he would live a better life.

Roberts also wrote one of the best historical novels about the frontier. It is called *The Great Meadow* (1930). However, this woman of quiet courage could not defeat the disease that she had, and she wrote for only a dozen or so years. Roberts died at the age of sixty, just before World War II started.

Many other good Kentucky writers followed her and gained success, starting in the 1930s. Some of them include

The home of author Jesse Stuart in Greenup County.

Cleanth Brooks of Murray, Caroline Gordon of Todd County, Janice Holt Giles of Adair County, Allen Tate of Winchester, A.B. "Bud" Guthrie of Lexington, Elizabeth Hardwick, also of Lexington, and James Still of Knott County. Some of the most powerful writing came from Harriette Simpson Arnow. Born in Wayne County in 1908, she grew up in Burnside. At first, no one supported her desire to write. After her marriage, she began to put pen to paper. With two small children, Arnow first wrote from four o'clock in the morning until seven o'clock, when they got up. In that way she wrote one of the hardest-hitting American novels, *The Dollmaker* (1954). It told of a mountain woman whose family moved to the North seeking a job and of the trials and tragedy they faced there.

For much of the last half of the twentieth century, the most popular writer among Kentucky readers was probably Jesse Stuart of W-Hollow in Greenup County. Stuart was the oldest of seven children. His father was an ex-miner who had turned to farming. Stuart hoed tobacco by the time he was six. He recalled getting one pair of shoes per year. He made it to college, then came back to teach for a time. Stuart wrote: "It took life beyond the hills to make one love life among the hills. I had gone beyond the dark hills to taste of life. It was not sweet like life in the hills." He stayed in Kentucky and told of his love for his native state:

> *I take with me Kentucky embedded in my brain and heart*
> *In my flesh and bone and blood,*
> *Since I am of Kentucky*
> *And Kentucky is part of me.*

In another poem he wrote:

> *Kentucky is neither southern, northern, eastern or western,*
> *It is the core of America*
> *If these United States can be called a body,*
> *Kentucky can be called its heart.*

Most experts do not consider Stuart's writing as good as that of some of the other authors of his time. All of them agree, however, that people liked to read Stuart's works. Most also agree that the greatest writer Kentucky has ever produced is Robert Penn Warren of Todd County in West Kentucky.

In fact, some believe he may be the greatest *American* writer of the twentieth century. He not only wrote stories, but he also wrote poetry. He won major prizes in both. The title of Poet Laureate of the United States is given to the person thought to be the greatest living American poet. Warren was the first person given that title. When he died in 1989, he was said to be America's greatest writer and poet.

Most of "Red" Warren's best books have Kentucky at the center of them. Such books include *Night Rider* (1939), *World Enough and Time* (1950), *Brother to Dragons* (1953), and *The Cave* (1959). His work usually deals with some human weakness, with the darker side of the human soul of Kentuckians. Warren shows how people realize their weakness. He loved history and saw it as a way for people to plan a better journey to the future. Warren wanted people to understand things past, the places around them, and themselves.

★ Modern Writers ★

When James Still died in 2001, he was the last of a group of writers. By then, a whole new group was continuing to make a name for Kentucky by their writing. Several of them happened to be in school together in the 1950s at the University of Kentucky—James Baker Hall of Lexington, Gurney Norman of Perry County, Ed McClanahan of Bracken County, Bobbie Ann Mason (see "Kentucky Faces" in chapter 3), and Wendell Berry.

Of that group, Wendell Berry has been called by some people the greatest living Kentucky writer. Others might point to Mason or other writers. Born in 1934 in Henry County, Berry still lives there and writes his poems and books by hand. He has written novels such as *The Memory of Old Jack* (1974), but is best known perhaps for his essays about the world around us. His book *The Unsettling of America* (1977) was termed "the most important book of the decade" by a California newspaper.

Berry does not think that all things that are new are good. Neither does he think that everything of the past is without fault. Berry wants us to remember that our place on the earth is but a temporary one, and

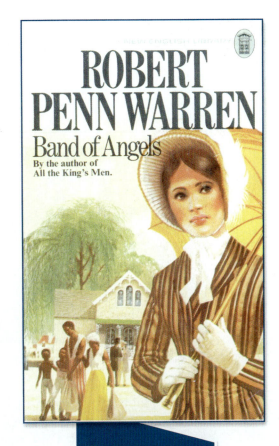

The cover of one of author Robert Penn Warren's books.

Wendell Berry of Henry County.

Harlan and Anne Hubbard in their Payne Hollow house.

Harlan Hubbard was born in Bellevue in northern Kentucky in 1900. Later he lived in New York City, then came back to Fort Thomas. In none of those places was he happy. After he married, at age forty-three, he and his wife Anna spent the rest of their lives away from people. They first lived on a small boat, then in a Payne Hollow house without electricity, phones, or an indoor toilet. They seldom went to a store or left their home. The Hubbards would paint, write, read to each other, and play music together by candlelight each night. In the modern world, they tried to live as people had lived centuries earlier. Here are some of the things Harlan Hubbard wrote in his daily journal:

JULY 5, 1932—The most important ties to the world would be art, painting, music, books. Without these my life would be empty and futile.

JUNE 2, 1945—Gardening is a battle. The insects and rabbits feed on our tender plants. A constant struggle is called for to bring in a crop and losses must be counted on, rather than gain.

MARCH 1, 1955—The key to it all is a love of nature. I want to feel a touch of the wilderness in the minutest acts. It must be like the air itself.

SEPTEMBER 8, 1955—By this time my feet are tough as leather, and I can walk anywhere barefoot. Those who are always shod [wear shoes] do not know the joy of walking on the earth, of wading in the water, of never thinking of what shoes to put on.

AUGUST 2, 1956—Caught a young 'possum in the trap last night, had it for dinner. Very good.

JULY 29, 1961—Sometimes I feel that the whole world is against me, and I have not one friend.

SEPTEMBER 7, 1962—Anna's birthday. We had a picnic. We grilled catfish and groundhog. Also had tomatoes and peppers, watermelon and milk.

NOVEMBER 22, 1962—Thanksgiving Day. Our dinner was liver, fresh from goat I butchered this morning.

APRIL 21, 1964—Cities are amazing places. Who would choose to live in them? They have no beauty; they are without hope.

JULY 10, 1966—The garden means to us all our vegetables for the whole year. Through the goats, we produce our own milk and meat. Fish from the river make up a good part of our food supply.

Anna Hubbard died in 1986; Harlan died two years later. Would you want to live like they did? Why do you think they wanted to live that way?

that we should take care of the world we leave to others. He wants each person to be an individual and to be respected as one of a kind. We do not have to be "one of the crowd."

His book *A Continuous Harmony* came out in 1972. In it, he warns us to care for our land: "In order to build a road, we destroy several thousand acres of farmland, forever, without regret, believing that we have gained much and lost nothing. In order to build a dam, which like all human things will be temporary, we destroy a forest. In order to burn cheap coal, we destroy a mountain forever. Great power has always been blinding to those who wield it." Berry wants us to be wise in our actions and to remember our place in the world.

There are many other fine Kentucky writers as well. If we tried to list them all, some good ones would still be left out. They write on a lot of topics and in different forms. Some, such as George Ella Lyon from Harlan County and Lexington, write excellent children's books. Others, such as Sue Grafton from Louisville, write best-selling mystery novels. A few, such as Barbara Kingsolver from Nicholas County, write books that make people want to read them and make others call them good writing.

✴ Writing History, Poetry, and Drama ✴

Writing can take many forms. Many authors write novels. Novels may or may not be based on fact, but they always include some made-up elements. The authors use their skill to present a story that takes us beyond the facts. Other writers may do the same thing, but their story is written as a play to be performed on a stage. They write drama.

In the days before television or movies, people saw plays on a stage in a theater or some other place. Plays were being presented in Kentucky even before statehood. More recently, Actor's Theater in Louisville has become nationally known for offering new stage plays. Marsha Norman of Louisville has won much success in that field.

Others have directed stage plays instead of writing them. George C. Wolfe is probably the best-known living Kentucky

Writer, producer, and director of plays, George C. Wolfe grew up in Frankfort.

Thomas D. Clark, famous Kentucky historian.

Poet Madison Cawein

stage director. He grew up in Frankfort at a time when African Americans could not go to the same school or see movies with whites. On a trip to New York when he was thirteen, he saw some plays and wanted to get into that field. He has directed such prize-winning plays as *Jelly's Last Jam* and *Angels in America.* Wolfe recently noted that "the older I get, the more I become Frankfort." As an adult, he has found it is hard to leave behind the things that shaped him in his youth.

Another kind of writing is done by historians. Those who write history cannot go beyond the facts. They must find out what happened, understand it, and then present it to their readers. There have been many fine writers of history in Kentucky, but the most important was Thomas D. Clark, who died in 2005 at age 101. He grew up happy but poor in Mississippi. As a youth, Clark spoke with ex-slaves and ex-Civil War soldiers who were still living then. He worked in cotton fields and on Mississippi River boats. Because he had to help on the farm, Clark did not finish high school until he was twenty-two. Later he would get the highest college degree in his field.

When people asked him about all the history books he wrote, Clark said: "I write because I wanted to write. I did research because I wanted to do it—I found it exciting." The thrill of a new discovery in history could be great. He tried to give readers that same feeling: "Writing is a lonely business," he wrote, "but I have from the start determined that what I wrote was going to have some style." It did.

Clark also helped build up libraries so others could research and write history. The University of Kentucky, the Kentucky Department for Libraries and Archives, and the Kentucky Historical Society all owe him much for what he did for them.

A very different way of creating images with words is poetry. Earlier we read some poems by Jesse Stuart. Many Kentucky writers of novels wrote poetry too, as Robert Penn Warren did. Others wrote chiefly poems. Joseph S. Cotter of Louisville and Effie Waller Smith of Pike County became the first major black poets in the state, for example. Madison Cawein of Louisville was one of the first state poets to receive national fame for his work.

DOCUMENT 9.2

Many Kentuckians died in the Mexican War. Theodore O'Hara wrote a poem to honor them for giving their lives for their country. His poem is still read all over the nation, as we remember the dead from that war and other wars.

As you read these verses, you should know that when he refers to a "tattoo," he means the blowing of a horn to tell soldiers to go to their tents for the night. The word "bivouac" in the last line means a place where people camped in their tents.

As you read this, think about the images of the dead soldiers that the poet wants us to see in our minds:

The muffled drum's sad roll has beat
The soldier's last tattoo:

No more as life's parade shall meet
The brave and daring few.
On Fame's eternal camping-ground
Their silent tents are spread,
And glory guards with solemn round
The bivouac of the dead.

A teacher and newspaper writer, O'Hara fought in the Mexican War and the Civil War. He did not live long after the Civil War ended, however. He died at the age of forty-seven. O'Hara had written this much-remembered poem when he was in his twenties. Some call it the greatest single poem penned by a Kentuckian.

Cawein grew up poor in a German immigrant family. He spent time in some nearby woods, where he learned to love nature. His poems often told of a fantasy world of elves and mystery, as he tried to forget his own real-world problems. In one he wrote of the beauty that we can hear around us, if we but listen:

There is no rhyme that is half so sweet
As the song of the wind in the rippling wheat;
There is no metre that's half so fine
As the lilt of the brook under rock and vine;
And the loveliest lyric I ever heard
Was the wildwood strain of a forest bird.

Many have followed him and have written excellent poetry.

Kentucky Faces

Frank X Walker

Frank Walker is one of a younger group of poets and artists who try to look at things in new ways. He was born in Danville in 1961 and later went to college at the University of Kentucky. Inspired by author Gurney Norman, he got his degree in English and art. Walker was the first member of his family to graduate from college. After school he worked at the Martin Luther King Center at the university and then in a similar job at Purdue University. As of 2004, he was director of the Kentucky Governor's School for the Arts. That school brings talented high school students together in the summer to learn and perform.

Most of all, however, Walker is an artist and poet. He feels that culture can be an important force in overcoming differences. Walker says: "Art is part of the solution. It is the perfect thing to learn to appreciate different cultures, to bring people together. They might all come to the same exhibit, or reading, or pick up the same book. I think that's powerful. I really believe that art has the capacity to induce healing."

Walker's first book of poetry was called *Affrilachia*. His title combines the words *Africa* and *Appalachia*. In it, he wanted to show what ties the people of the state together. He noted: "My parents were born in Kentucky, both sets of grandparents were born in Kentucky, my great-grandparents were born in Kentucky. Not just me, but there are a lot of people of color who belong to Kentucky, and who Kentucky belongs to."

Walker ends his poem "Kentucke" by making that point:

> *we are the amen*
> *in church hill downs*
> *   the mint*
> *in the julep*
> *we put the heat*
> *in the hotbrown*
> *   and*
> *gave it color*
> *   indeed*
> *some of the bluegrass*
> *   is black*

★ Newspapers ★

Works by Kentucky authors have been printed both in Kentucky and outside the state. The University Press of Kentucky remains the publisher of the greatest fame in the commonwealth. In Louisville the American Printing House for the Blind is the oldest such publisher in the United States and is the world's largest printer of books for the blind.

The form of the printed word most read by Kentuckians is not books or poetry or drama, however. It is the newspaper. The first one in Kentucky was *The Kentucke Gazette,* which was started in 1787—five years before statehood. Since then, many very good newspapers have told readers what is happening in their hometown and in the state, the nation, and the world. The two papers read by more Kentuckians than any other are the Lexington *Herald-Leader* and the Louisville *Courier-Journal.*

Newspapers print the news, but they also offer comments on matters in the news. Those printed comments are called **editorials.** The most famous Kentucky editorial writer was Henry Watterson of the *Courier-Journal.* (Watterson Expressway in Louisville is named for him.) He could take a dull fact and write about it in a way that would get people's attention. Watterson could be ahead of his time in some of the things he supported and behind the times on other matters. Often he made people

mad because he said openly how he stood. He did make the *Courier-Journal* a very strong paper in the state and in the South. After his death, the Bingham family made the paper even better known across the nation. A 1970 survey of all U.S. papers placed the *Courier-Journal* third best in the nation. Four years later, a national magazine ranked it in the top ten again. After that, the Binghams sold the newspaper, and its national standing declined .

In Lexington, the *Herald-Leader* had been both weak and strong at different times. However, it too was purchased by an outside group, and the paper became better as a result. Generally, it has the most readers in the central and eastern part of Kentucky. The *Courier-Journal* is read mostly by people in south-central and western Kentucky. In numbers of readers, the two rank among the top one hundred papers in the United States. Newspapers indirectly tied to Cincinnati cover northern Kentucky, while newspapers in Paducah, Owensboro, Frankfort, and other cities cover their parts of the state.

The highest American prize in newspapers, poetry, writing, and other fields is the Pulitzer Prize. Many Kentuckians have won the Pulitzer Prize, which shows the state's strength in many types of writing. For example, Henry Watterson won the Pulitzer Prize once, and his paper won it several times later. So too did people connected to the *Herald-Leader*. Reporter Arthur Krock from Glasgow won the Pulitzer Prize four times for his writing outside the state. Moneta Sleet Jr. of Owensboro became the first black American to win it in photography. Marsha Norman won it in drama, as had Kentuckian John Patrick earlier. Robert Penn Warren is the only person in U.S. history who has won the Pulitzer Prize for novels and also twice for poetry. A.B. Guthrie Jr. also won it for his writing. Kentucky has produced many prize-winning authors.

★ Music ★

Writers make books or poems out of their words and thoughts. Other people turn their words and thoughts into music. Each group tells a story or makes us think, but they do it in different ways. Just as people all over America read the books that people from Kentucky wrote, so too do many Americans listen to the songs Kentuckians play and sing. The state may not be known for its formal, classical music, but it is famous for its folk, country, and bluegrass music. Its music reaches all the people, not just a few.

When Europeans came across the ocean to America, long ago, they brought music with them. In frontier areas, settlers passed those songs on to others by singing them from memory, not from books. Over the years, many of the same songs, called folk songs, have become a part of the musical lives of Kentuckians. People such as John Jacob Niles of Louisville and then central Kentucky, Mary Wheeler of Paducah, and Jean Ritchie of Perry County in eastern Kentucky wrote down the words and the music to save them. They did not want the old songs to be forgotten. These songs told people about families long ago and times long past.

After the frontier period ended, some people began to write new songs and music. In the nineteenth century, the musician most often thought of in regard to Kentucky was probably Stephen Collins Foster. He wrote "My Old Kentucky Home." Foster's song "Oh! Susanna" has been called "the birth of pop music," and he wrote many

Born in Perry County, Jean Ritchie preserves and sings mountain ballads.

KENTUCKY FACES

Loretta Lynn

Loretta Webb Lynn wrote a book about her life called *Coal Miner's Daughter*. It tells about her early life, which was very hard. In a song of the same name, she said,

> *I was borned a coal miner's daughter,*
> *In a cabin on a hill in Butcher Holler*
> *We were poor, but we had love.*

Born in Johnson County in 1935, Loretta was one of eight children and slept on the floor until she was nine years old. "I remember being hungry too much," she writes in her book. Loretta Lynn never ate beef until after she was married. They had only pork, possum, squirrel, and chickens. She first got in a car when she was twelve. Some of her relatives had never been more than a dozen miles from home in their life. In the middle of the twentieth century, she lived first in a log cabin and then in a small frame house with a well out front and an outhouse in the back. From there she walked two miles to a one-room school. She says she got about a fourth-grade education.

Thinking she could get away from that harsh life, she got married at age fourteen. By the time she was eighteen, she had four children. Her life still was hard. She did not know how to cook. Some of the food she fixed was so bad her husband threw it outside. At least their dog got fat! Loretta was not much more than a child herself, and she had children and a husband. She cried many nights.

One day her husband bought her a guitar to play. She was twenty-four. He said she should express her feelings through songs. Nervous at first, she wanted to do just that. By 1960, when she was twenty-five, she went on the Grand Ole Opry in Nashville for the first time. Over the next eighteen years, she made forty-six single records. Thirty-nine of them became hits. She would be the first woman ever named Entertainer of the Year in country music. Her sister Crystal Gayle began to do well as a singer also.

Although she became a grandmother at the early age of twenty-nine, Loretta Lynn still sang and wrote songs. Often she would hear a word or a line and then write the words from there. Usually she added the music later. However she did it, Loretta Lynn became very important in the music field. She had come a long way from Butcher Holler.

other songs that we still sing today. However, Foster really had very few ties to Kentucky, except for the title of that one song. Later in the same century, sisters Patty and Mildred Hill of Louisville wrote the music for a song that may be sung more than any other one. The song is "Happy Birthday."

In the next century, Kentucky music really began to make its mark on the nation. Country music became popular, and Kentucky people helped make it popular. At least seven singers who were born in Kentucky or made their home here have been named to the Country Music Hall of Fame. That is

Bill Monroe (second from left) of Ohio County made bluegrass music popular.

considered to be the greatest honor for a country music singer. Those seven singers include "Red" Foley of Madison County; "Pee Wee" King, who lived in Louisville; Merle Travis of Muhlenberg County; "Grandpa" Jones of Henderson County; Loretta Lynn; and the Everly Brothers of Brownie, Kentucky. They came from all parts of the state, especially West Kentucky, and won fame in different ways. Red Foley's "Peace in the Valley" became the first gospel song to sell a million records. Merle Travis was named to the Hall of Fame as a guitar player. The Everly Brothers mixed country and pop styles.

Kentucky singers continue to be popular in the field of country music. Among those still performing are the Judds, Billy Ray Cyrus, Ricky Skaggs, the Osborne Brothers, John Michael Montgomery, Dwight Yokam, and Patty Loveless.

The Country Music Hall of Fame has one other member from Kentucky. He created a whole new sound, called bluegrass music. Bill Monroe was born in Rosine in Ohio County in the western part of the state. He and his Bluegrass Boys band made their music popular with songs such as "Blue Moon of Kentucky." Bluegrass music became one of Kentucky's most famous gifts to the national music scene.

At the same time, the state produced some fine musicians in the field of jazz. The so-called "Father of the Blues" was W.C Handy. He was not born in Kentucky, but he said he learned his music in Henderson. Other jazz musicians were Lionel Hampton, singer Helen Humes, and many others.

In short, music of all kinds has come from Kentucky—folk, gospel, country, bluegrass, and jazz. Music from the South and from the North met in the state, and new styles and songs were born.

Part of the reason for the growth of interest in music in the twentieth century and beyond came from the inventions of radio and television. One of the first important people in the nation in the field of radio was Nathan Stubblefield of Murray, Kentucky. He really did not invent the radio, as some people say. His invention could only work for short distances. Stubblefield was, however, the first person to send human voices through the air, not by wires as in the telephone. He set the stage for radio as we know it today.

DOCUMENT 9.3

The song "Kentucky Rain" became best known when Elvis Presley sang it. The words and music were written by Eddie Rabbit and Dick Heard, and the recording took place in 1969. As you read through the words to the song, think about what the story is, and try to see the visual images.

Seven lonely days
And a dozen towns ago
I reached out one night
And you were gone
Don't know why you'd run,
What you're running to or from
All I know is I want to bring you home
So I'm walking in the rain,
Thumbing for a ride
On this lonely Kentucky backroad
I've loved you much too long
And my love's too strong
To let you go, never knowing
What went wrong
Kentucky rain keeps pouring down
And up ahead's another town
That I'll go walking thru

With rain in my shoes,
Searchin' for you
In the cold Kentucky rain,
In the cold Kentucky rain
Showed your photograph
To some old gray bearded men
Sitting on a bench
Outside a gen'ral store
They said "Yes, she's been here"
But their memory wasn't clear
Was it yesterday,
No, wait the day before
So I fin'ly got a ride
With a preacher man who asked
"Where you bound on such a dark
*   afternoon?"*
As we drove on thru the rain
As he listened I explained
And he left me with a prayer
That I'd find you

Elvis Presley died on August 16, 1977. At the time, he was scheduled to sing in Rupp Arena in Lexington the next week.

How long do you think radio stations have been operating in Kentucky? A hundred years? A hundred and fifty years? Fifty years? The first radio station in Kentucky opened in Louisville in 1922. Soon other stations started. The next one was in Covington; then Paducah, Hopkinsville, Lexington, and Ashland followed. In those early days before television,

The first radio station in the state was WHAS in Louisville. This is a studio where live performances were aired.

people would sit around a radio and listen to programs. The radio provided entertainment for them.

That first radio station was WHAS in Louisville. It became the major station for the state. For a long time it put live music on the air. South of Richmond, Kentucky, in Rockcastle County, the "Renfro Valley Barn Dance" became known across the nation. WHAS radio played its music, and its sounds reached many states. As time went by, live radio performances stopped. The Louisville station would later be a radio station just for that city, not for the state. The change came partly because of television.

How long do you think it was after radio stations started that the first TV station began? Was it soon, or a long time later? The first radio station opened in 1922. The first TV station started twenty-six years later. It was WAVE in Louisville. For many years, television pictures were only in black and white. Color images came along mostly in the 1960s. As more and more people bought TVs, radio became less important to people. Once more, things had changed.

Covington's Frank Duveneck painted this young girl in 1891.

★ What the Eye Sees ★

People may express their feelings through words on a page or by singing a song. Many Kentucky people have had success in those areas. You can express yourself in other ways as well. One way is by painting, or by producing films, or by making objects for people to see, or by building new buildings. All of those can be called visual arts. Fewer Kentuckians have gained fame in these areas than in the ones we have already read about. There have been some people who have done well, however.

In the field of art, perhaps the best-known person from Kentucky was Frank Duveneck of Covington. His father died when Frank was only a year old, and when his mother remarried, he took his stepfather's name. Duveneck went to Europe to learn to paint better, and married an American girl there. She died when very young, and the sad Duveneck came back to northern Kentucky to live.

Probably the most popular painter within Kentucky is Paul Sawyier of Frankfort.

He studied under Duveneck and learned from him. Sawyier never had great success in his lifetime. Part of the time, he lived on a houseboat on the Kentucky River. He would paint a scene and sell the painting just to get money to buy food. Sawyier later moved to New York and died there when he was fifty-two years old. In his work, though, he had captured the spirit of Kentucky at his time.

Kentucky has had much more success in the field of folk art. Sawyier and Duveneck did formal paintings. But all people create art in some way. People may not learn to be artists at a formal school. They may learn from a family member or a person in their town. Such art can be passed on from one era to another, just like folk music can. It may take much skill, though the result may not look that way at times. That kind of art is called folk art. It may include carving wood, or making pottery, or weaving baskets, or painting, or quilting. Kentucky has many strengths in the area of folk art.

Making formal statues is not one of the state's strong points. A sculpture is a piece that has been carved or molded out of various materials, such as wood, or metal, or stone, or clay. A person who makes a sculpture is a sculptor. Not many Kentuckians have been nationally recognized in this area, but a few have. Perhaps the best of the early sculptors was Enid Yandell of Louisville. You can see an example of her work in the statue of Daniel Boone in Cherokee Park in Louisville. In modern times, Ed Hamilton, also of Louisville, has won

Edgar Tolson's *Rock Dog* would qualify as folk art.

"Spirit of Freedom" by Ed Hamilton of Louisville.

national praise for such work as his 1998 "Spirit of Freedom." That sculpture honors the black soldiers who fought in the Civil War. It was placed in the nation's capital.

Another form of making things is designing and constructing buildings. People who plan and then build buildings are called **architects.** In this area, the state has had some outstanding people, but not as many of them as in the areas of writing and music. In earlier times, Gideon Shryock of Lexington designed the beautiful Old Capitol. He was only twenty-five years old when he planned the famous double-curved stairs in that building.

If you look at old homes across Kentucky, you can see the beauty of many of them. From the simple log cabin to a mansion, each one has a story. Once they are torn down, that story is lost. Their special meaning is gone. As we build new homes or buildings that look like so many others, we must be careful not to destroy those old homes. They are a special part of our past.

Architect Gideon Shryock designed the beautiful curved staircase in the Old Capitol.

★ Motion Pictures ★

By the 1890s, motion pictures—or movies—had made their way to Kentucky. Those early films had no sound, were very short, and were not in color. People still loved them. They were a new form of entertainment. Almost everyone could afford to go to them. They were the show for all the people of the state.

One person from Kentucky had much to do with making movies look more like what we see today. A director of a movie tells people what to do. He tells the person behind the camera how to film a scene, and he tells an actor or actress what to do in the scene. Some people say that the greatest director of all time was D.W. Griffith, who grew up in Oldham County.

Griffith came from a poor family. To earn money, he acted in plays, worked in a steel factory, sailed on a ship, and did many other

jobs. Once when he had no money, he first got on a freight train, then begged for funds to get home. He returned to Louisville with his feet wrapped in rags for warmth. He was cold and hungry.

Griffith overcame his poverty and became the first great movie director. He made what is considered to be the first major film of the modern era, but it had in it many old, outdated ideas about some people of that time. In other movies, he showed great understanding of people, however. Griffith himself was a hard person to understand. He was great for a time, and his greatness lives on. But in his own time, he was almost forgotten after sound movies came on the scene. He returned to Kentucky and died as he started life—poor.

Other people from Kentucky went into acting. Just in recent times, for example, actors and actresses with Kentucky ties include Tom Cruise, George Clooney, Ashley Judd, and many others. Earlier, other people from Kentucky won major film awards. Griffith helped lead movies into the modern era. Since his time, Kentucky has not been at the forefront of film-making, but it still makes an impact on the motion picture screen.

We have looked at several types of culture and many of the people who make up the culture of Kentucky. Those examples show that the state is strong in some of those areas. We read about stereotypes earlier. Most people's stereotypes of Kentucky do not include great writers or perhaps even great singers. Yet such artists are a part of Kentucky. People of the state should feel proud of Kentuckians' success in different areas of culture.

Remember at the beginning of this chapter, we asked what causes a person to succeed in one of these areas. Have you seen any things that are the same in the lives of most of the people you have read about? Some of them had happy childhoods, but others did not. Some came from one area of the state, while others grew up in a different place. Some came from a city and some from a farm. Some had hard lives. Some had fairly regular ones. Are there things that are the same in their lives or not? You decide.

chapter 10

Kentucky in the Twentieth Century

The twentieth century is the century when your parents, grandparents, and great-grandparents were all born. Many things happened in that century. Some of them were good, and some were bad. Most of all, there were changes in the years from 1900 to 2000. Instead of trying to look at all the things that took place in those years, let's focus on the major changes. We have already read about some of them in other chapters, such as how people live much longer lives now. One change was the growing strength of Kentucky writing, which we read about in chapter 9. Another change had to do with how people make their living, as chapter 8 noted. People went from being part of a farming state to working in different jobs. We will read about changes in education in chapter 11.

In this chapter, let's look at seven of the major changes in the twentieth century.

✦ The Transportation Revolution ✦

A **revolution** is a very big change. Often we refer to revolution in regard to government, but revolutions can also occur in other areas. **Transportation** is how we get from one place to another. In the twentieth century, a transportation revolution took place.

In 1900, railroad travel was the best and fastest way of getting places. Kentucky had railroads early. Before the Civil War, railroad tracks tied Louisville to Nashville. Railroad trains could move coal or farm products to market faster and could take people from place to place so much more easily than before. You could go to the next town three or four times faster than by horse or stagecoach. As one Lewisburg man recalled, "We had trains, which were the life's blood of all the small towns in Kentucky."

Railroads brought the mail faster, took you on trips and vacations, and carried your farm products fresh to market. If you traveled on a train, you could eat in fancy dining cars and could rest in sleeping cars. Trains gave people more choices. Only one in every six Kentucky counties had railroads, though.

People who lived on large rivers, such as the Ohio, could make use of boat travel. The days of the great riverboats had passed, but you could still ship items by water. At a time when there were few good roads, rivers still helped people go places more easily.

If you lived near a railroad or a river in 1900, you had good transportation to use. If you did not, you had to travel pretty much as people had done for hundreds of years. You walked, rode a horse, or went in a wagon. Many people in Kentucky in 1900 had only those choices. It might take them all day to go to the nearest town and back—if the weather was good. In the summer, the dirt roads got dusty. In the winter, the roads looked like mud holes. Most people could not go places very easily.

In the days when people usually went long distances on trains, dining cars gave them a place to eat as they traveled.

As the twentieth century went on, two things changed all that. First, cars began to replace horses. The first cars did not go very fast and broke down often on the bad roads. They still could move people faster than horses, though. Kentucky slowly began to build better roads. In the 1950s, America started the interstate highway systems that allowed people to travel across the country even faster. In Kentucky, major interstates run north and south (I-65, I-71, and I-75) and east and west (I-64 and I-24). To be near an interstate road was like being near a railroad earlier. You had even faster ways to get places.

Old and new forms of transportation meet. Here a mule is getting ready to pull out a car stuck in a creek in the 1930s.

Because many towns were not on interstates, Kentucky built roads like the interstates and called them parkways. You had to pay a fee, or a toll, to travel on them at first. Once the parkways were paid for, no more toll was needed. These roads help connect different places in Kentucky and give it a very good transportation system now. Some of the major parkways are the Martha Layne Collins (Bluegrass) Parkway, the Hal Rogers (Daniel Boone) Parkway, the Bert Combs Mountain Parkway, the Louie Nunn (Cumberland) Parkway, the Wendell Ford Western Kentucky Parkway, the William Natcher (Green River) Parkway, the Audubon Parkway, the Edward T. Breathitt (Pennyrile) Parkway, and the Julian Carroll (Purchase) Parkway. Many other state roads have been expanded and are good highways also, such as Kentucky 80.

Now a person can drive across the state from east to west (or west to east) in less than a day. In 1900, if you tried to cross the state on horseback or by wagon, the trip would take many, many days. Cars gave people the freedom to move, whether or not they lived near a railroad or river.

Modern roads, such as the Bert Combs Mountain Parkway, opened up rural areas of the state.

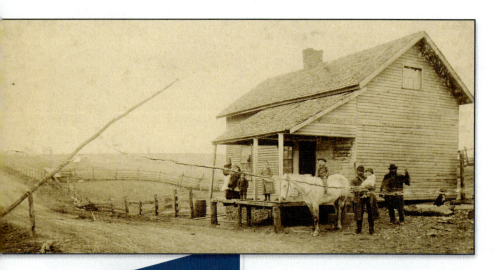

Cars changed how people do things. Good roads broke down the regional barriers dividing the state. People could drive places and see other parts of the state. They might now shop in a larger city instead of in a country store. They could go to the city from time to time but still enjoy farm life.

Cars also changed how people lived their lives. In earlier times, when a young man wanted to visit a young woman, he would go to her house and sit in the living room or on the porch. That might be how they dated. With cars, young people could leave their homes and go out on dates. For a time drive-in movies were popular as well. Cars made a big difference in people's lives.

The greatest transportation change, however, was the addition of air travel. After all, people had traveled on the earth for centuries. Horses, railroads, and cars all moved on the ground; they just moved in different ways. When the Wright Brothers made their first flight in 1903, something new had begun. To actually fly! That filled people with wonder. It was a great change, freeing people from the ground. You could fly over rivers and mountains, the barriers that had always slowed travel.

Toll roads have been a part of Kentucky life almost from the earliest times. People lived in this house and collected tolls.

This is how the Lexington airport looked in the 1930s.

Planes went faster and faster and became safer and safer. As cars and planes got better, people used them to go places. Trains were forgotten. Now, almost no trains in Kentucky carry people. That age has passed. Today, a person can go around the world in the time it used to take to ride a horse just a few miles. The world now seems much smaller because of planes.

Then came space travel in the 1960s. Once more there was a great change. People no longer were limited to the Earth. We could leave it and even land on the moon. Most of all, it showed us that more things could happen in the future. It opened up our imaginations.

From modern airports, like this one in northern Kentucky, people go all over the nation and the world.

★ The Communication Revolution ★

Let's think about all the ways you can find out what is going on in the world. What are those ways?

You may hear news on the radio. You might see things as they happen on television or watch a program on the state-wide network, Kentucky Educational Television (KET). You might read about something in a newspaper or magazine. You might use a computer to get information or even "chat" with other people. The telephone allows your relatives or others to tell you what is happening where they live. You might send or receive e-mail or pictures over the World Wide Web (www). Copies of documents can be instantly sent long distances by fax machines or by computer. Regular mail has become fairly fast as well. The way we exchange messages, ideas, feelings, and information is called **communication.** Communication too went through a revolution in the twentieth century.

In 1900, people on farms were just beginning to get mail delivered to their homes. Before that, to get their letters and packages, they had to go to the nearest post office, which might be many miles away. About the only source of news they had was newspapers. Because travel was so slow, the paper

Getting daily mail delivery meant a lot to people. But this Bowling Green postman seems to be carrying too much mail.

and its news might be a day or two old when you received it. People near railroads got their news faster. A few of the larger cities in 1900 had telephones. But they had no radio, no television, no fax, and no e-mail. Movies were just starting and were simple. No VCRs and videotapes existed, nor did any CDs or DVDs. People might play records on a record player, but they had few ways to hear the latest songs or see the newest trends.

People in 1900 had too little information to help them in making choices. Now, we have just the opposite problem. We may have too much information. Our problem is not getting information, for information is everywhere. Our problem is how to decide what is good information and what is worthless and bad. Just because you see something in a book or on a computer screen does not mean that it is right. The communication revolution has helped us in many ways, but like all change, it means we have to deal with new issues.

Computers have become an important part of the communication revolution.

✦ The New Deal ✦

About a third of the way through the twentieth century, the United States went through the Great Depression. A **depression** in business comes about when businesses start to lose money. They may fire some or all of their workers. Since the workers no longer are getting paid, they buy less, and more businesses have problems. Jobless people may not be able to pay off their loans and debts, and this creates more problems. Banks are usually a very safe place to keep money. In the Depression, some banks had to close their doors. If you had money saved over the years, it was gone. You might be suddenly broke and jobless. It was a hard time.

At the start of the Depression, many people said that government should not get involved in economic problems.

A Smithland family during the Great Depression of the 1930s.
Do they look worried or concerned?

They thought persons should only take care of themselves. Soon, however, it became clear that the Depression was so bad that something had to be done or people would starve or even turn to violence. President Franklin D. Roosevelt and Congress started what became known as the New Deal. It was begun to help people make it through the Depression. The New Deal also changed the views of many people. Now many agreed that the government should try to help people in hard times.

To protect people if a bank closed, the U.S. government said it would make sure that their money would be returned. If you see a bank that says it is "FDIC-insured," that is what that means. The New Deal also set up Social Security, which helps people as they get older as well as those of all ages who have special health needs.

In the Great Depression, many people lost their jobs. There was no work. With their money gone, their families had no food. It was a scary time for America. To try to keep people alive until times got better, the government set up programs that paid people to do work. If you look around your community, you probably will see something built by those workers in the 1930s. A lot of Kentucky courthouses and other public buildings went up then. Many schools were built, as were bridges and roads. The gold vault at Ft. Knox came about as part of those programs.

The government tried to help people without jobs during the Depression. One way was to pay them to construct buildings, such as this courthouse in Casey County, Kentucky.

DOCUMENT 10.1

The coming of electricity to rural homes changed people's lives so much. Here is how some women in West Kentucky remembered that change:

Mittie Dame of McLean County: *We got electricity and we thought we were living in New York. It was something we never dreamed of.*

Irene Taylor of Lewisport: *When we turned those lights on, we went over the house. You just couldn't believe it was the same place.*

Mattie Lou Thrasher of Hancock County: *You put away those kerosene lamps; you put away a lot of labor. You had to fill the lamp at least once a week. And you had to clean the glass. And then we had light that we could read by, so you could really see something.*

Dora Landrum of Ohio County: *One of the great things that hit the farms was the electricity. It just changed everything. The whole countryside was lighted. It was just a big change—from coal oil lamps, the old icebox or no ice at all.*

The New Deal helped bring these improvements about. In the 1930s only four of every one hundred farm families had electricity. By the end of the 1940s, some sixty of every one hundred did.

As you read over what those women felt about electricity, can you think of anything your parents saw that gave them the same sense of wonder?

If you have hiked or walked a trail at an older state park, the trail was likely built by New Deal workers. They also planted many trees across the state. The government funded the building of the dams that now form Lake Barkley and Kentucky Lake in the western part of the state. The dams helped produce cheap electricity. (See document 10.1.) People on farms began to get electric lights and electric appliances for the first time. Those lakes also gave people a place to fish or camp out. They helped make the area a vacation spot.

The New Deal did not solve all problems. Many problems remained. But at least it helped many people. It did not accept the idea that poor people would always be poor, or that hungry children would stay that way. It said to Americans that we are all a part of the nation and that we should try to help each other in times of need. One person wrote that the New Deal "was for a generation of people who had known nothing but poverty an introduction to possibilities." Life might be better. It gave them hope.

★ Wars ★

Unfortunately, a series of wars in the twentieth century destroyed not only the hopes of some but also the lives of thousands. Wars start when two sides cannot agree and one side or the other uses force to try to get its way. In the twentieth century, the United States (and Kentucky) sent soldiers to fight in World War I, World War II, the Korean War, the Vietnam War, and the Gulf War. America's part in those wars meant that we were fighting during about twenty of the century's one hundred years.

A World War I soldier.

In the course of these wars, about 12,500 people from Kentucky died. Not only did the state lose those young lives, but the deaths also deeply hurt each family who lost someone. Many more were wounded in war. Why did they fight for their country? Sometimes they went to war to protect an American freedom, or to aid a friendly country in need, or to protect a smaller country from a bigger one that wanted to take it by force, or to fight back when we were attacked first (as at Pearl Harbor). Whatever the reason, America and Kentucky went to war.

A man from Fleming County helped raise the American flag in a famous World War II battle. This picture is very famous.

In each of the wars, people from the state played an important role. In World War I, for example, the highest-ranking black American soldier was Colonel Charles Young of Mason County. The son of a former slave, he had served in

KENTUCKY FACES — Sarah Gertrude Knott

Many talented people migrated out of Kentucky in the twentieth century. Many also never could really leave behind the state of their birth.

Sarah Gertrude Knott was born in Ballard County in the Purchase area of Kentucky. She went to McCracken County High School and a school in Georgetown, Kentucky, then attended college outside the state.

At the start of the Great Depression, she moved to St. Louis, Missouri. There she began her new project. Knott became director of the National Folk Festival at its beginning in 1934 and stayed at her job until 1971. It became her life's work. She used experts in the field to help her and moved the festival from place to place to raise money for it.

That folk festival was different from others. For one thing, it was national. It also included Native Americans and African Americans, which was unusual for the time. Knott began it because "I got sold on the idea of rural drama, of simple natural drama that grew out of the lives of people."

Twice the festival met in Kentucky—in Covington and in Florence. By the time Knott turned over leadership of the festival to others, folk festivals had moved beyond her vision of them. She returned to live in Princeton, Kentucky. Like many others, she did come home again. Knott died in 1984. Her National Folk Festival continues to this day.

Kentucky has had many more of its people leaving the state than it has had people coming into the state to live. As a result, it has not grown as fast as many other states.

People left Kentucky for several reasons. African Americans moved north to get away from the way they were treated and to find better jobs. People from Appalachia left after the coal mines stopped hiring. They too were looking for good jobs. Those who lived in rural areas all over the state simply moved away to seek a better life.

Much of the out-migration took place during World War II and in the twenty-five years following the war. In eastern Kentucky, over three-fourths of a million people moved to other states. Such numbers compare to the great overseas migrations of people to the New World in an earlier century.

Those migrations meant a great loss for Kentucky. Who knows what strengths those who left could have brought to Kentucky if they had stayed? More recently, the trend of out-migration has not been as strong. The state now offers its citizens fairer treatment and more job choices than before.

★ Equal Rights ★

Another trend in the twentieth century and beyond has been to improve the rights of groups of people who did not have equal rights in 1900.

EQUAL RIGHTS FOR WOMEN

Women had just started to gain some of those rights in 1900. As late as a half-dozen years before 1900, a married woman in Kentucky had almost no rights. She could not keep any money she earned. It went to her husband. Anything she owned at the time of marriage became totally her husband's property. Women in the state could not sit on a jury or vote on most matters. Many people felt that women should stay in the home and be wives and mothers and do nothing else.

Others disagreed. They wanted women to have the same rights under the law as men. They did not say that women should not be wives and mothers. They just wanted women to be able to choose what they did.

Eliza Calvert Obenchain spoke out for women's rights.

DOCUMENT 10.3

Julia Ewan stood before other students in 1910. She was graduating from Miss Gordon's Training School in Maysville, Kentucky. Ewan spoke for the young women seeking more rights as she asked, "Has Woman Any Longer a Sphere?"

In the days of our grandmothers, woman certainly had a sphere or tread way in which she <u>must</u> walk. She had [few] choices of a career. She could take upon her self the duties of a domestic drudge. She could look pretty.

There were always two possible escapes; the one, an early demise [death]; the other, the finding of a master [husband] who was willing to set her over a home of her own, where, <u>second to him,</u> she might rule supreme.

But what a change! What a happy change! Woman is coming to her own. She is crowding into every calling, from college president to policeman; from land agent, to clergy man; from lawyer to laborer; from trained nurse to surgeon. She is bank president, merchant, farmer, editor, sculptor, reporter, lawyer, lobbyist. And a thousand other things.

She doesn't loaf; she doesn't swear; she doesn't use tobacco. There is just one thing she doesn't do that she wants to do, and means to do, and probably will do very soon—that is the right to vote. She means to have her rights on this vital point recognized, or know the reason why, and the legal male mind had better sit up and take notice.

Ten years after Ewan gave this talk, women in Kentucky finally got the right to vote.

If Julia Ewan gave a speech about women today, what do you think she would talk about?

As early as 1867, some women in Glendale in Hardin County set up the first group in the state that asked for the vote for women. A few years later, a statewide group formed. It was the first one in the South. Soon after that, Kentucky women asked not just for the vote but for additional rights. They formed the Kentucky Equal Rights Association. Over the years, people like Josephine Henry of Versailles and Eliza Calvert Obenchain of Bowling Green helped lead the fight for women's rights. Two other Kentucky women became major national as well as state leaders.

The first was Laura Clay of Lexington. She was the daughter of the antislavery leader Cassius Clay. He divorced her mother and later, when he was eighty-four, married a fifteen-year-old girl. Laura's mother was left with little after the divorce, due to Kentucky laws. That caused Laura Clay to seek justice for women. She and her sisters helped get some of the laws changed. By 1900, however, Kentucky women still could not vote. Another Kentuckian would lead the fight for voting rights in the twentieth century.

Madeline McDowell Breckinridge of Lexington was like Laura Clay in that she came from an old Kentucky family. The great-granddaughter of Henry Clay, "Madge" married into the famous Breckinridge family. Her husband's sister was also the first woman lawyer in the state. So when Madge Breckinridge spoke, people listened. They knew she was no newcomer but had the blood of Kentucky in her.

Madge had grown up much like other girls of the late nineteenth century. She played tennis, danced, rode horses, and enjoyed the things young girls did at the time. Then her world changed. A bone disease caused her to have part of her leg taken off. From then on, she could have been inactive and lived a quiet life. She did not. After her marriage, she worked hard to get public support for the cause of women's rights. She used her family ties to get private support.

Breckinridge got parks and playgrounds for the children of her city. She pushed the state to pass laws to keep very young children from working. Madge tried to make life better for the children she never had. She also worked with others and got Kentucky to support an amendment to the U.S. Constitution that would give women the right to vote. In 1920 that amendment became the law of the land. At the age of forty-eight, Madge Breckinridge voted for the first time. It was the only time, because she died that same year. But her cause lived on.

In 1920, Kentucky voted to support the effort to give women the right to vote. Here the governor approves that action.

Reformer Madge Breckinridge

Governor Martha Layne Collins

In some ways Kentucky continued to be a leader in women's rights in the South, for a time at least. Mary Elliott Flanery of Catlettsburg became the first woman elected to a state legislature in the South. Katherine Langley of Pike County became one of the first eight women elected to Congress in the United States. Later Kentucky would select Martha Layne Collins of Shelbyville and Versailles as governor. She would be only the sixth woman elected to that office in America. Collins was a teacher before going into politics.

In some other areas, however, Kentucky has not been a leader. It has not elected many women to the General Assembly. It ranks forty-seventh out of the fifty states in number of women legislators. Few women own businesses in Kentucky.

EQUAL RIGHTS FOR ALL RACES

Equal rights did not just mean equal rights for women. African Americans sought equal justice under the law as well. In the first half of the twentieth century, Kentucky law and custom kept blacks and whites apart most of the time. Black children and white children might play together when they were young, but by the time they got to high school, their parents would separate them. Black women and men might work in white homes and be beside whites all day, but they could not do that outside those homes. It was a strange time.

For a long time, laws and rules tried to keep whites and blacks apart and unequal.

African Americans lived in a second-class status. They were no longer slaves, but they did not have equal rights. The separation of the two groups was called **segregation.** By law or local rules, blacks could not eat in the same places as whites; they could not use the same swimming pools or bathrooms; they could not drink out of the same water fountains; they could not sit in the same area in movie theaters or train stations; they could not use the same parks; they could not go to the same library or touch the same books; they could not go to the same school or church; they could not play on the same sports team; they could not

Blyden Jackson

Blyden Jackson grew up black in Louisville in the early 1900s. He lived in a segregated society. African Americans could go only certain places and do only certain things. They could not go other places. In his later book, *The Waiting Years* (1976), he recalled, "In my Louisville, it was understood that Negroes had a place and should be kept therein." Jackson did say that the ugly, brutal side of segregation seldom was seen in the city.

He was born in Paducah in 1910. His mother worked in an African American library, and his father taught history in the black schools. They moved to Louisville when Blyden was four years old.

Jackson's Louisville "was a strong and rich community," despite segregation. People did the best they could with what they had. He remembered good teachers and noble citizens, who helped him grow. At the same time, Blyden Jackson could never forget the two worlds: "Through a veil I could perceive the forbidden city, the Louisville where white folks lived. It was the Louisville of the downtown hotels, the lower floors of the big movie houses, the high schools I read about, the restricted haunts I sometimes passed, like white restaurants and country clubs. On my side of the veil everything was black; the homes, the people, the churches, the schools, the Negro park with the Negro park police. I knew there were two Louisvilles."

Jackson overcame the handicaps of segregation and in his lifetime saw those barriers slowly break down. He went on to get the highest college degree in his field of English. Then Jackson became a college professor, teaching at Fisk University, Southern University, and the University of North Carolina, among other places. He became nationally known and wrote such books as *Black Poetry in America* (1974) and *History of Afro American Literature* (1989). This man who was the grandson of slaves became one of the most respected people in his field of study.

Blyden Jackson died in 2000, at the age of eighty-nine.

use the same hotels; and they could not be buried in the same cemeteries.

One African American man growing up in Louisville during that time recalled: "You couldn't even sit down to eat a White Castle [hamburger]. You had to buy the White Castle from the take-out window." Another man from Paducah told how white and black boys "shot at birds together. We played marbles together, and ball. Why did we have to go to different schools? I couldn't quite understand it."

He could not understand it because he believed in what American democracy meant—that all are created equal. As we noted earlier in this book, when one group thinks it is better

Louisville lawyer Charles Anderson Jr. became the first African American to sit in the Kentucky General Assembly. He is shown here with his mother.

than another group, that is a very dangerous idea. It goes against American ideals that say all people have equal worth as citizens.

Some black and white people finally began to question the rules of segregation. In the 1930s, Charles W. Anderson Jr. of Louisville was elected to the state General Assembly. It was the first time an African American had held that office in Kentucky and the first time a black man had served as a legislator in the South in the twentieth century. It came about because African Americans in the state continued to vote, unlike their situation in the Deep South. Voting was an important right.

Finally, in 1954, the U.S. Supreme Court ruled that segregation must end. Many people in southern states tried to fight the ruling with violent acts. At that time Americans saw Kentucky as a model for the South. In the next year, black students entered previously all-white schools in Lexington and Wayne County, and the process had started. People at Clay in Webster County and Sturgis in Union County protested, trying to keep segregation. The governor sent in troops and stopped their actions. Across Kentucky, change took place pretty quietly in the schools.

Martin Luther King Jr. led supporters of civil rights in a march in 1964 in Frankfort.

Shelby County's Whitney Young Jr. spoke out for black rights at the national level. Here he discusses issues with President Lyndon Johnson and Martin Luther King Jr.

It took longer for segregation to end in other areas. Students would "sit-in" at lunch counters to protest not being able to eat there. Usually the owners would finally give in. Stronger laws were still needed. In 1964, Martin Luther King Jr. came to Kentucky to lead a march of more than ten thousand people on the state capitol to plead for such a law. The General Assembly failed to pass the law. Two years later it did pass the Civil Rights Act. That was the first such state law passed in the South.

Several black leaders spoke out for the cause in the state. Frank Stanley Jr. of the black newspaper the *Louisville Defender* told of the need for change. Luska J. Twyman of Glasgow became the first African American mayor elected to a full term in a Kentucky city. At the national level, Whitney Young Jr. of Shelby County served as the head of the Urban League. That group pushed for black rights and asked people to try to understand each other. Because of Young's work, the president of the United States awarded him the nation's highest honor for a person not in the military.

Probably the best-known Kentuckian of the 1960s and 1970s was not Young, or even some white person. It was an African American man who first bore the same name as the early antislavery leader Cassius Clay. Do you know who that was? He later changed to another religion and changed his name. Cassius Clay became Muhammad Ali.

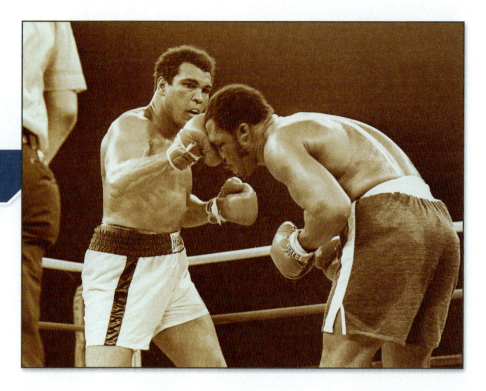

Boxer Muhammad Ali in a 1975 fight.

Ali grew up in Louisville and in 1960 won an Olympic gold medal in boxing. He got so upset about segregation, though, that he later threw his medal in the Ohio River. Ali became boxing champion of the world in 1964. He had to give up the title three years later when he was ordered to go to jail because he refused to go into the army. Ali refused to go because of his religion. Later the U.S. Supreme Court supported his stand. He won the title two more times, in 1974 and in 1978, and became world famous. More recently, he has made peace with the city where he threw away his medal, and Louisville has honored him in several ways.

Those changes in views about Ali show how the state has changed over the past fifty years. Things that could not happen a half century ago happen every day in Kentucky and hardly anyone thinks anything about it. It now seems natural for blacks and whites to eat together, swim together, and go to the same movies, libraries, parks, and hotels. It would seem strange if they did not play on the same sports teams and go to the same schools. People still separate from each other too much, and some people still judge by skin color, not by the person. New groups, such as Hispanics, face some of those same problems. But if you think about how segregation was not so long ago, Kentucky has come a long way. It still has a long way to go, but it has moved closer to the American ideal.

★ Politics ★

The last major change that we will look at in twentieth-century Kentucky involves politics. **Politics** is the process of winning and holding political office and then guiding the policies of government. Usually when we talk of politics, we also mention the two main political parties—the Democrats and the Republicans.

Each of those parties is made up of people who believe in some or all of the same things as the party itself does. They support with their votes the people who run for office from that party. At times, however, people do not vote for all the people of their party. A growing number of people in Kentucky have not joined either party. They are called Independents.

If you made a chart of which party won political races in Kentucky in the twentieth century, it would look like a roller coaster. Some counties tend to vote for one party, and some for another. Only a few are fairly evenly divided. However, if you look at elections to the General Assembly over the entire twentieth century, the Democrats generally won those races, as well as many local ones. For much of the twentieth century, Kentucky was said to be a Democratic state, but that is not true now. This change is one of the trends of the century.

In the governor's races, the same thing holds true, but with differences. In the first third of the century, the two parties were almost evenly divided in winning that office. The Great Depression and its effects, however, caused some people to move from the Republican to the Democratic party. That changed the balance. In fact, before 2003, Democrats had been elected governor fifty-two of the last fifty-six years. But in 2003, Republicans won the office of governor for the first time in thirty-six years.

In federal elections in Kentucky for president, for U.S. senator, and for the U.S. House of Representatives, a very different trend can be seen. Over the last fifty years, the two parties have divided U.S. Senate seats and the vote for president. Democrats tended to win most U.S. House elections for the first part of that period, while more recently Republicans have won most of them. In short, Kentucky has been divided. It has favored one party, then the other party, and has gone back and forth in how it votes.

One thing that has been the same across the years has been strong leaders in both parties. In the last half century, for

Republican U.S. Senator John Sherman Cooper of Somerset.

example, for many years the Republicans elected John Sherman Cooper of Somerset as U.S. senator. In 1960, national newspaper people named him the best Republican senator in Washington, D.C. Besides Governor Louie Nunn, more recently the party leader has been U.S. Senator Mitch McConnell of Louisville.

The best-known Democratic leaders have included A.B. "Happy" Chandler, who was born in Corydon in western Kentucky and lived in Versailles in the central Bluegrass. In addition to serving as governor and U.S. senator, he was the head of major league baseball for a time. Twenty years after he first won the governor's race, he won again. His slogan was "Be like your pappy, and vote for Happy." Other leaders include Alben W. Barkley (see "Kentucky Faces," page 223); Governor and Senator Earle Clements of Union County, who really was the first modern governor of the state; Bert Combs (See "Kentucky Faces" in chapter 4); and Wendell Ford of Owensboro. After being governor, Ford entered the U.S. Senate and held several key posts there. When Ford left the Senate, he had served longer there than any other Kentuckian.

In politics, Kentucky has changed several times over the years of the twentieth century. How do you think it will be in your lifetime in the twenty-first century?

The most important question, however, is this one: When you are old enough, will you vote? About half of the people who can vote in Kentucky do not. We are below average in that regard. If you do not vote, you are not carrying out your duty as a citizen. You are letting others have a voice in selecting leaders and giving up your own right to do so.

One other question to think about: Will Kentucky ever have a year as special as 1949? That is when President Truman was sworn in. His grandparents came from Kentucky. He was being sworn in by Chief Justice Fred Vinson—from Kentucky. The vice president taking the oath of office was Alben Barkley—of Kentucky. He was sworn in by another Supreme Court Justice, Stanley Reed—of Kentucky. Yet another Kentucky-born justice watched.

In sports that same year, Adolph Rupp of the University of Kentucky won another basketball championship, and Calumet Farm of Lexington had a horse that won the Derby. In professional basketball, Joe Fulks from Marshall County set a new

Alben W. Barkley

Would you vote for someone named Willie Alben Barkley? That was the name Barkley was given by his parents, but he decided it was not a good name for a politician. He changed it to Alben W. Barkley.

Barkley was born in a log house in Graves County in the Purchase area of Kentucky. He later made his home in Paducah and rose to political greatness from there. During his entire career, he lost only one race—for governor in 1923. After that, he became the most important Kentucky political figure of the twentieth century.

Barkley served fourteen years in the U.S. House and then as U.S. senator for twenty-four years. During part of that time, he held the key job of Majority Leader of the Senate. In that post he helped get important New Deal and then wartime acts passed. Later, he became vice president under President Harry Truman. People called him "the Veep."

Barkley might have been president if he had not held fast to his beliefs. In 1944

President Roosevelt was going to choose a new vice president to run with him for office. At that time Roosevelt was not in good health, and people knew it.

That year the president sent a tax bill to the Senate. Barkley finally got it passed but had to accept many amendments to do so. Roosevelt then turned the bill down by vetoing it. Barkley felt betrayed. He had done the best he could, but the president had not supported him. In protest, he resigned as Majority Leader. The senators re-elected him the next day and passed the bill over the president's veto. Barkley had done "what he thought was what honor required." However, that action made Roosevelt mad. Barkley had been a leading choice to be vice president, but now Roosevelt picked Harry S. Truman. Only months after the election, Roosevelt died, and Truman became president. Had Barkley just done what Roosevelt wanted, he might have been the vice president and then the president.

Barkley continued to serve the nation well. Witty and warm, he was an excellent speaker. One man heard him and recalled: "He was nearly irresistible. When he got going [as a speaker] he carried everything with him like a windstorm."

Senator Barkley was giving one of his speeches at a college in 1956. He ended his talk with these words: "I would rather be a servant in the house of the Lord, than sit in the seats of the mighty." He then fell over dead from a heart attack. But those last words came to be some of the most famous ones in Kentucky history. He had died as a servant of the people of the state.

Vice President Alben Barkley (right) of Paducah, with President Harry Truman.

In 1949 Kentucky seemed to be everywhere you looked—in politics, sports, and even in the movies.

record by scoring sixty-three points in one game. Baseball's "Pee Wee" Reese of Kentucky led his team into the World Series.

In the arts, Kentuckian Robert Penn Warren saw a movie based on one of his books win the major motion picture prize, the Oscar, as the best movie of the year. Covington-born Robert Surtees won an Oscar as well for the way he filmed another movie. In Lexington, A.B. Guthrie's second book came out that year and won the Pulitzer Prize a year later. Another movie of 1949 starred actor John Wayne as "The Fighting Kentuckian." Kentucky seemed to be everywhere a person looked.

When the twentieth century ended, people could look back and see much change and many trends. The transportation revolution, the communication revolution, the New Deal, wars, out-migration, the fight for equal rights, politics—all showed how much had changed. Some have said that more changes took place in the twentieth century than in all the centuries before. Whether or not that is true, if a person was born in the first decade of the twentieth century and still lived in the last year of that century, that person had seen vast change. Will you see as much change, or even more, in your lifetime?

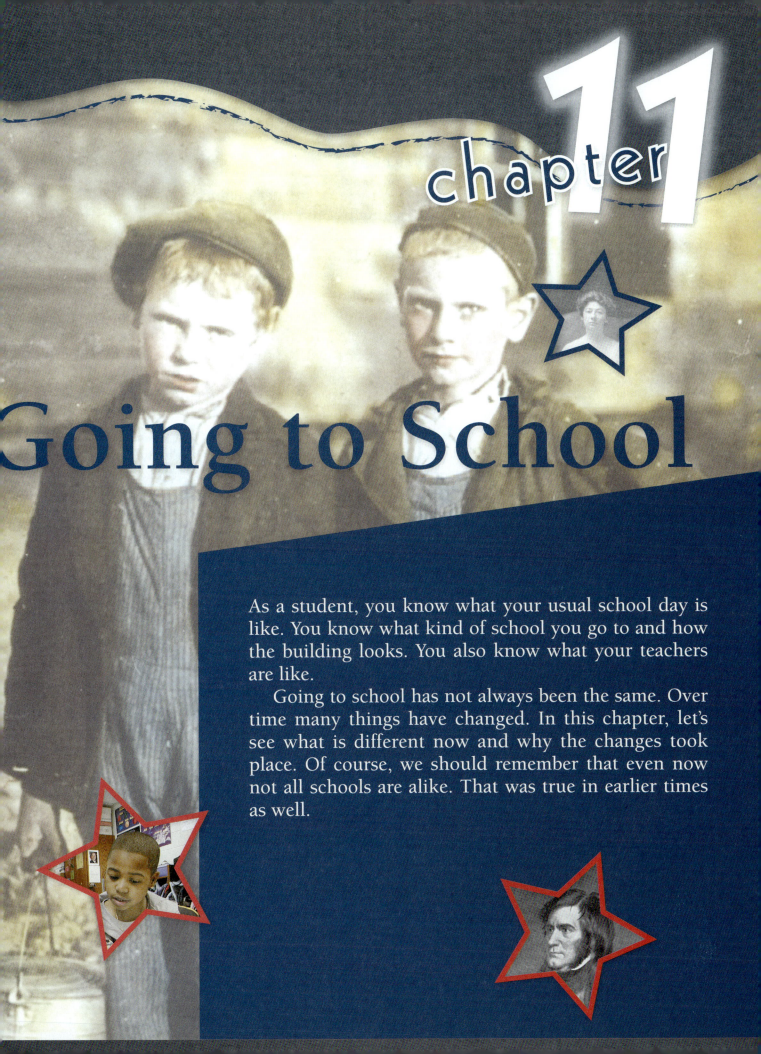

chapter 11

Going to School

As a student, you know what your usual school day is like. You know what kind of school you go to and how the building looks. You also know what your teachers are like.

Going to school has not always been the same. Over time many things have changed. In this chapter, let's see what is different now and why the changes took place. Of course, we should remember that even now not all schools are alike. That was true in earlier times as well.

★ Early Kentucky Schools ★

One historian wrote that frontier Kentucky "was a battlefield not a schoolground." Frontier people had to fight for their lives. Setting up schools did not seem so important. Yet, from almost the first year of the settlements, students were being taught, in forts and then in rough schools. People knew that children needed to learn, even with danger all around them.

At that time, adults had a different idea about school than most have today. They thought that education should only be a private matter. Even after Kentucky became a state, they did not think the state should pay for public schools, except in a very indirect way. That view held Kentucky education back for a time.

Instead of public schools, they started private schools, called academies. Anyone who went to an academy had to pay to attend. The state tried to encourage those schools by giving them some land to get started. They hoped that the money from the sale of that land would allow the schools to grow. Probably about 250 schools were started that way in a one-hundred-year period.

The plan did not work very well. Many of the academies went broke and closed. Others gave only a weak education. The ones that continued still only served people who could pay. But most people could not afford to send their children to a private school. In fact, nearly forty years after Kentucky became a state, fewer than one of every five children in Kentucky went to any school. If the state wanted its future citizens to be educated, something different had to be done.

At a time when men and women usually did not attend school together, Shelbyville Female College was a place where women could study.

While Kentucky was trying to find an answer to that question, private groups opened their own schools. Soon after statehood, a Lexington paper noted in 1798 that a Sunday School would be opened "for the use of the People of Color. Those who wish their servants taught, will please send a line." Unlike most other slave states, Kentucky did not keep slaves from learning to read and write. Not many schools for African Americans started, but some did.

At the same time, schools only for girls opened up as well. Remember Julia Tevis and Science Hill? (See "Kentucky Faces" in chapter 6.) Catholic religious groups also started girls' schools in Nelson and Marion Counties—these were the first such schools west of the mountains. Other schools for girls came along over time, such as Potter College in Bowling Green.

Still, almost all the schools served only a small portion of the children of school age. Finally, in 1838, Kentucky set up a system of public schools. The U.S. government had extra money and sent it back to the states. Kentucky pledged to "forever set apart [that money] to funding and sustaining a general system of public instruction." The first person to head the system told why it was so important. (See document 11.1.)

About ten years later, the Reverend Robert J. Breckinridge of Danville and Lexington was in charge of Kentucky schools. He found out that few schools had been set up and few children went to school. A typical school went for only three months, and, with fifty students and one teacher in it, could expect to get a total of only fifteen dollars from the state. That was not enough. Breckinridge got a tax passed to provide needed money. He got more schools started. When he left office, nine of every ten children were in school, at least for a time. Most of all, he made people believe "that the work can be done and shall be done." Breckinridge came to be known as the "father of Kentucky public schools."

Robert J. Breckinridge was called the father of the public school system.

★ Life in School ★

Most Kentucky schools were one-room schools. Even as late as 1920, about seven thousand of the eight thousand elementary schools in the state still had only one room. That meant

DOCUMENT 11.1

Reverend J.J. Bullock was the head of the new public school system at its beginning in 1838. He was twenty-six years old. Bullock left after a year, due to his health. When he got better, he went back to preaching and later became the chief minister to the U.S. Senate. His first report to the General Assembly told why public schools should be well funded:

The great object of the school law is to give every child in the commonwealth a good education; to develop the whole intellect of the state. The great principle of the system is that of equality; the rich and the poor are placed on the same footing.

That the education of all the children of the state will cost much, I do not wish to conceal; but it should be obtained at any cost. Nothing is so wasteful as ignorance. The elevation of an entire people is beyond all price.

To provide for the education of all the children of the state is the most economical expenditure of money that can possibly be made. Ignorance keeps inactive the mind and leads to poverty.

that they also had only one teacher. The school children would take turns working with the teacher. If lessons were done out loud, everyone could hear what was said.

Daniel Drake of Mason County went to a very early frontier school. It was sixteen feet wide, twenty feet long, and made of logs. The space between the logs often was poorly filled and failed to keep out the wind and cold. One boy recalled that "the ink cannot be kept from freezing." The only light in Drake's one-room school came through holes covered with oiled paper. There was no glass to use for windows. Water had to be brought from a stream three hundred yards away. Drake remembered his teacher as a person who could teach spelling, reading, and a little writing, but that was all the teacher knew.

School buildings seemed to change very little over the years. A few years after the Civil War, a Kentucky governor gave this view of the average schoolhouse: "A little, square, squatty, unhewed log building, blazing in the sun, standing upon the dusty highway or some bleak and barren spot that has been robbed of every tree, without yard, fence, or other surroundings suggestive of comfort, is the fit representative of the district schoolhouses of the commonwealth."

"The benches," he said, were "slabs with legs in them so long as to lift the little fellows' feet from the floor, and without support for the back." The governor called them places "full of foul air." Here, he noted, the lack of funding "condemns childhood to pass its bright young days." The governor went on to say that such a school "seems to have been built simply as a pen for prisoners, at the smallest outlay of money. It stands an offense to justice, kindness, taste, [a] blot upon the site."

That lack of proper funding continued for nearly one hundred years after he wrote. In fact, just twenty or so years later, a man wrote of the problems he faced: "The difficulty I meet in the work of improving our [school] house is to get the people to understand that a Woodford County child is worth as much as a race horse and is entitled to as good a home." About forty years after that, another man wrote that the problem still existed, in the age of roads: "Apparently Kentuckians are building $500 school houses along million dollar highways." He noted that every other state in the union had spent more on school buildings from 1920 to 1930 than Kentucky had.

So, throughout much of the state's history, children went to schools that were not supported as they should have been. What was a typical day like for a student of about a century ago?

One man in the Purchase area recalled that his school started at eight and went to four o'clock. Students had recess in the morning and afternoon, and an hour for lunch and more play. In his school, everyone read out loud, and each student learned

Small schools, like this 1909 one in Ohio County, were very common in Kentucky. Notice the bell to call students to class.

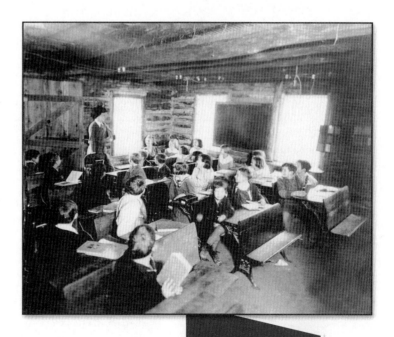

Interior of a rural school in Leslie County in the 1930s.

DOCUMENT 11.2

In 1921 the Kentucky Education Commission gave its report on the state's schools. Here is what they said about the buildings:

The great majority of rural schoolhouses—9 out of 10—have in the main, a single classroom.

Approximately 50 percent of these schoolhouses are painted and in good repair. The other half never even had a coat of paint, and are in ill repair. The roofs leak, the boarding is off here and there; doors are broken, knobs gone, window panes out, walls stained, floors uneven and cracked, seats broken, and a pall of dust over all.

A stove furnishes heat, the fire being started by the first person who reaches school. A bucket with the common drinking cup takes the place of a sanitary drinking fountain; [bathroom] facilities are nonexistent. The blackboard usually consists of a front wall and a few side walls painted black.

About half of the rural schools have wells or cisterns; at the other half, water is carried from a nearby spring or well.

Of the city school buildings, 40 percent are old structures. They are, as a rule, inadequately lighted and ventilated.

Remember how the Kentucky governor said Kentucky school buildings were in bad shape? That was forty-seven years before this time. Read the governor's comments again and compare the two. Had things changed much?

How would you describe your classroom? How have things changed since 1921? What would you like to see in schools in the future?

some things well but other subjects not at all. He noted that in geography he knew the states and countries, "but knew nothing about people and their ways of living" in those countries.

A few years later, a Lyon County man told of getting ready for school. His father bought his clothes for the year—two pairs of overalls and two blue shirts. He did not need shoes yet, for everyone went barefoot until the first frost came. His school ran for seven months, from July through January. The school day started at eight. Students had a twenty-minute morning recess and then an hour for lunch. Like almost all school children until more recently, the children brought their own lunch. They usually put it in a lard bucket or a shoe box.

Later they might use a paper sack or, even later, a lunch pail or bucket. After lunch, they went back to classes until school let out at three.

In the 1920s, Lyde Simpson went to a small school in Jessamine County in central Kentucky. She remembered, "We had 18 to 23 students in all eight grades, only about two or three per class. School lasted from 8:30 in the morning until 3:00 in the afternoon. Most students walked to school; some rode horses. The building was heated by an old coal and wood stove. There was a well. We would draw water from it and use tin cups or a dipper to drink from. For lunch we brought sack lunches."

A teacher in that same school recalled that before she came, "Several teachers had been driven off from there. The students had the reputation of being a wild bunch, and the teachers couldn't manage them." Other teachers in other schools across the state told similar stories of students bringing guns and knives to school and of school violence. Unfortunately, that problem is not new in our day.

Teachers more than earned their little pay. The average teacher got $215 a year in 1900, $340 in 1910, and $410

in 1920. The teacher at the Jessamine County school we read about earned $72 per month for a seven-month school term, or a little over $500 a year in 1925. At that time, a cheap new car cost $800. Now, most teachers make more in a year than a new car costs. Their salaries have gone up, but they had a long way to go. For many years, Kentucky teachers were not paid well. The very first person to head the Kentucky school system wrote that for teaching to attract good people—who would stay in it—it had to offer more than a person could make working on a farm. For a long time that was not the case.

In those early days, teachers also "boarded around." To try to get people to teach, different families would give teachers "room and board." That is, they would let a teacher live and eat with them for a month. Then another family would do the same. That helped teachers save money and stay in the profession.

Still, teaching was hard work with low pay. One person said teachers needed only a few things to run a school—a bell, a water bucket, a blackboard, and a stove. He forgot to mention a love for children, knowledge of the subjects, and much else. Teachers had to start the fire in the morning and clean the building after the children left. Most of them taught by themselves in a one-room school with a lot of students. Despite all the problems, though, many teachers taught well, and learning did take place in many cases. A good teacher and willing students can overcome problems.

Going to school in Mercer County before there were school buses.

Cora Wilson Stewart

In 1900, one out of every six people in Kentucky could not read or write. In the prisons, six out of every ten could not read or write. That was a real problem for Kentucky. Cora Wilson Stewart tried to do something about it.

She grew up in Rowan County and began teaching school there when she was twenty years old. At age twenty-six, she was in charge of the whole county school system. Soon she became the first woman president of the state teachers' organization.

Night classes to teach adults to read and write were called moonlight schools.

Stewart decided to start night schools so that adults who wanted to learn to read and write could go to school after work. She called them Moonlight Schools because people walked or rode to school by the light of the moon. They became very popular. She wrote a series of schoolbooks for her schools as well. Stewart became a world-famous speaker on the subject of education for adults.

Stewart's success won her much praise. For six years, the state gave her group money to expand Moonlight Schools over the state. But then the funds stopped coming. She still tried to aid people, but with less success.

Because of her efforts, Kentucky was, for a time, a leader in trying to help people learn to read and write. It lost that place, however. By 1940, only one state had more people who could not read or write. When Stewart died in 1958, she knew that the education fight would still need to go on.

★ Special Schools ★

Certain groups supported schools with different purposes. For instance, at Great Crossing in Scott County, a school for Indians opened in 1825 and had students for twenty-three years. It was called Choctaw Academy. Choctaw was the name of one of the tribal nations that gave money to support the school. Indians from many other tribal groups went there too. One odd thing

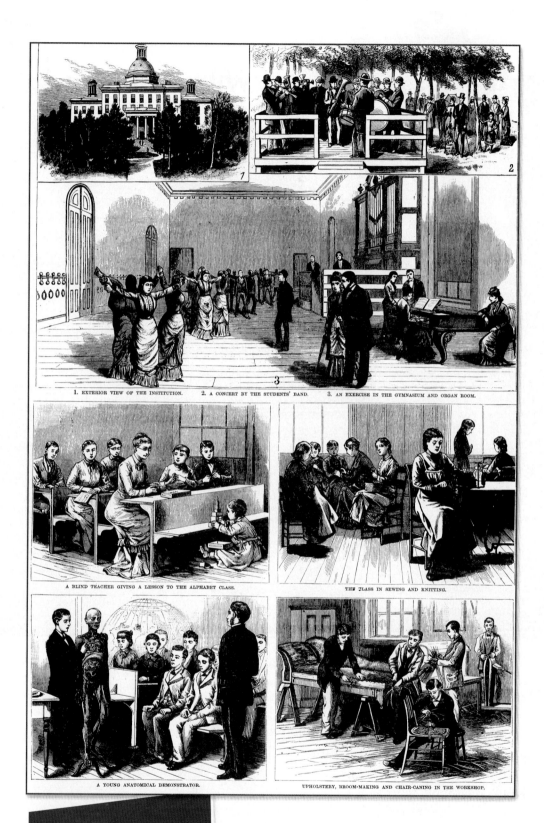

1. EXTERIOR VIEW OF THE INSTITUTION.　　2. A CONCERT BY THE STUDENTS' BAND.　　3. AN EXERCISE IN THE GYMNASIUM AND ORGAN ROOM.

A BLIND TEACHER GIVING A LESSON TO THE ALPHABET CLASS.　　THE CLASS IN SEWING AND KNITTING.

A YOUNG ANATOMICAL DEMONSTRATOR.　　UPHOLSTERY, BROOM-MAKING AND CHAIR-CANING IN THE WORKSHOP.

Scenes of education at the Kentucky Institution for the Education of the Blind, in Louisville in 1880.

about the school is that it was run by Richard M. Johnson, who later became vice president. Remember him? He gained much of his fame for killing the Native American chief Tecumseh. Now he ran a school to help Indians.

Some years before Kentucky supported free public schools for all children, it began to support a school to help educate hearing-impaired children. In 1823 the Kentucky School for the Deaf in Danville became the first state-supported school of the kind in the United States. Less than twenty years later, Kentucky also set up a school for the vision-impaired. The Kentucky School for the Blind in Louisville was the third state-supported one in the nation and the sixth such school overall. Kentucky was a leader in those areas.

Settlement schools were schools that mostly had church support or were independent. They started near the end of the nineteenth century. There were many parts of Kentucky, especially in the eastern region, that did not have schools even then. Women teachers would go into those places and set up, in many cases, the first school the people had. They not only taught school subjects, but they helped people learn other things as well. Some of the best-known settlement schools were Hindman in Knott County, Pine Mountain in Harlan County, and what became Alice Lloyd College in Knott County. At a time when there were no public schools in some parts of the state, these schools met a need. Later, most settlement schools became part of the public school system, closed, or changed in other ways. For a time they were an important part of Kentucky education.

Other kinds of private schools continue to exist. But most Kentucky students, except for those living in a few places, go to public rather than to private schools.

★ Schools in the Twentieth Century and Beyond ★

For students in elementary, middle, and high schools, the twentieth century had a mixed record. In the first half of the century, schools fared poorly. In the last part of the second half of the century, things got better. By then, however, the

Before 1954, these two students could not have been in the same classroom, as they are now.

Under segregation, these students at State Street School in Frankfort could not attend school with white students.

state had fallen way behind, and catching up with other states would take time.

In 1900, Kentucky seemed to be a pretty good place in the South. The state ranked high among southern states in the number of people who could read and write, in the length of the school year, and in the amount of money it spent per child in school. As the century went on, however, the state dropped more and more behind. That trend continued for a long time. The hopes of 1900 faded.

Three major events took place in Kentucky education in the twentieth century. The effects of all three are still felt. They all helped the states' schools move forward. Kentucky needed to do even more, however.

The first big change in Kentucky schools came in 1908. In that year the General Assembly passed a law that improved the whole system. It said that every county in the state must set up a public high school within its borders. Money from a tax gave the schools five times what they had had before. The law also made it harder for students not to attend school.

Education professionals knew that the people of Kentucky needed to support the law year after year. So they carried out what they called "the Whirlwind Campaign." Like a whirlwind, speakers went all over Kentucky supporting the law. At one level, they seemed to be succeeding. High schools jumped in number from fifty-four in 1910 to more than two hundred some ten years later. Money per student more than doubled. People felt good about what they had done.

Remember when we read about perspective—looking at things in different ways? In this case, the people of Kentucky had a narrow perspective. They did not see that other states were moving forward even faster than they were. By 1940, Kentucky stood last in the nation in the number of people who had finished high school. It took the state a long time to get out of that educational hole.

The second major change in Kentucky schools in the twentieth

Lyman Johnson

Lyman Johnson and some others were going through a small Kentucky town. It was late, and they were hungry. Johnson had a college degree and was a high school teacher by that time. When he went to the restaurant, the owner saw that Johnson was African American and said, "You can't eat in the dining room." He sent Johnson around to the kitchen. Johnson said they gave him good food. In fact, he said, "They gave us everything but respect." Respect was what Johnson wanted most of all.

Johnson's grandparents had been slaves. He grew up as one of nine children of a family in Tennessee. His father was the principal of a black school there. Johnson went away to college in Michigan and found himself the only black person in all-white classes. After college he came to Louisville and taught for about forty years at Louisville Central High School.

He found that some things in Kentucky were like they were in Tennessee. Segregation ruled. If you went to a dentist, he had separate chairs for whites and blacks. Black women could go to some stores to buy dresses, but they could not try them on. When Johnson went on vacation once to another state, he found out that the rules said African Americans could use the beach and swim in the ocean only at night. He thought such rules were stupid. Johnson once said, "Don't pity me because I live in the slums. Pity yourself that you permit a slum to be."

Johnson decided to change the rules. He applied to enter the University of Kentucky. At that time, all Kentucky schools were segregated. A judge ordered in 1949 that Johnson should be allowed to attend the university. After that other colleges opened their classrooms to people of all races. Years later, the University of Kentucky honored Johnson for breaking down those barriers. In Louisville, a school was named for him. Johnson had made a difference. He had earned respect.

century occurred when the U.S. Supreme Court ruled that black and white students could go to school together. Separating them in different schools was illegal, it said.

The third change came in 1990. That year the state passed the Kentucky Education Reform Act, or KERA for short. The old system had not worked very well. Schools in poor counties, especially, had a hard time. Finally the state supreme court agreed that the system was not fair. They did away with it and said that a new one must be set up. (See document 4.3 in chapter 4.) KERA included several new ways of doing things to try to make public schools better.

People knew that the problems had been building for many, many years. Some of the problems could not be solved quickly. Slowly, the changes started to have some effect, however. The differences between Kentucky and the U.S. average became smaller. The state rankings got a little better, year after year. Not everything that was tried worked, and more changes took place. Still more may be needed in the future. The key thing was that people were talking about Kentucky schools and how they could improve. That was better than just ignoring them, as had happened before. The question for the future is whether state and local support will keep coming at a high level. Remember the 1908 reform and the Whirlwind Campaign? After that died down, people did not support schools enough. It was a good beginning that did not finish well. A strong system of schools requires continuing support—from students, teachers, parents, leaders, local groups, and state organizations. Everyone has to be a part of it.

Looking back at how people went to school in early times, let's compare those times to today:

How do you get to school? How did they?

What is your school building like? What was theirs like?

What kinds of things do you have in your classroom? What did they have?

What do you do at lunch time, and what do you eat? What did they do and eat?

Do you learn about the same things in your lessons?

What are the biggest changes? What has changed the least?

What changes do you think will take place in Kentucky schools during your life?

★ Colleges and Universities ★

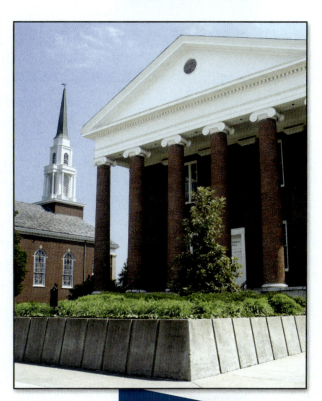

Would students have been running to catch a school bus a hundred years ago? How have schools changed over time?

Schooling does not have to end after high school. More and more people are continuing to go to school after that. They may go to technical schools to learn special skills or to two-year community colleges. Those are now part of the Kentucky Community and Technical College System. Others may go to schools (colleges) that offer four years of higher education. If a college also has classes beyond the four years, it is usually called a university. From the early times, Kentucky has had colleges and universities.

The first school offering college-level classes was what is now called Transylvania University in Lexington. It started with classes in a log cabin in Danville in 1785 and later moved to Lexington. For some years, Transylvania was one of the best schools in the nation. At a time when there were only ten medical schools in the United States, one of them was at Transylvania. The college had a school of law, a fine library, and talented teachers. Before the Civil War, it was the best college in the South, and many

Georgetown College

Berea College

famous people went there. However, problems grew up. A good president was forced to leave. Some of the teachers went to another school. Its funding decreased, and the state support ended. By the time of the Civil War, Transylvania had closed its school of medicine and was not nearly as strong as before. It became better again in the twentieth century.

Before the Civil War and for much of the nineteenth century, most people who went to colleges went to private ones. Most were either all-male or all-female. That situation did not change until late in the century.

Two other private colleges that were started before the Civil War remain as outstanding schools in Kentucky. Centre College in Danville had Presbyterian Church support, and Georgetown College was the first Baptist college west of the mountains and the fifth one in the nation.

Berea College only offered high-school-level classes before the Civil War and had its first college students four years after the war ended. It was different from other schools at the time because black and white students attended classes together. In 1904 the state ordered the school to separate the races. For almost a half century after that time, only segregated classes were permitted in Kentucky.

During that period, African American schools grew up. In Louisville, Simmons University, a private school for blacks, was the first Kentucky college run by African Americans. It was taken over by the University of Louisville and later become part of the university. Meanwhile, the state also set up a public college for African Americans. Now called Kentucky State University, in Frankfort, it opened in 1887 and at first mostly trained people to be teachers.

Other private schools began to open their doors. Some did not last very long; others continue to offer classes today. At the beginning of the twenty-first century, these were the private colleges and universities in Kentucky: Alice Lloyd College in Pippa Passes, Asbury College in Wilmore, Bellarmine University in Louisville, Berea College, Brescia University in Owensboro, Campbellsville University, Centre College, Cumberland College in Williamsburg, Georgetown College, Kentucky Christian College in Grayson, Kentucky Wesleyan

College in Owensboro, Lindsey Wilson College in Columbia, Midway College, Pikeville College, Spalding University in Louisville, Thomas More College in Crestview Hills, Transylvania University, and Union College in Barbourville. More than a half dozen other schools gave college-level classes for those who sought to become preachers. Private colleges remain strong in the state.

A view of one of the buildings at Kentucky State University.

Private colleges filled a real need in the educational system of Kentucky and still do so. However, they never have trained large numbers of students. As higher education grew in importance, a different kind of school was needed. People wanted schools where larger numbers could go and for lower costs. An early leader told of his dream: "We want a university giving education of the highest order to all classes." He sought a people's college.

Out of that need grew what is now the University of Kentucky. It was the first fully state-supported college in the state. It started in 1865, at the end of the Civil War. About twenty years later, it gave its first degree to a woman. A law school opened early in the twentieth century, and the university became larger and larger as the years went on.

After Kentucky State University was created, other state-supported colleges were set up around the commonwealth. In 1906, the state formed what became Eastern Kentucky University in Richmond and Western Kentucky University at Bowling Green. The year 1922 saw the creation of Morehead State University and Murray State University. Northern Kentucky University at Highland Heights came into the system in 1968. The University of Louisville had first been supported by that city as a kind of private college. In 1970 it too gained state support. Over the years, the state has built a system of higher education that offers students many choices.

Murray State University

An early dorm room for students at the University of Kentucky.
What is the item on the table, in the middle? Would you want to sleep on the top bunk?

Compare today's dorm room with the early one.
What has changed most?

In the future, the level of education may be one of the keys to success both for a person and for a state.

Kentucky schools helped three people rise to the very top of their field. The Nobel Prize is the world's top award. Three times a person with ties to Kentucky has won that prize: Thomas Hunt Morgan of Lexington in 1933; William N. Lipscomb Jr., who grew up in Lexington, in 1976; and Phillip A. Sharp, a native of Falmouth, in 1993.

chapter 12

Today and Tomorrow in *Kentucky*

One of the reasons we look at the past is to help us understand where we may be going in the future. History can help us to plan for what is to come in the unknown years ahead. We also have to know about where we are right now and who we are as a people— our strengths and weaknesses. That way we can try to bring the best parts of the past and the present into the future. We can also try to cast aside those things that have hurt our state's growth. Finally, we can look at what might be some issues in Kentucky's future and make plans to deal with them.

⋆ A Typical Kentuckian ⋆

To try to piece together what the typical Kentucky person was like at the start of the twenty-first century means we have to use numbers. We will present the **average** person. Many will be above and below that average. For example, in 2000, 51 percent of the people in Kentucky were women and 49 percent were men. So if you wanted to say who the average Kentuckian was in 2000, you would say a woman, since more people were women. Of course, many of the people in Kentucky were men. What we will do, then, is to describe the average, typical person, based on numbers. Once we know that, then we can look at where we might need to be going in the future.

The typical person in Kentucky in the year 2000 was a thirty-six-year-old white woman who was likely born in the state. (Kentucky had few foreign immigrants compared to the United States as a whole.) On the average, people in Kentucky did not earn as much as the typical American, but it cost less to live here also. Kentuckians were more likely to own their home than the average American and made smaller house payments as well. An income gap existed between earnings in Kentucky compared to earnings of people in the entire country, but that difference has been getting smaller in recent years.

Kentucky in the year 2000 was still a poor state compared to other states. It ranked forty-fifth of the fifty states in people living in poverty. Almost one in six people in Kentucky lived below the poverty line, compared to one in eight in the whole United States. The state also had a very large gap between rich and poor people, compared to the nation.

In health matters, people in Kentucky tended to be overweight, with high blood pressure. More of them died from heart disease, cancer, and accidents than did people across the nation. The state had more people who smoked than any other state except one (Nevada). On the positive side, very few people in the state had AIDS, and Kentuckians felt very safe in their homes, compared to the whole United States.

In the area of religion, Kentucky was above average in church members, though it did not rank particularly high. Half of those who were members were Baptists. In politics, more people said they were Democrats, though many of them voted Republican. On matters of the environment, Kentucky stood in the middle of the states in air quality. People used a

One of Kentucky's many faces.

lot of gasoline—the state was ninth highest—but overall did well in using energy. In short, at the start of the twenty-first century, there were both good and bad aspects of living in Kentucky.

★ Saving Parts of the Past ★

As you look over what the typical person was like long ago and now, and as you recall what you have read about in this book, what are some of the things in Kentucky that are the state's strengths? What things should we try to take with us into the future?

We do not want, for example, to continue to be an unhealthy, poor state with low education levels in the future.

What are some things we want to keep as a part of Kentucky life, then? Each person may have different answers. Some, for instance, point to a sense of place, a love for their home place, as one thing to keep. More than 170 years ago, someone wrote that "Wherever the Kentuckian travels, he earnestly remembers his native hills and plains." A hundred years after that, a book told of "the Kentuckian's love of family."

People have pointed to Kentucky writing, music, and folk culture as important things to continue in the future. One person asked: "Are we seriously intent on becoming a region of fast food, or will we eventually learn to cherish and preserve our folk culture?"

Some people stress as important the fact that Kentucky is different. In a world where things are more and more alike, people will be attracted to places that are different. The state's horse farms, forests, parks, waterways, friendly people, rich history, and so much more can make it a special place in America's future. As one writer noted, though, "Distinctiveness may easily slip through our fingers."

Saving those things that have made Kentucky different is not easy. Someone wrote that we must protect past strengths "from what has proved to be the greatest threat to everything in this planet—ourselves." That does not mean we should preserve all that is old, just because it is a part of our past. Many parts should be forgotten and left behind. Instead, as we go into the future, we should remember the things that have made Kentucky special. How the future unfolds is partly in our hands. We must use that power well.

★ Future Issues ★

A person once said, "Predictions are hard, especially about the future."

Trying to decide what might be the issues in the future is hard because conditions change. Something that we expect to be a problem in the future may suddenly no longer be a problem because of a new invention or some other change. At the same time, however, we must look forward. We cannot just wait for the future; we have to plan for it, no matter how uncertain our planning might be. Most of all, we have to have our minds ready for the future. As one person wrote: "We must learn to embrace change and become more flexible and less afraid of the new." Yet we must not be afraid of keeping the best parts of the old. Finding the right balance may be the hard part.

What do you think will be important issues of the future? At the beginning of the twenty-first century, a number of people were asked that question.

Some people pointed to our use of the land. Will we pollute it or protect it? Others noted the rapid growth of technology— computers and other things. Technology can move us forward into whole new areas. As a high school student stated, though: "We must control technology and not let it control us, or we will destroy ourselves."

Some said we must prepare Kentucky better to be a part of a "New Economy." They said the old ways people earn a living will change. Education is a key to adjusting to that change. Many say that in the future you will have to continue learning after you leave school. That way you can keep up with great changes in technology, information, and the global market-place. States will prosper if their people are educated and can learn well in a changing economy.

Other people spoke of issues that have been with us for a long time, saying that there are challenges we still need to deal with in the future. For example, we must work to treat all people as equals, we must do more to try to end hunger and poverty, and we must work even harder to resolve conflicts

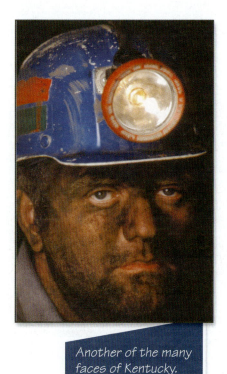

Another of the many faces of Kentucky.

John Uri Lloyd

Science fiction is writing that shows the impact of science on something real or made up. Often it is about time travel, or the future, or worlds far away. The *Star Wars* movies are examples of science fiction.

One of the first science fiction novels written in America was by a Kentuckian. John Uri Lloyd came to the state when he was four years old and grew up in Boone and Grant counties in northern Kentucky. Later he wrote a series of novels about that area. The most famous one was called *Stringtown on the Pike*. It came out in 1900.

Lloyd went to work at age fourteen. He worked in a drug store and later became a famous druggist himself. Lloyd also wrote many books about how to use plants and other natural things as medicine. The money he made from those books was used to build a large library, which still exists in Cincinnati.

His life had unhappy times. Only eleven days after he married, his wife died. Lloyd went back to work to try to forget.

His first novel, *Etidorhpa*, was published in 1895. It was very unusual for the time because almost no one wrote science fiction then. It told of a man's journey to some deep caves near Smithland, Kentucky. From there he went down to the center of the earth. Lloyd presented the story as if someone else had written it and had given it to him. He was simply putting those words into book form, he said.

In his novel, an eyeless, faceless, blue-skinned guide leads the hero downward. He finds a strange underground world of giant mushrooms, huge lakes, odd animals, and new rules of motion. At the earth's center, he also finds the mother of love—Etidorhpa.

The book was not great writing by our standards today, but it was one of the first attempts to make people think about things unknown or in the future.

If you were writing a science fiction novel now, what would you write about? What would your vision of the future be like?

John Uri Lloyd's science-fiction vision of the interior of the earth.

DOCUMENT 12.1

In 1992—two hundred years after statehood—Kentucky created the Long-Term Policy Research Center. It was formed to give people information and perspective so that they could make better decisions in the future.

After getting comments from a lot of people, the Research Center set up these twenty-six goals for the future:

Goal 1: Kentucky communities will be safe and caring places that enable all citizens to lead productive, fulfilling lives.

Goal 2: Kentucky's communities and citizens will share responsibility in helping families succeed.

Goal 3: Kentuckians will have decent, safe, and affordable housing.

Goal 4: All Kentuckians will be able to afford high-quality health care.

Goal 5: Kentucky communities will have high levels of trust, civic pride, and citizen involvement.

Goal 6: Kentucky communities will value and respect all individuals, whatever their culture, race, religion, or gender.

Goal 7: Kentuckians will have an excellent education system of lifelong learning.

Goal 8: Kentuckians will have equal opportunity to get that education.

Goal 9: Kentucky's children will come to school ready and able to learn.

Goal 10: Kentucky children will have safe, stable learning environments.

Goal 11: Kentuckians will look to partnerships among parents, schools, and communities to help children develop socially and academically.

Goal 12: Kentuckians will have opportunities to appreciate, participate in, and contribute to the arts and history.

Goal 13: Kentucky will end poverty.

Goal 14: Kentucky will have long-term development that stresses competitiveness and higher living standards for all citizens.

Goal 15: Kentucky will benefit from the global economy.

Goal 16: Kentucky will keep and improve a strong farm economy.

Goal 17: Kentucky will develop ways to support economic development and a high quality of life.

Goal 18: Kentucky technology will aid learning and help Kentucky compete in the world economy.

Goal 19: Kentucky will establish a fair tax system.

Goal 20: Kentucky will help businesses in the New Economy.

Goal 21: Kentucky will protect and improve its environment.

Goal 22: Individuals, communities, and businesses will use resources wisely and reduce waste through recycling.

Goal 23: Kentucky communities will promote care of the environment and reduce pollution.

Goal 24: All levels of government will respond to the changing needs of Kentuckians.

Goal 25: Kentucky will ensure a fair, equal, and effective system of justice.

Goal 26: Citizens should work to understand the issues, to improve their communities, and to understand how important it is that they participate.

and have peace and not war in American life. Some told of the need to find new power sources, such as solar or hydrogen power. Others stressed the need for better health care for longer lives. All of them agree with one study of the future that said, "Change has been the one constant in our lives."

✦ Your Future ✦

What will the future be? We do not know. We can try to make it a better future, though. A few years ago, one group asked people in Kentucky what needed to be done to make things better in the future. They came up with twenty-six goals. (See document 12.1.) Can we reach these goals? What can we all do as citizens of Kentucky to try to make them a reality?

We may hear some people say how bad things are now, or how one person alone cannot do anything to change things. Those people do not have the right perspective on our times. As one person at a college said: "Our ancestors faced worse. And I think no matter what trials we face, somebody born today always has a chance to effect some positive change, to find their place in the world and do something good."

One person *can* make a difference. Think of the forgotten young boy who saved Abraham Lincoln from drowning in a Kentucky creek, and handicapped Madge Breckinridge working for women's rights. The way to make the future better is to work to make it better. A student near Louisville said in the year 2000: "We should be a nation of doers. We should be out there and we should be doing stuff."

A high school student in Nelson County said it very clearly: "If we want these things to change, that's the only way it's going to happen—if we do it ourselves."

For year after year, century after century, people faced problems and issues in their future. Some were the same problems we still face; some were different. Some they solved; some they did not. But they tried. We now have more things to help us deal with issues than ever before, if we only work and try.

The future awaits you.

What would your vision of the future be like?

A New Kentucky Face

If your face were in this spot in the future, what would people be writing about you? What part will you play in Kentucky's future?

KENTUCKY COUNTIES

County	County Seat	When Created	2000 Population	Origin of County Name
Adair	Columbia	1801	17,244	Governor John Adair
Allen	Scottsville	1815	17,800	John Allen, killed in Indian wars
Anderson	Lawrenceburg	1827	19,111	Richard C. Anderson Jr., public official
Ballard	Wickliffe	1842	8,286	Bland W. Ballard, Indian fighter
Barren	Glasgow	1798	38,033	The Barrens, name of a section of the state
Bath	Owingsville	1811	11,085	Healthy springs there
Bell	Pineville	1867	30,060	Joshua F. Bell, political leader
Boone	Burlington	1798	85,991	Daniel Boone
Bourbon	Paris	1785	19,360	Royal family of France
Boyd	Catlettsburg	1860	49,752	Linn Boyd, Speaker of U.S. House of Representatives from Kentucky
Boyle	Danville	1842	27,697	Chief Justice John Boyle
Bracken	Brooksville	1796	8,279	William Bracken, area pioneer
Breathitt	Jackson	1839	16,100	Governor John Breathitt
Breckinridge	Hardinsburg	1799	18,648	U.S. Attorney General John Breckinridge of Kentucky
Bullitt	Shepherdsville	1796	61,236	Lt. Governor Alexander S. Bullitt
Butler	Morgantown	1810	13,010	General Richard Butler, killed in Indian wars
Caldwell	Princeton	1809	13,060	Lt. Governor John Caldwell
Calloway	Murray	1822	34,177	Pioneer Richard Calloway
Campbell	Alexandria and Newport	1794	88,616	Pioneer John Campbell
Carlisle	Bardwell	1886	5,351	U.S. Secretary of the Treasury John G. Carlisle of Kentucky
Carroll	Carrollton	1838	10,155	Charles Carroll, signer of Declaration of Independence
Carter	Grayson	1838	26,889	William G. Carter, state senator
Casey	Liberty	1806	15,447	Pioneer William Casey
Christian	Hopkinsville	1796	72,265	William Christian, killed in Indian wars
Clark	Winchester	1792	33,144	General George Rogers Clark
Clay	Manchester	1806	24,556	Pioneer Green Clay
Clinton	Albany	1835	9,634	New York Governor DeWitt Clinton
Crittenden	Marion	1842	9,384	Governor John J. Crittenden
Cumberland	Burkesville	1798	7,147	Cumberland River
Daviess	Owensboro	1815	91,545	Joseph H. Daveiss,* killed in Indian wars
Edmonson	Brownsville	1825	11,644	John Edmonson, killed in Indian wars
Elliott	Sandy Hook	1869	6,748	Judge John M. Elliott
Estill	Irvine	1808	15,307	James Estill, killed in Indian wars
Fayette	Lexington	1780	260,512	General Lafayette of France
Fleming	Flemingsburg	1798	13,792	Pioneer John Fleming
Floyd	Prestonsburg	1799	42,441	Pioneer John Floyd
Franklin	Frankfort	1794	47,687	Benjamin Franklin
Fulton	Hickman	1845	7,752	Steamboat inventor Robert Fulton
Gallatin	Warsaw	1798	7,870	U.S. Secretary of the Treasury Albert Gallatin
Garrard	Lancaster	1796	14,792	Governor James Garrard

Grant	Williamstown	1820	22,384	Samuel Grant, killed by Indians
Graves	Mayfield	1823	37,028	Benjamin Graves, killed in Indian wars
Grayson	Leitchfield	1810	24,053	William Grayson, Virginia senator
Green	Greensburg	1792	11,518	General Nathanael Greene* of Rhode Island
Greenup	Greenup	1803	36,891	Governor Christopher Greenup
Hancock	Hawesville	1829	8,392	John Hancock, signer of Declaration of Independence
Hardin	Elizabethtown	1792	94,174	John Hardin, killed in Indian wars
Harlan	Harlan	1819	33,202	Silas Harlan, killed in Indian wars
Harrison	Cynthiana	1793	17,983	Benjamin Harrison, legislator
Hart	Munfordville	1819	17,445	N.G.T. Hart, killed in Indian wars
Henderson	Henderson	1798	44,829	Richard Henderson, landowner
Henry	New Castle	1798	15,060	Virginia Governor Patrick Henry
Hickman	Clinton	1821	5,262	Paschal Hickman, killed in Indian wars
Hopkins	Madisonville	1806	46,519	General Samuel Hopkins
Jackson	McKee	1858	13,495	President Andrew Jackson
Jefferson	Louisville	1780	693,604	President Thomas Jefferson
Jessamine	Nicholasville	1798	39,041	Settler Jessamine Douglas
Johnson	Paintsville	1843	23,445	Vice President Richard M. Johnson of Kentucky
Kenton	Independence and Covington	1840	151,464	Pioneer Simon Kenton
Knott	Hindman	1884	17,649	Governor J. Proctor Knott
Knox	Barbourville	1799	31,795	Revolutionary War General Henry Knox
Larue	Hodgenville	1843	13,373	Pioneer John Larue
Laurel	London	1825	52,715	Laurel River
Lawrence	Louisa	1821	15,569	Naval officer James Lawrence
Lee	Beattyville	1870	7,916	Probably General Robert E. Lee of Virginia
Leslie	Hyden	1878	12,401	Governor Preston Leslie
Letcher	Whitesburg	1842	25,277	Governor Robert Letcher
Lewis	Vanceburg	1806	14,092	Meriwether Lewis of Lewis and Clark exploring party
Lincoln	Stanford	1780	23,361	General Benjamin Lincoln of Virginia
Livingston	Smithland	1798	9,804	Robert Livingston of N.Y., signer of Declaration of Independence
Logan	Russellville	1792	26,573	Pioneer Benjamin Logan
Lyon	Eddyville	1854	8,080	Congressman Matthew Lyon
McCracken	Paducah	1824	65,514	Virgil McCracken, killed in Indian wars
McCreary	Whitley City	1912	17,080	Governor James McCreary
McLean	Calhoun	1854	9,938	Judge Alney McLean
Madison	Richmond	1785	70,872	President James Madison
Magoffin	Salyersville	1860	13,332	Governor Beriah Magoffin
Marion	Lebanon	1834	18,212	General Francis Marion of South Carolina
Marshall	Benton	1842	30,125	U.S. Supreme Court Chief Justice John Marshall
Martin	Inez	1870	12,578	Congressman John P. Martin
Mason	Maysville	1788	16,800	Virginia legislator George Mason
Meade	Brandenburg	1823	26,349	James Meade, killed in Indian wars
Menifee	Frenchburg	1869	6,556	Congressman Richard Menefee*
Mercer	Harrodsburg	1785	20,817	General Hugh Mercer of Virginia
Metcalfe	Edmonton	1860	10,037	Governor Thomas Metcalfe
Monroe	Tompkinsville	1820	11,756	President James Monroe
Montgomery	Mt. Sterling	1796	22,554	General Richard Montgomery, killed in Revolutionary War
Morgan	West Liberty	1822	13,948	General Daniel Morgan of Virginia
Muhlenberg	Greenville	1798	31,839	Revolutionary War General Peter Muhlenberg

Nelson	Bardstown	1784	37,477	Revolutionary War General Thomas Nelson of Virginia
Nicholas	Carlisle	1799	6,813	Lawyer George Nicholas
Ohio	Hartford	1798	22,916	Ohio River
Oldham	LaGrange	1823	46,178	William Oldham, killed in Indian wars
Owen	Owenton	1819	10,547	Abraham Owen, killed in Indian wars
Owsley	Booneville	1843	4,858	Governor William Owsley
Pendleton	Falmouth	1798	14,390	Congressman Edmund Pendleton of Virginia
Perry	Hazard	1820	29,390	Navy hero Oliver Hazard Perry
Pike	Pikeville	1821	68,736	Explorer Zebulon Pike
Powell	Stanton	1852	13,237	Governor Lazarus Powell
Pulaski	Somerset	1798	56,217	Revolutionary War General Joseph Pulaski of Poland
Robertson	Mt. Olivet	1867	2,266	Kentucky Judge George Robertson
Rockcastle	Mt. Vernon	1810	16,582	Rockcastle River
Rowan	Morehead	1856	22,094	Kentucky Judge John Rowan
Russell	Jamestown	1825	16,315	Colonel William Russell
Scott	Georgetown	1792	33,061	Governor Charles Scott
Shelby	Shelbyville	1792	33,337	Governor Isaac Shelby
Simpson	Franklin	1819	16,405	John Simpson, killed in Indian wars
Spencer	Taylorsville	1824	11,766	Spears Spencer, killed in Indian wars
Taylor	Campbellsville	1848	22,927	President Zachary Taylor
Todd	Elkton	1819	11,971	John Todd, killed in Indian wars
Trigg	Cadiz	1820	12,597	Stephen Trigg, killed in Indian wars
Trimble	Bedford	1836	8,125	U.S. Supreme Court Judge Robert Trimble of Kentucky
Union	Morganfield	1811	15,637	Uncertain
Warren	Bowling Green	1796	92,522	Revolutionary War General Joseph Warren
Washington	Springfield	1792	10,916	President George Washington
Wayne	Monticello	1800	19,923	General "Mad Anthony" Wayne
Webster	Dixon	1860	14,120	Senator Daniel Webster of Mass.
Whitley	Williamsburg	1818	35,865	Pioneer William Whitley
Wolfe	Campton	1860	7,065	Louisville lawyer Nathaniel Wolfe
Woodford	Versailles	1788	23,208	General William Woodford of Virginia

*The spelling of the county name is different from the spelling of the person's name.

KENTUCKY'S GOVERNORS

Isaac Shelby: 1792–1796 and 1812–1816; of Lincoln County; native of Maryland; surveyor and soldier; active in the American Revolution and frontier campaigns against the Indians; counties in nine states named in his honor.

James Garrard: 1796–1800 and 1800–1804; of Bourbon County; born in Virginia; Revolutionary War soldier; first to live in Governor's Mansion (today the residence of the lieutenant governor); only Kentucky governor to serve two full successive terms until Paul Patton.

Christopher Greenup: 1804–1808; of Mercer and Fayette counties; born in Virginia; soldier; one of the first two Kentucky representatives in Congress after Kentucky entered the union; elected governor in 1804 without opposition.

Charles Scott: 1808–1812; of Woodford County; born in Virginia; soldier; officer in Braddock expedition (1755); represented Woodford County in Virginia Assembly.

George Madison: 1816; of Franklin County; born in Virginia; Revolutionary War soldier; Indian fighter; hero of War of 1812; captured at River Raisin; elected governor in 1816 but died the same year.

Gabriel Slaughter: 1816–1820; of Mercer County; born in Virginia; farmer; regimental commander at Battle of New Orleans; twice lieutenant governor; became governor upon Madison's death.

John Adair: 1820–1824; of Mercer County; born in South Carolina; Revolutionary War soldier; fought in Indian wars; aide to Governor Isaac Shelby in 1813 Battle of the Thames; elected to U.S. House of Representatives for one term, 1831–1833.

Joseph Desha: 1824–1828; of Mason County; born in Pennsylvania; soldier in Indian campaigns; commander in Battle of the Thames (1813); state legislator; served in U.S. House of Representatives, 1807–1819.

Thomas Metcalfe: 1828–1832; of Nicholas County; born in Virginia; stonemason; nicknamed "Old Stonehammer"; soldier in the War of 1812; served ten years as U.S. Congressman and Senator; died during cholera epidemic of 1855.

John Breathitt: 1832–1834; of Logan County; born in Virginia; lawyer; previously served in Kentucky legislature and as lieutenant governor; died in office after two years.

James Turner Morehead: 1834–1836; of Logan County; as lieutenant governor succeeded to the governorship in 1834 upon death of Breathitt; served two years; U.S. Senator, 1841–1847; political ally of Henry Clay, a fellow Whig.

James Clark: 1836–1839; of Clark County; born in Virginia; served in Kentucky legislature; as judge, rendered decision that started Old and New Court fight; died in office in 1839.

Charles Anderson Wickliffe: 1839–1840; of Nelson County; lawyer; six-term U.S. Congressman; became governor in 1839 upon death of Clark; postmaster general for President John Tyler, 1841–1845; grandfather of Governor J.C.W. Beckham.

Robert P. Letcher: 1840–1844; of Mercer (later Garrard) County; Whig; born in Virginia; lawyer; served in state legislature and U.S. Congress; American minister (ambassador) to Mexico, 1849–1852.

William Owsley: 1844–1848; of Lincoln County; born in Virginia; Whig; lawyer; served in state legislature; long service as justice of Kentucky Court of Appeals.

John Jordan Crittenden: 1848–1850; of Woodford County; Whig; lawyer; saw service in War of 1812 as aide to Shelby and was present at Battle of the Thames: resigned governorship after two years to become U.S. Attorney General; served total of twenty years in U.S. Senate.

John L. Helm: 1850–1851 and 1867; of Hardin County; succeeded Crittenden his first term; elected in his own right sixteen years later; state legislator; openly sympathetic to Confederate cause.

Lazarus W. Powell: 1851–1855; of Henderson County; Democratic lawyer; state legislator; U.S. Senator; favored Kentucky neutrality during Civil War.

Charles Slaughter Morehead: 1855–1859; of Nelson County; lawyer; two-term Whig member of Congress; elected governor on American (Know-Nothing) party ticket.

Beriah Magoffin: 1859–1862; of Mercer County; Democrat; lawyer; after being permitted to name his successor as governor, resigned because of his Confederate sympathies.

James F. Robinson: 1862–1863; of Scott County; lawyer; Whig state senator, staunch Unionist Democrat.

Thomas E. Bramlette: 1863–1867; of Cumberland (now Clinton) County; lawyer and circuit judge; commissioned in Union army.

John W. Stevenson: 1867–1871; of Kenton County; born in Virginia; Democrat; as lieutenant governor, became governor upon Helm's death; U.S. senator, 1871–1877.

Preston H. Leslie: 1871–1875; of Clinton County; Democrat; lawyer and state legislator; accepted appointment in 1887 as governor of Montana Territory, where he died in 1907.

James Bennett McCreary: 1875–1879 and 1911–1915; of Madison County; Democrat; lawyer; soldier with Generals Morgan and Breckinridge in Confederate service; served eighteen years in U.S. House and Senate; first to occupy new Governor's Mansion (1914).

Dr. Luke P. Blackburn: 1879–1883; of Woodford County; Democrat; first physician to serve as Kentucky governor; volunteer in cholera and yellow fever epidemics in Kentucky and throughout the South; prison reformer.

J. Proctor Knott: 1883–1887; of Marion County; Democrat; lawyer, congressman, and noted orator; attorney general of Missouri before returning to Kentucky in 1862; one of the framers of the present Kentucky constitution.

Simon Bolivar Buckner: 1887–1891; of Hart County; Democrat; West Point instructor; served in Mexican War and later with Confederacy; editor of *Louisville Courier.*

John Young Brown: 1891–1895; of Hardin County; Democrat; lawyer; congressman; his "three-year legislature" adjusted laws to the new constitution.

William O. Bradley: 1895–1899; of Garrard County; lawyer; first Republican governor; U.S. senator, 1909–1914.

William S. Taylor: 1899–1900; of Butler County; lawyer; Republican; Kentucky attorney general; lost the governorship to William Goebel in a contest decided by the legislature.

William Goebel: 1900; of Kenton County; born in Pennsylvania; Democrat; lawyer; state senator; declared governor after being shot by assassin on the ground of the Old Capitol; only governor in U.S. history to die in office as result of assassination.

John Crepps Wickliffe Beckham: 1900–1903 and 1903–1907; of Nelson County; Democrat; lawyer and state legislator; speaker of Kentucky House; elected lieutenant governor on Goebel ticket and succeeded to governorship upon his death; U.S. senator, 1915–1921; grandson of Governor Charles Anderson Wickliffe.

Augustus E. Willson: 1907–1911; of Jefferson County; born in Mason County; law partner of John Marshall Harlan; five-time unsuccessful Republican nominee for U.S. House or Senate.

Augustus Owsley Stanley: 1915–1919; of Henderson County; born in Shelby County; Democrat; lawyer; served six terms in U.S. House; elected to U.S. Senate in 1918; resigned as governor in 1919; later chaired International Joint Commission to mediate disputes arising along the U.S.-Canadian border.

James D. Black: 1919; of Knox County; Democrat; lawyer; state legislator; assistant attorney general of Kentucky; as lieutenant governor, succeeded Stanley as governor; defeated for election (1919) in his own right.

Edwin Porch Morrow: 1919–1923; of Pulaski County; Republican lawyer; soldier in Spanish-American War; U.S. District Attorney; nephew of Governor William O. Bradley.

William J. Fields: 1923–1927; of Carter County; Democrat; resigned after almost thirteen years in Congress to become governor; called "Honest Bill of Olive Hill."

Flem D. Sampson: 1927–1931; of Knox County; born in Laurel County; Republican lawyer; circuit judge; chief justice of Kentucky Court of Appeals.

Ruby Laffoon: 1931–1935; of Hopkins County; Democrat; lawyer; chairman of first Insurance Rating Board in Kentucky; Hopkins County Judge.

Albert Benjamin Chandler: 1935–1939 and 1955–1959; of Woodford County; born in Henderson County; Democrat; lawyer; state senator; lieutenant governor; U.S. Senator; commissioner of baseball; nicknamed "Happy."

Keen Johnson: 1939–1943; of Madison County; born in Lyon County; Democrat; publisher of *Richmond Daily Register*; lieutenant governor; became governor upon resignation of Chandler, who went to U.S. Senate; elected in own right that same year.

Simeon Willis: 1943–1947; of Boyd County; born in Ohio; lawyer; appointed to state Court of Appeals; member of Republican National Committee.

Earle C. Clements: 1947–1950; of Union County; Democrat; served in U.S. Army during World War I; sheriff; county clerk; county judge; state senator; Congressman; resigned governorship in 1950 to assume seat in U.S. Senate.

Lawrence W. Wetherby: 1950–1951 and 1951–1955; of Jefferson County; Democrat; lawyer; judge of Jefferson County Juvenile Court; lieutenant governor on Clements ticket; became governor upon Clement's resignation; was elected to the office in his own right in 1951.

Bert T. Combs: 1959–1963; of Floyd County; born in Clay County; Democrat; served in World War II; lawyer; judge of Kentucky Court of Appeals, 1951–1955; judge of U.S. Court of Appeals, Sixth Circuit, 1967–1970.

Edward (Ned) T. Breathitt Jr.: 1963–1967; of Christian County; lawyer; served in state legislature, 1952–1958; later a railroad executive.

Louie B. Nunn: 1967–1971; of Barren County; Republican; lawyer; elected county judge of Barren County; city attorney of Glasgow.

Wendell H. Ford: 1971–1974; of Daviess County; Democrat; state senator; lieutenant governor; resigned governorship in 1974 to assume seat in U.S. Senate.

Julian M. Carroll: 1974–1975 and 1975–1979; of McCracken County; Democrat; member of Kentucky House of Representatives, 1962–1971; speaker of Kentucky House; lieutenant governor; became governor in 1974 upon resignation of Governor Ford; elected to the office in his own right in 1975.

John Young Brown Jr.: 1979–1983; of Fayette County; attorney; successful business executive (Kentucky Fried Chicken); involved in the ownership of professional sports.

Martha Layne Collins: 1983–1987; of Shelby and Woodford counties; public school teacher and home economist; Democrat; elected clerk of Kentucky Court of Appeals in 1975 and lieutenant governor four years later; first woman to be elected governor of Kentucky.

Wallace Wilkinson: 1987–1991; of Casey and Fayette counties; Democrat; prominent businessman and real estate developer; instrumental in revitalization of downtown Lexington.

Brereton Jones: 1991–1995; born in Ohio; of Woodford County; Democrat; West Virginia legislation; Kentucky horse-farm owner; lieutenant governor.

Paul Patton: 1995–1999 and 1999–2003; born in Lawrence County; of Pike County; Democrat; engineer and businessman.

Ernest L. Fletcher: 2003– ; born in Montgomery County; of Fayette County; medical doctor; Republican member of Kentucky House of Representatives; U.S. Congress.

Adapted from James C. Klotter, ed., *Our Kentucky: A Study of the Bluegrass State*. (Lexington: University Press of Kentucky, 2000).

☆ Appendix 3 ☆

These Kentuckians have served on the United States Supreme Court:

Thomas Todd of Danville and Frankfort

Robert Trimble of Paris

John McKinley* of Frankfort and Louisville

Samuel Miller* of Richmond and Barbourville

John Marshall Harlan of Danville, Harrodsburg, and Frankfort

Horace Lurton* of Newport

James McReynolds of Elkton

Louis Brandeis* of Louisville

Stanley Reed of Maysville

Wiley Rutledge* of Cloverport

Fred Vinson of Louisa

Either born in Kentucky or lived here for a period of time, but named to the court while living in another state.

The cover of the sheet music for "My Old Kentucky Home."

My Old Kentucky Home (Modern Version)

The sun shines bright on my old Kentucky home,
' Tis summer, the people are gay;
The corn-top's ripe and the meadow's in the bloom,
While the birds make music all the day.

The young folks roll on the little cabin floor,
All merry, all happy, and bright.
By'n-by hard times comes a-knocking at the door,
Then my old Kentucky home, good-night!

Weep no more my lady, Oh weep no more today!
We will sing one song for my old Kentucky home
For my old Kentucky home far away.

[Two more verses follow these.]

KENTUCKY INFORMATION

Area: 40,395 square miles

Population: 4,041,769 in 2000

Capital: Frankfort

Counties: 120

U.S. Representatives: 6

U.S. Senators: 2

State Representatives: 100

State Senators: 38

State Song: "My Old Kentucky Home"

Nickname: The Bluegrass State

Statehood Date: June 1, 1792 (15th state)

State Motto: "United we stand;
                divided we fall"

State Musical Instrument:
Appalachian Dulcimer

State Bird: Kentucky Cardinal

State Horse: Thoroughbred

State Flower: Goldenrod

State Tree: Tulip Poplar

State Animal: Gray Squirrel

State Fish: Kentucky Bass

State Insect: Viceroy Butterfly

State Fossil: Brachiopod

State Mineral: Coal

State Gemstone: Freshwater Pearl

These books contain a wealth of information about Kentucky:

Harrison, Lowell H., and James C. Klotter. *A New History of Kentucky*. Lexington: University Press of Kentucky, 1997.

Kleber, John, editor. *The Kentucky Encyclopedia*. Lexington: University Press of Kentucky, 1992.

Ulack, Richard, and Karl Raitz, editors. *Atlas of Kentucky*. Lexington: University Press of Kentucky, 1998.

Other general books include:

Clark, Thomas D. *History of Kentucky*. Revised edition. Ashland: Jesse Stuart Foundation, 1992.

Irvin, Helen. *Women in Kentucky*. Lexington: University Press of Kentucky, 1979.

Kleber, John, editor, *The Encyclopedia of Louisville*. Lexington: University Press of Kentucky, 2001.

Klotter, James C., editor. *Our Kentucky: A Study of the Bluegrass State*. 2nd edition. Lexington: University Press of Kentucky, 2000.

Lewis, R. Barry, editor. *Kentucky Archaeology*. Lexington: University Press of Kentucky, 1996.

Lucas, Marion B., and George C. Wright. *A History of Blacks in Kentucky*. 2 volumes. Frankfort: Kentucky Historical Society, 1992.

Rennick, Robert M. *Kentucky Place Names*. Lexington: University Press of Kentucky, 1984.

Ward, William S. *A Literary History of Kentucky*. Knoxville: University of Tennessee Press, 1988.

For more in-depth study of different time periods, see:

Friend, Craig, editor. *The Buzzel about Kentuck: Settling the Promised Land*. Lexington: University Press of Kentucky, 1999.

Harrison, Lowell H. *The Civil War in Kentucky*. 2nd edition. Lexington: University Press of Kentucky, 1987.

Klotter, James C. *Kentucky: Portrait in Paradox, 1900–1950*. Frankfort: Kentucky Historical Society, 1996.

Tapp, Hambleton, and James C. Klotter. *Kentucky: Decades of Discord, 1865–1900*. Frankfort: Kentucky Historical Society, 1977.

Two historical journals have many good articles on Kentucky. They are:

Ohio Valley History (formerly the *Filson Historical Quarterly*, which started in 1926). Brief listing of articles is in a 1987 issue, and online.

The Register of the Kentucky Historical Society (printed from 1903 on). General index is in a 1989 issue.

(*The Kentucky Explorer* has reprints of old articles and some modern-day memories of past times but should be used with care.)

Online sources:

Among the many, check the Kentucky Virtual Library, with its Digital Library, at www.kyvl.org.

☆ Acknowledgments ☆

In truth, to thank all those who helped make this book possible would involve going back to our own elementary school days, for as adults we bear the imprint of the learning received from teachers then, and ever since. Raising our own children often helped us understand better the mind of a young child—though on occasion, it must be noted, their actions also confused us. We both have used our experience as teachers and educators over the years in shaping this work. That time in the classroom also has made us recognize that books are not perfect, and we call on those who use this volume to let us know their reactions—good or bad—so we can keep the strong points and improve any weak ones in the future.

More specifically, we do want to thank Andy Anderson, Nancy Baird, Sharon Bidwell, Bonnie Curnock, Nancy DeMarcus, Keith Dykes, Jason Flahardy, Linda Friend, Sarah Hardin, Leigh Anne Hiatt, Joy Lyons, William Marshall, Margaret Mattingly, Rebecca Rice, Lisa Rolfe, Melissa Shown, Gerald Smith, Bob Ward, and Mary Winter for their help with illustrations. Several people also read drafts and made comments and suggestions. Educators Linda Hargan of Louisville, Mary Anne Lock and Larry Lock of Russellville, and Nancy Huffstutter of Princeton all aided in that regard. College professors in history and education did yeoman and excellent work as well. Our special thanks go to Lindsey Apple and Sarah Marshall of Georgetown College, and Thomas H. Appleton Jr. of Eastern Kentucky University.

We especially want to thank the staff at the University Press of Kentucky for their hard work and dedication to this project. We would also like to thank the staff at Shepherd Incorporated for all of the effort that went into the design and production of this book.

And perhaps most of all, we acknowledge the role our grandchildren played. We wanted them to have a Kentucky studies book appropriate for a younger audience so that they too could learn more about the place their grandparents call home. This book is dedicated to them, but in truth, it is for all the children who make up Kentucky's future.

⋆ Credits ⋆

COVER

Front   (from the top) Courtesy of the Kentucky Historical Society; Photo by Thomas G. Barnes; Courtesy of the Kentucky Historical Society; Courtesy of the Kentucky Department of Travel*; Courtesy of the Kentucky Historical Society; Photo by Thomas G. Barnes; (main image) Courtesy of the Anschutz Collection.

Back   (from the top) Courtesy of the Kentucky Historical Society; Courtesy of the Kentucky Historical Society; Courtesy of the Kentucky Department of Travel; Courtesy of the Kentucky Library, Western Kentucky University; Courtesy of Shaker Village of Pleasant Hill, Kentucky.

CHAPTER 1

2   (top) Image courtesy of NASA Marshall Space Flight Center (NASA-MSFC), (bottom) Courtesy of the Kentucky Library, Western Kentucky University.

3   Courtesy of the Kentucky Historical Society.

4   Courtesy of the Kentucky Historical Society.

6   (top) Courtesy of the Kentucky Historical Society, (bottom) Photo courtesy of Richard Jefferies.

8   Copyright Kentucky Heritage Council, design and artwork by Jimmy A. Railey.

9   (top) Image from Kentucky Heritage Council poster titled "Kentucky Before Boone," (bottom) Drawing by Jim A. Railey.

10   (top left) Adapted from R. Barry Lewis, ed., *Kentucky Archaeology* (1996), (top right) Copyright Kentucky Heritage Council, design and artwork by Jimmy A. Railey, (bottom) Copyright Kentucky Heritage Council, design and artwork by Jimmy A. Railey.

11   Courtesy of Martin Pate.

12   Copyright Kentucky Heritage Council, design and artwork by Jimmy A. Railey.

13   Images courtesy of Photo Researchers, Inc.

14   Photo by Thomas G. Barnes.

CHAPTER 2

19   Map by Dick Gilbreath.

21   Illustration courtesy of the National Geographic Society.

22   From Z. F. Smith, *The History of Kentucky* (1886).

23   Courtesy of the Bell County Historical Society, from David M. Burns, *Gateway: Dr. Thomas Walker and the Opening of Kentucky* (2000).

24   Courtesy of the Kentucky Department of Travel.

25   Image courtesy of Cumberland Gap National Historical Park.

26   From Walter W. Spooner, *The Back-woodsman, or Tales of the Borders* (1883).

28   From Clay Lancaster, *Antebellum Architecture of Kentucky* (1991).

29   Courtesy of the Kentucky Department of Travel.

30   Map by Dick Gilbreath.

31   Courtesy of the Kentucky Historical Society.

32   Illustration courtesy of the National Geographic Society.

33   Courtesy of the Filson Historical Society, Louisville, Kentucky.

Every reasonable effort has been made to secure permission for and appropriately credit all images in this text.

* Information obtained from the Kentucky Department of Travel is subject to change. The department is not liable for the accuracy of any information published outside its editorial control. For up-to-date Kentucky travel information, call 1-800-225-TRIP, or write Kentucky Travel, P.O. Box 2011, Frankfort, KY 40602. www.kentuckytourism.com.

34	(top) Courtesy of the Kentucky Historical Society, (bottom) George Caleb Bingham, *Daniel Boone Escorting Settlers through the Cumberland Gap*, 1851–52. Oil on canvas, 36 ½" × 50 ¼". Mildred Lane Kemper Art Museum, Washington University in St. Louis. Gift of Nathaniel Phillips, 1890.
35	Courtesy of the William Whitley House, Kentucky Department of Parks.
37	Courtesy of the Kentucky Historical Society.
38	(top) Courtesy of the Massachusetts Historical Society, (bottom) Courtesy of the Kentucky Historical Society.
39	(top) From Z. F. Smith, *The History of Kentucky* (1886), (bottom) Illustration courtesy of the National Geographic Society.
40	(top) Image courtesy of Fort Boonesborough State Park, (bottom) Courtesy of the Missouri Historical Society, St. Louis.
41	Courtesy of the Filson Historical Society, Louisville, Kentucky.
42	(top) Courtesy of the Kentucky Historical Society, (bottom) Map by Dick Gilbreath.
43	(top) Courtesy of the Woolaroc Museum, (bottom) Photo by Dan Dry.

CHAPTER 3

46	Photo by Rick McComb, Kentucky Department of Education.
48	Map by Dick Gilbreath.
50	Map by Dick Gilbreath.
51	Courtesy of the Kentucky Library, Western Kentucky University.
52	Map by Dick Gilbreath.
53	Courtesy of the Kentucky Library, Western Kentucky University.
54	Map by Dick Gilbreath.
55	Map by Dick Gilbreath.
56	Map by Dick Gilbreath.
58	(top) Courtesy of Bonnie Curnock, (center) Courtesy of Charles J. DeCroix, Mammoth Cave National Park.
59	(center) Photo by Thomas G. Barnes, (bottom) Courtesy of the Kentucky Department of Travel.
60	Photo by Thomas G. Barnes.
61	(top) Courtesy of the West Virginia State Archives, Division of Culture and History, (bottom) Courtesy of the Kentucky Library, Western Kentucky University.
62	Courtesy of Paul Tenkotte, Ph.D.
63	(top) Courtesy of the Kentucky Historical Society, (bottom) Courtesy of Shaker Village of Pleasant Hill, Kentucky.
64	(top) Photo by Dan Dry, (bottom) Photo by Ron Garrison.
65	(top) Photo by Thomas G. Barnes, (bottom) Courtesy of the Kentucky Department of Travel.
66	Map by Dick Gilbreath.
67	(top) Courtesy of the Kentucky Library, Western Kentucky University, (bottom) Courtesy of the Kentucky Department of Travel.
68	(top) Map by Dick Gilbreath, (bottom) Photo by Dan Dry.
69	Map by Dick Gilbreath.
70	(top) From the Library of Congress Prints and Photographs Division, reproduction #LC-USZ62-11250, (center) Courtesy of the Kentucky Historical Society.
71	Photo by Roger Rawlings.
72	Photo courtesy of the Tennessee Valley Authority.
74	Courtesy of the Kentucky State Parks.

CHAPTER 4

76	(both) Courtesy of the Kentucky Historical Society.
77	Courtesy of the Kentucky Historical Society.

78	(top) Courtesy of the University of Louisville Special Collections Rare Books & Photographic Archives, (bottom) Photo by Ila McEntire, courtesy of Harp Enterprises.
80	Map by Dick Gilbreath.
81	Map by Dick Gilbreath.
82	(top) Image courtesy of Kentucky Office of Creative Services, (bottom) Courtesy of the Kentucky Historical Society.
83	Courtesy of Brian Moore, Director, Division of Creative Services, Kentucky Division of Historic Properties.
84	Courtesy of the Kentucky Historical Society.
85	Courtesy of the Administrative Office of the Courts, Frankfort, Kentucky.
87	(top) Courtesy of the Administrative Office of the Courts, Frankfort, Kentucky, (bottom) Courtesy of the University of Kentucky Special Collections and Archives.
88	(top) From the Library of Congress Prints and Photographs Division, reproduction #LC- USZ62-112954, (bottom) Courtesy of the Legislative Research Commission Public Information.
89	Courtesy of the Kentucky Historical Society.
90	Courtesy of the Legislative Research Commission Public Information.
91	Courtesy of the Legislative Research Commission Public Information.
92	Courtesy of the University of Kentucky William T. Young Library.

CHAPTER 5

94	Courtesy of the University of Louisville Special Collections Rare Books & Photographic Archives.
95	Courtesy of the Kentucky Historical Society.
96	Courtesy of the Kentucky Historical Society.
97	(top) Collection of the Speed Art Museum, Louisville, Kentucky. Chester Harding, 1792 1866, oil on canvas, 100 in. × 78 in., gift of William Stucky, (bottom) Courtesy of the Lexington Public Library, Kentucky Room.
98	(left) Courtesy of the Kentucky Historical Society, (right) From the Library of Congress Prints and Photographs Divison, reproduction #LC-D41-77.
99	Courtesy of the Kentucky Historical Society.
100	Courtesy of the Kentucky Historical Society.
101	Courtesy of the University of Kentucky Special Collections and Archives.
103	Photo by Dan Dry.
105	(top) Photo courtesy of Linda Scott DeRosier, (bottom) Courtesy of the Kentucky Library, Western Kentucky University.
106	Collection of the Speed Art Museum, Louisville, Kentucky. Aurelius O. Revenaugh, 1840–1908, oil on canvas, 43 in. × 27 in., gift of Mrs. Silas Starr.
107	Courtesy of the University of Louisville Special Collections Rare Books & Photographic Archives.
108	"Dawn of Abdominal Surgery" by Dean Cornwell, reproduced with the permission of Wyeth Pharmaceuticals.
109	(top) Courtesy of the University of Louisville Special Collections Rare Books & Photographic Archives, (bottom) Photo courtesy of Kentucky Youth Soccer Association.
110	(top) Courtesy of the Kentucky Historical Society, (bottom) Courtesy of the University of Kentucky Special Collections and Archives.
111	Collection of the Speed Art Museum, Louisville, Kentucky. Robert Brammer, Augustus A. von Smith, oil on canvas, 28 ¼ in. × 35 ¾ in., purchase, Museum Art Fund.
112	Courtesy of the Kentucky Historical Society.
114	(top) The Filson Historical Society, Louisville, Kentucky, (bottom) Image courtesy of Georgetown College.
115	(top) Courtesy of the Kentucky Library, Western Kentucky University, (bottom) Photo by Tim Downer.
116	(top) Courtesy of the University of Kentucky Special Collections and Archives, (bottom left) Courtesy of the Kentucky Library, Western Kentucky University, (bottom right) Copyright by *The Courier-Journal*.
117	Courtesy of Chad Allen Harpole.

118	Basilica of St. Joseph Proto-Cathedral, courtesy of Bardstown Convention and Visitor's Bureau.
119	Courtesy of the Kentucky Historical Society.
120	Courtesy of Gerald Smith.
121	Photograph of Thomas Merton by Sibylle Akers. Used with permission of the Merton Legacy Trust.
122	Courtesy of the Kentucky Historical Society.

CHAPTER 6

126	Courtesy of the Colorado Historical Society, F3714; F21164 BPF—Brown, Clara 10027902.
127	Courtesy of the University of Kentucky Special Collections and Archives.
129	Courtesy of the Kentucky Historical Society.
130	Courtesy of the University of Kentucky Special Collections and Archives.
131	Courtesy of the Kentucky Historical Society.
133	Courtesy of the Kentucky Historical Society.
134	(top) Courtesy of the Kentucky Historical Society, (bottom) Courtesy of Bard and Gina Prentiss.
135	(top) From the Library of Congress Prints and Photographs Division, reproduction #LC-USZ62-76206, (bottom) Courtesy of the Kentucky Historical Society.
136	Courtesy of the Kentucky Historical Society.
137	Courtesy of the Kentucky Historical Society.
138	From the Library of Congress Prints and Photographs Division, reproduction #LC-USZCN4-149.
139	Painting by Joseph H. Bush, courtesy of the White House Historical Association.
140	(top) From the Library of Congress Prints and Photographs Division, reproduction #LC-DIG-CWPBH-00879, (bottom) Courtesy of Farmington Historic Home.
141	From the Library of Congress Prints and Photographs Division, reproduction # LC-USZ6-176.
142	The Filson Historical Society, Louisville, Kentucky.
143	From the Library of Congress Prints and Photographs Division, reproduction #LC-USZ62-8341.
144	Courtesy of the Kentucky Historical Society.

CHAPTER 7

146	Courtesy of the Kentucky Historical Society.
147	Map by Dick Gilbreath.
148	(left) From the Library of Congress Prints and Photographs Division, reproduction #LC-USZ62–15567, (right) From the Library of Congress Prints and Photographs Division, reproduction # LC-DIG-cwpb-05595.
149	(top) Courtesy of the Kentucky Library, Western Kentucky University, (bottom) Courtesy of the Ketucky Historical Society.
150	Courtesy of the Kentucky Department of Travel.
151	Courtesy of the University of Kentucky Special Collections and Archives.
152	(top) Courtesy of the University of Kentucky Special Collections and Archives, (bottom) Courtesy of the Kentucky Historical Society.
154	Wood engraving from *Harper's Weekly,* August 30, 1862, from a drawing by Thomas Nast.
155	Courtesy of the Kentucky Historical Society.
156	(top) Courtesy of the University of Kentucky Special Collections and Archives, (bottom) Copyright 2005 by Adam Jones.
157	Courtesy of the Kentucky Historical Society.
158	From A. B. Lipscomb, ed., *The Commercial History of the Southern States: Kentucky* (1903).
159	Courtesy of the Kentucky Historical Society.
160	Courtesy of the Kentucky Historical Society.
162	Courtesy of the Kentucky Historical Society.

CHAPTER 8

164   (top) Courtesy of the Kentucky Library, Western Kentucky University, (bottom) From James F. Hopkins, *A History of the Hemp Industry in Kentucky* (1951).

165   (both) Courtesy of the Kentucky Department of Travel.

167   Image courtesy of Doe Anderson, Inc.

168   (top) Courtesy of the Kentucky Library, Western Kentucky University, (center) Courtesy of the Kentucky Library, Western Kentucky University, (bottom) Photo courtesy of the Daviess County Public Library.

169   (top) Courtesy of the Kentucky Library, Western Kentucky University, (bottom) Courtesy of the Kentucky Historical Society.

171   (top) Courtesy of the Kentucky Historical Society, (bottom) Photo courtesy of Humana, Inc.

173   (top) From the authors' collection, (bottom) Photo courtesy of Toyota Motor Manufacturing, Kentucky, Inc.

174   (top) Copyright by *The Courier-Journal*, (bottom) Photo courtesy of Toyota Motor Manufacturing, Kentucky, Inc.

175   (top) Courtesy of the GM Bowling Green Assembly Plant, (bottom) Courtesy of the Kentucky State Parks.

176   Map by Dick Gilbreath.

177   Map by Dick Gilbreath.

178   Courtesy of UPS Creative Media.

CHAPTER 9

180   Courtesy of the Kentucky Historical Society.

181   Courtesy of the Kentucky Historical Society.

182   Courtesy of the Kentucky Historical Society.

183   Courtesy of the Kentucky Historical Society.

184   Courtesy of the Jesse Stuart Foundation.

185   (top) Courtesy of the Kentucky Library, Western Kentucky University, (bottom) Photo by Dan Carraco.

186   From Wendell Berry, *Harlan Hubbard* (1990).

187   Photo by Julia Maloof, courtesy of George C. Wolfe.

188   (top) Photo by Richard Stone, (bottom) From Otto A. Rothert, *The Story of a Poet: Madison Cawein* (1921).

190   Courtesy of Frank X Walker.

191   Courtesy of the Filson Historical Society, Louisville, Kentucky.

192   Photo by George Pickow, courtesy of Jean Ritchie and the Kentucky Historical Society.

193   Photo by Russ Harrington.

194   Courtesy of the Kentucky Historical Society.

196   (top) Copyright by *The Courier-Journal*, (bottom) Courtesy of the Kentucky Historical Society.

197   (top) Courtesy of the Kentucky Historical Society, (bottom) Edgar Tolson, "Rock Dog," circa 1945, carved and painted limestone, 30 in. × 15 ½ in. × 24 in., Milwaukee Art Museum, The Michael and Julie Hall Collection of American Folk Art, M1989.312.

198   (top) "Spirit of Freedom," bronze, 1998. Located at Tenth and U Street, Washington, D.C. Sculpted by Ed Hamilton, photograph by Richard Pace, Baltimore, Md., (bottom) Courtesy of the Kentucky Historical Society.

199   Courtesy of the Academy of Motion Pictures Arts and Sciences.

CHAPTER 10

202   Louisville & Nashville Railroad Records, University of Louisville Archives and Records Center, Louisville, Ky.

203   (top) Library of Congress, Prints & Photographs Division, FSA-OWI Collection, LC-USF34-055773-D, (bottom) From the authors' collection.

204   (both) Courtesy of the Kentucky Historical Society.

205   Courtesy of the Cincinnati/Northern Kentucky International Airport.

206   (top) Courtesy of the Kentucky Library, Western Kentucky University, (bottom) Image courtesy of Kentucky State University.

207   (top) Library of Congress, Prints & Photographs Division, FSA-OWI Collection, LC-USF3301-006077-M2, (bottom) Courtesy of the University of Kentucky Special Collections and Archives.

209   (top) Courtesy of the Kentucky Library, Western Kentucky University, (bottom) Photo by Joe Rosenthal, courtesy of AP/Wide World Photos.

211   Photo by First Sergeant Joseph P. Simpson, courtesy of the Kentucky Historical Society.

212   Copyright by *The Courier-Journal*.

213   (top) Courtesy of the University of Kentucky Special Collections and Archives, (bottom) Courtesy of the Kentucky Library, Western Kentucky University.

215   (top) Courtesy of the University of Kentucky Special Collections and Archives, (bottom) Courtesy of the Kentucky Historical Society.

216   (both) Courtesy of the Kentucky Historical Society.

217   Courtesy of the University of North Carolina, Chapel Hill.

218   (top) Courtesy of the Kentucky Historical Society, (bottom) Copyright by *The Courier-Journal*.

219   Courtesy of the LBJ Library, photo by Yoichi Okamoto.

220   Courtesy of AP/Wide World Photos.

222   Courtesy of the University of Kentucky Special Collections and Archives.

223   Courtesy of the Kentucky Library, Western Kentucky University.

224   Image from the Kentucky Historical Society.

CHAPTER 11

226   Courtesy of the Kentucky Historical Society.

227   Courtesy of the Kentucky Historical Society.

229   (top) Courtesy of the Kentucky Historical Society, (bottom) Courtesy of the University of Kentucky Special Collections and Archives.

231   (left) Foote lantern slide 0024 "Mountain boys on way to school," courtesy of the Lexington Public Library Kentucky Room, (top right) Courtesy of the Kentucky Historical Society, (bottom right) Library of Congress, Prints & Photographs Division, FSA-OWI Collection, LC-USF34-055854-D.

232   (top) Photo by Rick McComb, Kentucky Department of Education, (bottom) Courtesy of the Kentucky Library, Western Kentucky University.

233   (top) Courtesy of the University of Kentucky Special Collections and Archives, (bottom) Courtesy of the Kentucky Historical Society.

234   From Martin Schmidt, *Kentucky Illustrated* (1992).

236   (top) Photo by Rick McComb, Kentucky Department of Education, (bottom) Courtesy of the Kentucky Library, Western Kentucky University.

237   Courtesy of the Kentucky Historical Society.

239   (top) Photo by Rick McComb, Kentucky Department of Education, (bottom) Photo courtesy of Georgetown College.

240   Photo courtesy of Berea College.

241   (top) Photo courtesy of Kentucky State University, (bottom) Photo courtesy of Murray State University.

243   Copyright by *The Courier-Journal*.

244   (top) Courtesy of the University of Kentucky Special Collections and Archives, (bottom) Photo courtesy of the University of Kentucky.

CHAPTER 12

246   Photo by Dan Dry.

248   Photo by Dan Dry.

249   From John Uri Lloyd, *Etidorpha* (1895).

Appendix

262   University of Kentucky Photographic Archives.

263   (both) Courtesy of the Kentucky Department of Travel.

264   (top) Photo by Thomas G. Barnes, (remaining) Courtesy of the Kentucky Department of the Travel.

265   (all) Courtesy of the Kentucky Department of Travel.

266   (top) Courtesy of Kentucky Geological Survey, (bottom) Photograph by Jeb DeKalb, State of Tennessee Photographic Services. Courtesy of www.tennesseeriverpearls.com.

☆ Index ☆

A

A&W, 172
academies or private schools, 226–27, 235
actors, 199–200
Adair County, 17, 65, 116, 184, 241
Adams, Henry, 130
Affrilachia (Walker), 190
African Americans, 212
  after the Civil War, 158–59
  Ali, Muhammad (Cassius Clay), 219, 220
  Anderson, Charles W., Jr., 218
  basketball, 116–17
  Bibb, Henry, 135
  Bishop, Stephen, 58
  Brown, Clara, 126
  Brown, William Wells, 134–35
  churches, 120
  colleges and universities, 240
  equal rights for all races, 216–20
  Estill, Monk, 39
  first school, 130
  Fitzbutler, Henry, 158
  Free Frank, 29, 127, 131–32
  Harper, Nathaniel, 158
  Hawkins, Sam, 170
  Henson, Josiah, 133, 134
  Jackson, Blyden, 217
  Johnson, Lyman, 237
  King, Martin Luther, Jr., 218, 219
  Marrs, Elijah, 159
  Meyzeek, Albert E., 158
  Murphy, Isaac, 112
  poets, 188, 190
  populations in Kentucky, 47
  Powers, Georgia Davis, 89
  schools for, 158, 159, 227
  segregation, 188, 236–37
  settling in Kentucky, 15, 20, 29
  Sleet, Moneta, Jr., 192
  soldiers in the Civil War, 155, 159
  soldiers in WWI, 209–10
  sports teams, 114
  Stanley, Frank, Jr., 219
  State University in Louisville, 159
  Twyman, Luska J., 219
  Uncle Tom's Cabin (Stowe), 133
  Underground Railroad, 133–34
  voting, 158
  Wolfe, George C., 187–88
  York, 131
  Young, Charles, 155, 209
  Young, Whitney, Jr., 219
  see also slavery; slaves
agriculture, 9–12, 70–71, 102, 103–4, 155, 164–67
air-conditioning, 95
airplanes, 94, 95
air transportation, 173, 177, 204–5
Ali, Muhammad, 112, 219, 220
Alice Lloyd College, Knott County, 235
Allen, James Lane, *The Choir Invisible*, 180–81
Allen County, 171
All That Is Kentucky (Combs), 73
amendments to constitutions, 79
American Indians, 7
  see also Indians; Native Americans
American Printing House for the Blind, 190
American Revolutionary War, 36, 40, 41, 42, 67, 111
Anderson, Charles W., Jr., 218
Anderson, Robert, 146
Anderson County, 71
animals in Kentucky, 24
antislavery, 135–36
Appalachia (Eastern Kentucky), 61–62, 169, 212
Appalachian Mountains, 18
  map, 19
appeals, 85
archaeologists, 6, 8
Archaic Period, 9–10
architects, 198
Arnow, Harriette Simpson, *The Dollmaker*, 184
arrowheads, 9
art, 197–98
Asbury, Bishop Francis, 118
Ashland, 61
  basketball, 117
  radio in, 195
  steel-rolling mills, 171
Ashland Oil, 62, 171, 172
astronauts, 1–2

Athens, Kentucky, 74
Atlatl (weapon), 9, 10
atomic energy plant, 175
Audubon, John James, 70, 71
Audubon Parkway, 203
automobiles, 94, 95
average Kentuckian, 94, 246–47
axes, stone, 9, 10

B

Badin, Stephen T., 118
Ballard County, 55, 74, 212
banks, 207
Baptist churches, 118, 120
Bardstown, 65, 121, 130
    Federal Hill, 74
    National Guard troops, 211
    St. Joseph Cathedral, 118
Barkley, Alben W., 222, 223
Barren County, 65, 74, 192, 219
Barren River State Park, 65
Barrett Manual Training School, 115
barter and trade, 16, 20
baseball, 112–14, 224
basketball, 115–17, 222, 224
Bath County, 36, 37, 153
Battle of Blue Licks, 40
Battle of Mill Springs, 149
Battle of Perryville, 149–51
Battle of Richmond, 149
Bellarmine University, 70
Bell County, 61, 117, 160, 175
Berea, 136
Berea College, 240
Berlin, Kentucky, 74
Berry, George W., 148
Berry, Wendell, 185, 187
Bert Combs Mountain Parkway, 203
Bibb, Henry, 135
Big Black Mountain, 49
Big Bone Lick, 18
Big Sandy River, 51
    map, 52
Big South Fork National River and Recreation
    Area, 175
Bill of Rights, 78
bills becoming laws, 89–91
birds in Kentucky, 24
Birds of America, The (Audubon), 70, 71

Bishop, Stephen, 58
Black Poetry in America (Jackson), 217
blacksmiths, 103
Blazer, Paul, 171, 172
Bluegrass Boys, 194
Bluegrass music, 192, 194
Bluegrass region, 27, 59, 63–65
boat travel, 202
bonnets or hats, 98
Boone, Daniel, 28, 32–41
    on buffalo herds, 23
    capture and rescue of daughter, Jemima, 36–38
    and the coonskin cap, 20
    death of son, Israel, 40
    Filson's history of, 31
    Indian name, 40
    leaving for Missouri, 41
    painting of, 38
    research sources on, 5
    and slaves, 127
    statue in Louisville, 197
    as symbol, 41
    wife of, 32
Boone, Israel, 40
Boone, Jemima, 36–38
Boone, Rebecca Bryan, 32
Boone County, 18, 62, 212, 249
Boonesborough, 63, 118, 127
borders of Kentucky, 51, 52
Bourbon County, 63, 80, 118, 167, 181
bourbon whiskey, 67, 167
bow and arrow, 10
Bowling Green, 1, 65, 109, 159, 214
    capital of Confederate State of Kentucky, 147
    Corvette sports cars, 173
    description of, 125
    Duncan Hines, 173
    postman, 206
    Potter College, 227
    Western Kentucky University, 241
boxing, 112
Boyd, Linn, 137
Boyd County, 61, 171–72, 195
Boyle County, 63, 64, 88, 98, 108, 149, 151, 190,
    235, 239–40
Bracken County, 134, 136, 185
branches of government, 79–91
Brandeis, Louis, 87
Breathitt County, 53, 160, 231

Breckinridge, John C., 137, 144, 148
Breckinridge, Madeline "Madge" McDowell, 215, 251
Breckinridge, Mary, 109
Breckinridge, Robert J., 227
Brewers, 117
Brooks, Cleanth, 184
Brothers' War (Civil War) in Kentucky, 147–49
Brown, William Wells, 134–35
Brown-Forman, 171
Brown Hotel, Louisville, 173
Brownie, 194
Bryan's Station, 40
Buckhorn, 210
buffalo, 23–24, 26, 41
Buford, Martha McDowell, 157
Bugtussle, 74
Bullock, J.J., 228
Bunning, Jim, 114
burial mounds, 10
Burlington, 62
Burnside, 184
Butler, Laurence, 26
Butler, Lorine L., *My Old Kentucky Home*, 73

C

Cadiz, Kentucky, 74
Caldwell County, 44
California (battleship), 210
Callaway, Betsy, 36–38
Callaway, Fanny, 36–38
Calloway County, 55, 72, 73, 184, 194, 241
Calumet Farm, Lexington, 222
Campbell County, 62, 114, 171, 186, 241
Campbellsville University, 65
camp meetings, 119
Camp Nelson, 155, 156, 159
Camp Taylor, 107
Cane Ridge, 63, 118–19
capitol building of Kentucky, 82
card playing, 110, 120
Carlisle County, 55
car racing, 117
Carr Creek, 117
Carroll County, 156
cars, 203–4
Casey County, 150, 207
Catholic Church, 118, 120, 121
Catlettsburg, 216

Caudill, Harry, *The Mountains, the Miner, and the Lord*, 170
Cawein, Madison, 188–89
central heat, 95
Centre College, Danville, 64
    Centre College versus Harvard University in football, 114–15
Chandler, A.B. "Happy," 53, 114, 222
Check and balances in government, 90
Cherokee Indian Nation, 44
Chickasaw Indians, 55, 80
Chief Blackfish, 38, 40
Choctaw Academy, 233
Choir Invisible, The (Allen), 180–81
cholera, 107
Christian County, 43, 71, 125, 167, 195
The Christian Traveller, 73
Churchill Downs, 67, 68
Cincinnati, Ohio, 62
Cincinnati and Northern Kentucky International Airport, 62, 173
circuit courts, 85
circuses, 111
Civil Rights Act, 219
Civil War, 145–58, 189
    battles in Kentucky, 149–53
    beginning of, 125
    Brothers' War, 147–49
    Confederate defense line map, 147
    deaths in, 156–57
    end of, 158
    flags of, 146
    and geography, 146
    guerrillas, 153–55
    Kentucky in the Union, 55, 146, 147
    lawlessness after, 155
    neutrality in, 146, 147
    results of, 155–58
    see also Confederacy; slavery; Union
Clark, George Rogers, 28, 41–42
Clark, Thomas D., 188
Clark, William, 131
Clark County, 13, 63, 142
Clay, Cassius (Muhammad Ali), 219, 220
Clay, Cassius M., 84, 135, 136, 215
Clay, Henry, 137–38, 142, 144, 146, 215
Clay, Laura, 213, 215
Clay, Lucretia Hart, 138
Clay, Webster County, 218

Clay County, 84, 160, 167
Clements, Earle, 222
climate of Kentucky, 53
    map, 54
Clooney, George, 200
clothes and fashion, 15, 97–99
Coal Miner's Daughter (Lynn), 193
coal mining, 60, 62, 70, 169–71, 212
Cobb, Irvin S., 183
Coleman, "King" Kelly, 117
colleges and universities, 64, 239–44
Collins, Josiah, 36
Collins, Martha Layne, 216
colonies, map of original thirteen, 42
Columbia, 17, 65
Columbus, Christopher, 12
Columbus, Confederate defense line map, 147
Combs, Bert, 84, 222
Combs, Earle, 114
Combs, Josiah, *All That Is Kentucky*, 73
Combs, Sara Walter, 86, 87
commonwealths, 76
communication revolution, 205–6
computers, 178, 205, 206
Confederacy, 145
    Confederate State of Kentucky, 147, 155
    Davis as president of, 139
    flag of, 146, 147
    see also Civil War
conflict resolution, 16, 248, 251
constitutions of Kentucky, 76–79, 92
Cooper, John Sherman, 222
Corbin, 61
corn (maize), 11, 12, 164, 167
corsets, 99
Corvette sports cars, Bowling Green, 173
Corydon, 114, 222
Cotter, Joseph S., 188
country music, 192, 193–94
country stores, 101, 102
county health departments, 109
Courier-Journal, Louisville, 105, 191
court of appeals, 85
courts, 85–87
Covington, 51, 62, 63, 73, 162, 224
    National Folk Festival, 212
    radio in, 195
Crawford, Jane Todd, 108
Crittenden, George Bibb, 148

Crittenden, John J., 137, 146
Crittenden, Thomas Leonidas, 148
Cruise, Tom, 200
Crum, Denny, 116
cultural or human regions, 60–72
    Appalachia (Eastern Kentucky), 61–62
    Bluegrass, 63–65
    Jackson Purchase, 72
    Louisville, 67–70
    Northern Kentucky, 62–63
    South–Central Kentucky, 65–67
    West Kentucky, 70–72
    see also geographical regions of Kentucky;
        Kentucky
culture defined, 60
culture of Kentucky, 179–200
    motion pictures (movies), 198–200, 224
    music, 192–96
    newspapers, 190–92
    visual arts, 196–98
    see also writing and writers
Cumberland Falls, 60
Cumberland Gap, 18–19, 21, 25, 49
    Boone leading group through, 34
    Confederate defense line map, 147
    national historical park, 175
Cumberland River, 51, 72
    Cumberland Falls, 60
Cyrus, Billy Ray, 194

D

daily life, 93–124
    basketball, 115–17
    clothes and fashion, 97–99
    food, 99–102
    fun and games, 109–15
    health, 106–9
    religion, 117–21
    work, 103–6
Dame, Mittie, 208
dams, 51, 72
dancing, 120
Danville, 43, 63, 77, 131, 134, 190, 227
    Centre College, 64, 240
    Kentucky School for the Deaf, 235
"Dark and Bloody Ground," 14, 144
Daviess County, 71, 116, 133, 167, 192, 222, 240
Davis, Jefferson, 139, 140, 141, 144, 146
Declaration of Independence, 36, 67

Delta Airlines, 173
democratic government, 76
Democrats, 84, 221, 222, 246
depressions, 206
Derby Pie, 173
DeRosier, Linda Scott, 105
Dewees, Mary, 25
Diddle, Ed, 116
Dippin' Dots Ice Cream, 172
Disciples of Christ or Christian Church, 119
Discovery, Settlement, and Present State of Kentucke, The (Filson), 31, 32
diseases
    in early days, 106–7
    and Native Americans, 13–14, 16
dissents, 88
district courts, 85
documents, reading, 27
dogs in frontier Kentucky, 34
Dollar General Stores, 171
Dollmaker, The (Arnow), 184
Doram, Dennis, 131
Doram, Diademia Taylor, 131
Dorman, James H., 153
dormitory rooms, 244
Drake, Daniel, 37, 228
dressmaking businesses, 168
drive-in movies, 204
drought, 53
drug use, 108
drying food, 101
Dupee, George, 120
Duveneck, Frank, 196, 197

E

earthquake, New Madrid, 57
Eastern Coal Fields (mountains), 59–60
Eastern Kentucky University, 115
economy of Kentucky, 163, 179
    barter and trade, 16
    see also Work
editorials, 191
Edmonson County, 11
education and schools in Kentucky, 86, 225–44, 248
    Choctaw Academy, 233
    college life, 242–44
    colleges and universities, 239–41
    early schools, 226–27, 231

high schools, 236
Kentucky Education Reform Act (KERA), 237–38
Kentucky Institution for the Education of the Blind, 234, 235
Kentucky School for the Deaf, 235
life in school, 227–32
Moonlight Schools (night schools), 233
one-room schools, 227–29
private colleges and universities, 240–41
private schools or academies, 226–27, 235
public colleges and univesities, 241
public schools, 226, 227, 228, 236
religious groups, 227, 235, 240
schools for females, 227
schools for slaves, 227
schools in the twentieth century, 235–38
segregation, 236–37
settlement schools, 235
special schools, 233–35
teachers in early schools, 231–32, 235
technical schools, 239
two-year community colleges, 239
violence in schools, 231
"Whirlwind Campaign," 236, 238
Edward T. Breathitt (Pennyrile) Parkway, 203
Eighty-Eight, 74
elections, 221, 222
electricity, 94, 96, 100
    to rural areas, 208
Elizabethtown, 65, 67, 118
Elkton, 114
e-mail, 205
"Endless Mountains," 18
Energy production, 175
English explorers, 15, 16, 17, 19–21
English settlers, killed in Indian conflicts, 27–28
environment, 246, 248
equal rights, 213–20
Erlanger, 62
Eskippakithiki, 13
Estill, James, 39
Estill, Monk, 39
Estill's Defeat, 39
Estill's Station, 39
Etidorhpa (Lloyd), 249

Europeans
    as adopted captives of Indians, 16
    exploring Kentucky, 2, 7, 13, 15–17
    settling Kentucky, 36
Everly Brothers, 194
Ewan, Julia, 214
executive branch (governor), 82–85
exports, 178

F

Fairbank, Calvin, 134, 135
fairs, 111
Fairview, 139
Falls City, 168
Falls of the Ohio, Ohio River, 67
Falmouth, 243, 244
family photographs, 4
Fancy Farm, 72
farming, 9, 10, 11, 12, 103–4, 164–67
    Civil War effects on, 155–56, 159
Farmington, Louisville, 140
fashion, 97
fast-food businesses, 172–73, 178
Fayette County, 80, 167
Fazoli's, 172
FDIC-insured banks, 207
Federal Hill, Bardstown, 74
Fee, John G., 136
Ferrill, London, 120
feuds, 61, 160–61
Fifth Street Baptist Church, Louisville, 130
Fighting Kentuckian, The, 224
Filson, John, 180
    Discovery, Settlement, and Present State of
        Kentucke, The, 32
First African Baptist Church, Lexington, 120
fishing, 100, 111
Fisk University, Tennessee, 217
Fitzbutler, Henry, 158
flags
    American, 76
    of the Union and the Confederacy, 146, 147
Flanery, Mary Elliott, 216
Fleming, 170
Fleming County, 211
floods and flood control, 51–52
Florence, 62, 212
Floyd County, 84, 86
Foley, "Red," 194

folk art, 197
folk culture, 247
folk songs, 110, 192
food, 99–102
food industry, 172–73
football, 114–15
Ford, Wendell, 222
Ford plants, Louisville, 173
Fort Ancient Culture, 12
Fort Boonesborough, 32, 34, 35, 40
Fort Harrod, 28–29, 127
Fort Knox, 67, 207
forts, 29
    map, 30
Fort Thomas, 62, 114, 186
Foster, Stephen Collins, 133, 192–93
Fox, John, Jr.
    Kingdom Come, 181
    Little Shepherd, The, 181
    Trail of the Lonesome Pine, The, 181
Frankfort, 43, 51, 63, 64, 137, 173
    civil rights march, 218
    Kentucky History Center, 4, 63
    Kentucky State University, 240
    State Street School, 236
Franklin County, 4, 23, 43, 51, 63, 64, 82, 88,
        116, 137, 149, 157, 162, 188, 196, 198,
        218, 236, 240
freedom from slavery, 131–35
free enterprise system, 163
Free Frank (slave), 131–32
French explorers, 15, 16, 17
Frontier Nursing Service, 109
frontiers, 1–3
    end of the Kentucky frontier, 41
    in Kentucky, 27–28
    of the mind, 2–3
Fulks, Joe, 222, 224
Fulton County, 49, 55, 57
future issues, 245–52
    conflict resolution, 248, 251
    education, 248
    global marketplace, 248
    health care, 251
    land use, 248
    Long-Term Policy Research Center twenty-six
        goals for the future, 250, 251
    "New Economy," 248
    poverty and hunger, 248

power sources, 247, 251
saving parts of the past, 247–48
technology, 248
a typical Kentuckian, 246–47
your future, 251–52

G

Gallatin County, 48, 107, 117
Garrard County, 160
Gaspar River, 118
Gayle, Crystal, 193
General Assembly, 87–91, 236
General Electric, 171
geographic regions of Kentucky, 53–60
    Bluegrass, 27, 59
    Jackson Purchase, 55–57
    the Knobs, 55, 59
    maps of, 55, 56
    Mountains (Eastern Coal Fields), 59–60
    Pennyroyal (or Pennyrile), 58
    Western Coal Fields, 59
    see also cultural or human regions; Kentucky
geography of Kentucky, 18–19, 22, 27,
        49–53
    and Civil War, 146, 149
Georgetown, 63, 173, 212
Georgetown College, 64, 114, 115, 116, 239,
        240, 242
German immigrants, 47, 159
Gettysburg Address, 67
Giles, Janice Holt, 184
Giovanni's Pizza, 172
Girty, Simon, 16–17
Gist, Christopher, 20, 21, 127
Glasgow, 65, 192
Glendale, 214
Global Kentucky, 175–78, 248
Goebel, William, 162
Gold Vault at Fort Knox, 67
Golden Triangle, 63, 73
Gordon, Caroline, 184
government of Kentucky, 75–92
    branches of government, 79–91
    change in governments, 78–79
    constitutions of Kentucky, 76–79, 92
    executive branch (governor), 82–85
    government defined, 76
    judicial branch (the courts), 85–87
    legislative branch (General Assembly), 87–91

levels of government, 79
    Tate, "Honest Dick," 75, 76, 91–92
governor of Kentucky, 82–85
Grafton, Sue, 187
Graham, Sarah, 35
Grand Ole Opry, 193
Grant County, 249
Graves County, 53, 55, 71, 72, 223
"Graveyard Quilt," 95
Great Crossing, Scott County, 233
Great Depression, 206–7, 210, 212
"Great Dying," The, 12–14
Great Meadow, The (Roberts), 183
Great Revival, 63, 118, 119
Green County, 108
Green River, 51
Greenup County, 13, 184
Griffith, D.W., 198–99, 200
Guerrant, Edward O., 153
guerrillas in the Civil War, 153–55
Gulf War, 209
Guthrie, A.B. "Bud," 184, 192, 224

H

Hall, James Baker, 185
Hall, Joe, 116
Hall, Wade, The Kentucky Book, 73
Hal Rogers (Daniel Boone) Parkway, 203
Hamilton, Ed, "Spirit of Freedom," 197–98
Hamlin, Jim, 210
Hampton, Lionel, 194
Hancock County, 51, 208
Handy, W.C., 194
Hardin, Lizzie, 152
Hardin County, 65, 66, 207, 214
Hardwick, Elizabeth, 184
Harlan, 210
Harlan, John Marshall, 87, 88
Harlan County, 49, 169, 171, 187, 210, 235
Harper, Nathaniel, 158
Harrison County, 148, 155
Harrod, James, 28–29, 32, 41, 42
Harrodsburg, 35, 63, 152
Harrodstown, 28–29
Hart County, 41
Hatfield–McCoy Feud, 61, 160
Hawkins, Margaret, 170
Hawkins, Sadie, 170
Hawkins, Sam, 170

hay, 167
Hayden, Lewis, 134, 135
Hazard, 61
health, 106–9, 246, 251
Heard, Dick, 195
hemp, 129, 164, 165
Henderson, 70, 115, 125, 194
Henderson, Richard, 34
Henderson County, 70, 71, 114, 128, 167,
    194, 222
Henry, Josephine, 214
Henry County, 159, 185
Henson, Josiah, 133, 134, 135
Herald-Leader, Lexington, 191, 192
Hickman County, 55
Highland Heights, 241
high schools, 236
Hill, Mildred, 193
Hill, Patty, 193
"hillbilly" image, 62
Hindman School, Knott County, 235
Hines, Duncan, 173
Hispanics, 46, 220
historians, 188
history, 3–6
    perspective from, 3–4, 152, 172
    and planning, 245
    saving parts of the past, 247–48
    timeline, 7, 8
    writing about, 4–6, 188
    see also future issues; research
History of Afro American Literature (Jackson), 217
Hodgenville, 67, 139
hogs, 164
home canning, 101
hookworms, 107
Hopkins County, 71
Hopkinsville, 43, 129, 195
horse farms, 63, 64, 165, 166
horse or stagecoach travel, 202
horse racing, 111, 112, 120
Hot Brown sandwich, 173
House of Representatives of Kentucky,
    82, 87–91
Hubbard, Anne, 186
Hubbard, Harlan, 186
human regions. *See* cultural or human regions
Humana, Louisville, 171

Humes, Helen, 194
hunting, 9, 10, 100, 111
Hyden, 109

I

IBM, Lexington, 171
ice age, 8, 9
iceboxes, 101
ice factories, 101
ice houses, 100
Imlay, Gilbert, 26
immigrants, 46, 47, 159, 246
In Country (Mason), 71
Independence, 62
Independent, 84
Indian mounds, 39
Indians, 2
    see also American Indians; Native Americans
industries, 171–75
Ingles, Mary, 18
interstate highway system, 168, 203
Intolerance (motion picture), 199
inventories after death, 123, 124
Irish immigrants, 47, 159
Iwo Jima, 209, 211

J

Jackman, John, 156–57
Jackson, Andrew, 55
Jackson, Blyden, 217
    Black Poetry in America, 217
    History of Afro American Literature, 217
    Waiting Years, The, 217
Jackson Purchase, 55–57, 72, 183
jazz, 194
Jefferson, Thomas, 137
Jefferson County, 48–49, 80
Jessamine County, 63, 155, 156, 159, 231,
    232, 240
Jewish faith, 118
jockeys, 112
Johnson, Ambrose, 130
Johnson, Annie Fellows, *The Little Colonel*,
    181–82
Johnson, Eddie, 130
Johnson, Henry V., 102
Johnson, Isaac, 130
Johnson, Lyman, 237

Johnson, Lyndon, 219
Johnson, Richard M., 136–37, 144, 235
Johnson County, 105, 193
Jones, "Grandpa," 194
Jones, Martha McDowell Buford, 157
Jones, Willis Field, 157
Judd, Ashley, 200
Judds, 194
judicial branch (the courts), 85–87
Julian Carroll (Purchase) Parkway, 203
justices of Supreme Court of Kentucky, 86

K

Keeneland Race Course, Lexington, 63, 165
Kenlake, 72
Kenton, Simon, 28, 32, 33, 36, 38, 41, 42
Kenton County, 47, 51, 53, 62, 78, 162, 196,
    212, 224
"Kentucke" (Walker), 190
Kentucke Gazette, The, 191
Kentuckians Are Different (Morton), 73, 166
Kentucky
    after the Civil War, 158–60
    animals and birds in, 23–24
    borders of, 51
    climate of, 53
    Confederate State of Kentucky, 147
    counties from 1912 to present, 81
    counties in 1792, 80
    counties of, 48–49
    culture of, 179–200
    early days in, 15–44
    early political leaders, 136–38
    education and schools, 86
    feuds and murders, 160–62
    geography of, 18–19, 22, 27, 49–53
    global, 175–78
    latitude and longitude map, 50
    location in the U.S. and North America, 176
    map of location in the world, 177
    map of most populous cities, 69
    names of towns, 74
    origin of the name, 14
    people and population of, 46–47
    presidents from, 139–43
    regionalism, 72–73
    state capitol building, 82
    statehood, 41–44, 76–77, 125

stereotypes of, 61, 161
Supreme Court of, 85–87, 90
Trail of Tears, 43–44
trails or traces, 22–24
a typical Kentuckian, 246–47
and written records, 13
see also Civil War; cultural or human regions;
    future issues; geographic regions of Kentucky;
    government of Kentucky; settling Kentucky;
    twentieth-century changes
Kentucky Book, The (Hall), 73
Kentucky Community and Technical College
    System, 239
Kentucky Dam, 72
Kentucky Dam Village, 72
Kentucky Department for Libraries and
    Archives, 188
Kentucky Derby, 67, 68, 112, 166, 222
Kentucky Educational Television (KET), 205
Kentucky Education Commission, 230
Kentucky Education Reform Act (KERA), 86,
    237–38
Kentucky Equal Rights Association, 214
Kentucky General Assembly, 221
Kentucky Governor's School for the Arts, 190
Kentucky Historical Society, 188
Kentucky History Center, Frankfort, 4, 63
Kentucky Horse Park, Lexington, 63, 112
Kentucky Institution for the Education of the Blind,
    234, 235
Kentucky Lake, 72, 208
"Kentucky Rain" (Rabbit and Heard), 195
Kentucky River, 51, 167
    Palisades, 59
    travel in Kentucky, 19
Kentucky School for the Deaf, 235
Kentucky State University, 64, 116,
    240, 241
Kentucky Wesleyan, 116
KERA. See Kentucky Education Reform Act
KFC (Kentucky Fried Chicken), 172, 174
King, Martin Luther, Jr., 218, 219
King, "Pee Wee," 194
Kingdom Come (Fox), 181
Kingsolver, Barbara, 187
Knobs, The, 55, 59
Knott, Sarah Gertrude, 212
Knott County, 74, 171, 184, 235

Knox County, 174, 241, 243
Korean War, 209
Krock, Arthur, 192

L

LaGrange, 159
Lake Barkley, 72, 175, 208
Lake Cumberland, 65
Lakes of Kentucky, 51, 52
Land Between the Lakes, 72, 175
land use, 248
Landrum, Dora, 208
Larue County, 66, 139, 175
Late Prehistoric Period, 12
Laurel County, 132
lawlessness after Civil War, 155, 159
Lawrence County, 87
laws and bills, 89–91
legislative branch (General Assembly),
      87–91
Leslie County, 109, 169, 210, 229
Letcher County, 170
Lewis and Clark trip, 131
Lewisport, 51, 208
Lexington, 43, 63, 64, 111, 112, 184, 185, 187,
      215, 218, 224, 227
   airport in the 1930s, 204
   airports at, 173
   Calumet Farm, 222
   Clay, Henry, in, 138
   description of, 125
   First African Baptist Church, 120
   Herald-Leader, 191, 192
   IBM, 171
   Keeneland Race Course, 63, 165
   Kentucky Horse Park, 63, 112
   Lexmark, 171
   radio in, 195
   Rupp Arena, 195
   slaves being sold, 127
   Transylvania University, 64, 239, 240
Lexmark, 64, 171
Licking River, 51
life expectancy, 106, 108
Lincoln, Abraham, 139–43, 251
   born in Kentucky, 67, 137, 175
   and Civil War, 146, 155
   favorite poem, 144
   Gettysburg Address, 67

   sculpture and photograh of, 144
   sworn in as president, 145
Lincoln, Mary Todd, 142, 143, 148
Lincoln, Thomas "Tad," 141
Lincoln County, 31, 35, 43, 80, 111
Lindsey Wilson College, 65
Lipscomb, William N., Jr., 244
Little Colonel, The (Johnson), 181–82
Little Shepherd, The (Fox), 181
Livingston County, 207
Lloyd, John Uri
   Etidorhpa, 249
   Stringtown on the Pike, 249
local governments, 79
Logan, Benjamin, 28, 31, 32, 42
Logan County, 1, 63, 71, 118–19, 137, 147, 154
Logan family feud, 161
Logan's Fort, 31
London, Kentucky, 61, 65, 74
Long Hunters, 20, 33
Long John Silver's, 172
Long Knives (people from Virginia), 17
Long-Term Policy Research Center, 250, 251
Loretto, 167
Louie Nunn (Cumberland) Parkway, 203
Louisa, 87
Louisville, 1, 19, 63, 67–70, 111, 168, 187, 188,
      194, 217, 222
   Actor's Theater, 187
   airports at, 173–74
   American Printing House for the Blind, 190
   Brown Hotel, 173
   Camp Taylor, 107
   Courier-Journal, 105, 191
   cultural events, 70
   Daniel Boone statue in, 197
   description of, 125
   Farmington, 140
   Fifth Street Baptist Church, 130
   Flood of 1937, 51
   Ford plants, 173
   General Electric, 171
   growth of, 156
   Humana, 171
   Kentucky Derby, 67, 68, 112
   Kentucky Institution for the Education of the
      Blind, 234, 235
   map of urban expansion, 68
   Oakland Race Course, 111

plow factory in, 168
Presbyterians, 120–21
radio in, 195, 196
Simmons University, 240
Slugger Museum, 114
State University in, 159
Taylor's home in, 139
television, 196
United Parcel Service (UPS), 174, 177
University of Louisville, 240
Yum!Brands, 171, 172
Louisville Defender, 219
Louisville Eagles (baseball club), 114
Louisville Gas and Electric (LG&E), 171, 175
Louisville Slugger brand bats, 114
Loveless, Patty, 194
Lower Shawneetown, 13
Lynn, Loretta, 193, 194
Lyon, George Ella, 187
Lyon County, 230

M

Madison County, 32, 34–37, 39–40, 63, 80, 97,
    120, 136, 149, 194, 240, 241
mail, 205, 206
Mammoth Cave, 58, 65, 175
   Woodland Indian, 11
mammoths, 8, 9
Man o' War (horse), 112
manufacturing, 171
   see also Industries
maps
   Appalachian Mountains, 19
   climates similar to Kentucky's, 54
   forts and stations, 30
   geographic regions, 55, 56
   Jackson Purchase, 55
   Kentucky counties from 1912 to
     present, 81
   Kentucky counties in 1792, 80
   Kentucky's location in the U.S. and North
     America, 176
   Kentucky's location in the world, 177
   Kentucky's most populous cities, 69
   largest and smallest counties of Kentucky, 48
   latitude and longitude of Kentucky, 50
   original thirteen colonies, 42
   rivers and lakes of Kentucky, 52
   state parks and resort areas, 66

urban expansion in Louisville, 68
   The Wilderness Road, 30
Marcum, Julia, 150
Marion County, 227
Marshall County, 55, 117, 222, 231
Martha Layne Collins (Bluegrass) Parkway, 203
Martin family feud, 161
Martin Luther King Center, University of
   Kentucky, 190
Mason, Bobbie Ann, 71, 185
Mason County, 37, 80, 209, 214, 228
Mayfield, 71, 72
Mayslick, 37, 155
Maysville, 19, 118, 214
McChord, William, 151
McClanahan, Ed, 185
McConnell, Mitch, 222
McCormack, Arthur, 109
McCormack, Joseph N., 109
McCracken County, 44, 51, 55, 72, 83, 118, 175,
   183, 192, 212, 217, 223
McCracken County High School, 212
McDowell, Ephraim, 108
McKinney, "Wildcat" John, 36
McLean County, 208
Medal of Honor, 210
media, 205
medicine. *See* health
Mercer County, 26, 28–29, 36, 63, 80, 88, 119,
   152, 232
Merton, Thomas, 121
Metcalf County, 123–24
Methodist churches, 118, 120
Mexican War, 138, 139, 140, 146, 189
Meyzeek, Albert E., 158
Middle East, 175
Middlesboro, 61, 117
migration, 211
   see also out-migration
Miss Gordon's Training School, 214
Mississippi River, 49, 51, 146
   map, 52
   New Madrid Bend, 55, 57
   New Madrid Bend map, 55
   New Madrid Earthquake, 57
Mississippian Indians, 11, 12
Monkey's Eyebrow, 74
Monroe, Bill, 194
Monroe County, 74

Montgomery, John Michael, 194
Montgomery County, 39, 153
moonbows, 60
Moonlight Schools (night schools), 233
moonshine, 61
Morehead, 61, 161
Morehead State University, 161, 241
Morgan, John Hunt, 150, 151, 152, 154
Morgan, Mattie, 151
Morgan, Thomas Hunt, 244
Morton, Marmaduke B., *Kentuckians Are Different*, 73, 166
motion pictures, 120, 198–200, 206, 224
motor vehicles, 178
"Mountain Family," 97
Mountains (Eastern Coal Fields), 59–60
Mountains, the Miner, and the Lord, The (Caudill), 170
Mousie, 74
movies. *See* motion pictures
Mt. Sterling, 39, 153
Muddy River, 118
Muhlenberg County, 194
mules, 164
multicultural society, Kentucky as, 15
Murphy, Isaac, 112
Murray, 72, 184, 194, 211
Murray State University, 72, 73, 241
Musgrave, Story, 1–2
music, 192–96
My Old Kentucky Home (Butler), 73
"My Old Kentucky Home" (Foster), 67, 133, 192, 210
My Old Kentucky Home State Park, 74

N

names of towns in Kentucky, 74
Nast, Thomas, 154
National Folk Festival, 212
National Guard, 211
Native Americans, 2, 7–14, 212
    and African Americans, 131
    Archaic Period, 9–10
    Choctaw Academy, 233
    conflicts with, 15–17, 19, 27–28
    and diseases, 13–14, 16
    early days in Kentucky, 15
    Fort Ancient Culture, 12
    the Great Dying, 12–14

Late Prehistoric Period, 12
    Mississippian Culture, 12
    the name "Kentucky," 14
    Paleoindians, 8–9
    religion of, 117
    Tecumseh (Indian chief), 137, 235
    Trail of Tears, 43–44
    views on owning land, 17
    Woodland Period, 10–11
Natural Bridge, 59
Nelson County, 65, 66, 74, 80, 118, 121, 130, 211, 227, 251
Neville, Linda, 109
New Castle, 159
New Deal, 206–9, 223
    banks, 207
    electricity in rural areas, 208
    Great Depression, 206–7, 210, 212
    jobs, 207
"New Economy," 248
New Madrid Bend, Mississippi River, 55, 57
New Madrid Earthquake Fault Line, 57
Newport, 62
    steel-rolling mills, 171
newspapers, 190–92, 205
    for historical research, 3, 4
New World, 2, 12
Nicholas County, 187
Nicholasville, 63
Niles, John Jacob, 192
Nobel Prizes, 243, 244
Norman, Gurney, 185, 190
Norman, Marsha, 187, 192
Northern Kentucky, 62–63
Northern Kentucky University, 62, 115
Nunn, Louie, 222
nurse-midwives, 109

O

Oakland Race Course, Louisville, 111
Obenchain, Eliza Calvert, 213, 214
O'Hara, Theodore, 189
Ohio County, 194, 208, 229
Ohio River, 51, 146, 167, 202
    Falls of the Ohio, 67
    and Jackson Purchase, 57
    map, 52
    in travel to Kentucky, 19, 21, 25, 26, 49
Old State Capitol, 63, 198

Oldham County, 159, 181, 198, 199
one-room schools, 227–29
oral history, 4
original thirteen colonies map, 42
Orphan Brigade, 156–57
Osborne Brothers, 194
outhouses, 96, 107
out-migration, 211–12
Owen County, 153
Owensboro, 116, 133, 167, 168, 192, 222
Owsley County, 74, 95, 114

P

Paducah, 51, 72, 118, 175, 183, 192, 217, 223
    radio in, 195
Paleoindians, 8–9
Palisades, Kentucky River, 59
Papa John's Pizza, 172
Paris, Kentucky, 74
parkways, 203
the past. *See* history
Patrick, John, 192
Pearl Harbor, 209, 210
Pendleton County, 243, 244
Pennyroyal (or Pennyrile), 58
Perry County, 61, 160, 185, 192, 210
perspective from history, 152, 172, 251
Peter, Frances Dallam, 152
photographs, 4, 6
Pike County, 48, 49, 61, 73, 86, 160, 171, 188,
    216, 241
Pikeville, 61, 73
Pine Mountain School, Harlan County, 235
Pitino, Rick, 116
Pizza Hut, 172
Pleasant Hill, 63, 119
Poet Laureate of the United States, 185
poetry, 188
political leaders, 136–38, 222, 223
political parties, 84, 221, 222, 246
politics, 221–24
    before Civil War, 136–44
    Democrats, 84, 221, 222, 246
    federal elections, 221
    governor's races, 84, 88, 162, 221
    Kentucky General Assembly, 221
    Republicans, 84, 221, 222, 246
    voting, 222
    the year 1949, 222, 224

Polk, James K., 108
pollution, 171, 204
Potter College, Bowling Green, 227
pottery, 10, 12
poverty and hunger, 248
Powell County, 84, 86
power plants, 174
Powers, Georgia Davis, 89
power sources, 247, 251
Presbyterians, 120–21
preserving food, 100–101
presidents from Kentucky, 139–43
    Davis, 139, 140, 141, 143
    Lincoln, 139–43
    Taylor, 139, 140, 143
Presley, Elvis, 195
primary sources in research, 5–6, 27
Princeton, 212
private colleges and universities, 240–41
private industry, 163
    see also work
private schools or academies, 226–27, 235
privies, 96
public colleges and univesities, 241
public schools, 226, 227, 228, 236
public worship, 117–18
Pulaski County, 53, 131, 150, 222
Pulitzer Prizes, 191–92
Purdue University, 190

Q

Quakers, 32
quilts, 95–96

R

Rabbit, Eddie, 195
race horses, 61, 176
racetracks, 63, 67, 68
Radcliff, 65
radio, 194, 195, 196
Rafferty's, 172
railroads, 94, 95, 159–60, 168, 169, 202
Rally's, 172
Red River, 118
Red River Gorge, 59
Reed, Stanley, 222
Reelfoot Lake, 57
Reese, "Pee Wee," 114, 224
regionalism, 72–73

religion, 117–21, 246
religious schools, 227, 235, 240
Renfro Valley Barn Dance, 196
Republicans, 84, 221, 222, 246
research, 4–6
    archaeologists, 6, 8
    primary sources, 5–6, 27
    secondary sources, 5
    see also history
resort areas map, 66
revolution, 202
Revolutionary War, 36, 40, 41, 42, 67, 111
Richmond, 63, 196, 241
Ritchie, Jean, 192
riverboat travel, 202
rivers and lakes of Kentucky, 51, 52
roads, 22–24
Roberts, Elizabeth Madox
    Great Meadow, The, 183
    Time of Man, The, 182
Robertson County, 40, 48
rock or stone fences, 64
Rockcastle County, 196
Roosevelt, Franklin D., 207, 223
Rose v. Council for Better Schools, 86
Rosine, 194
Rowan County, 53, 160, 161, 233, 241
"running the gauntlet," 33
Rupp, Adolph, 115–16, 222
Rupp Arena, Lexington, 195
rural areas, 48, 49, 212
Russellville, 1, 137, 147
rye, 164

S

salt licks, 38
salt production, 167
Sampson, Terah, 151, 153
Sanders, Harland, 174
Sandlin, Willie, 210
Saudi Arabia, 175–76
sawmills, 168
Sawyier, Paul, 197
schools. *See* education and schools in Kentucky
science fiction writing, 249
Science Hill Female Academy, 142, 227
Scott County, 63, 64, 102, 114–16, 136, 173, 233, 240, 242
Scottsville, 171

sculpture, 144, 197–98
secondary sources in research, 5
Secretariat (horse), 112
segregation, 216–20
    in schools, 236–37
senate of Kentucky, 82, 87–91
settlement schools, 235
settling Kentucky, 15–44
    barter and trade, 16, 20
    conflict resolution, 16
    end of the frontier, 41
    the first explorers, 20–24
    the first non-Indian woman in, 18
    the first west, 17–20
    hard times and choices, 35–40
    leaders in, 28–31
    settlements, 27–32
    statehood, 41–44
    travel to Kentucky, 25–26
    see also Boone, Daniel; Kentucky
Seven Storey Mountain, The (Merton), 121
Severns Valley, 118
Shakers, 63, 119
Shakertown, 63
Sharp, Phillip A., 243, 244
Sharpsburg, 153
Shawnee Indians, 16
    Boone's capture by, 38–40
    Kenton's capture by, 33
Shel-Tow-y (Big Turtle), Boone's Indian name, 40
Shelby, Isaac, 42–43, 55
Shelby, Susannah Hart, 42
Shelby County, 70, 135, 142, 151, 159, 167, 216, 219, 226
Shelbyville, 70
Shelbyville Female College, 226
Shyrock, Gideon, 198
Simmons University, Louisville, 240
Simpson, Lyde, 231
Simpsonville, 159
Sixty Years in a Schoolroom (Tevis), 142, 227
Skaggs, Ricky, 194
slavery, 126–28, 216
    antislavery, 135–36
    ending, 155
    and freedom, 131–35
    Kentucky as slave state, 146
    Lincoln on, 143
    see also African Americans; Civil War; slaves

slaves, 20, 39, 102
  culture of, 126–27
  life in Kentucky, 129–30
  markets for selling, 127, 130, 133
  music of spirituals, 130
  population in Kentucky, 128
  schools for slaves, 227
  voting, 77
  see also African Americans; Civil War; slavery
Sleet, Moneta, Jr., 192
Slugger Museum, Louisville, 114
smallpox virus, 13
Smith, C.C., 124
Smith, Effie Waller, 188
Smith, Eliza Clay, 97
Smith, John Speed, 97
Smith, Sallie Ann, 97
Smith, Tubby, 116
Smithland, 207, 249
soccer, 115
Social Security, 207
Somerset, 65, 118, 222
Sousley, Franklin R., 211
South-Central Kentucky, 65–67
Southern University, 217
South Union, 63, 119
soybeans, 167
space flights, 1–2
Spalding University, 70
Spanish-American War, 160
Spanish explorers, 15, 16, 17
Spanish flu epidemic, 107
Speaking of Operations (Cobb), 183
spear points, 9
special schools, 233–35
Speed, Joshua, 140, 141
spirituals, 130
sports, 109
  baseball, 112–14, 224
  basketball, 115–17, 222, 224
  boxing, 112
  car racing, 117
  football, 114–15
Springfield, 182
squash, 9
stagecoach travel, 202
Stanford, 31, 35
Stanley, Frank, Jr., 219
St. Asaph's, 31

state parks, 175
  map, 66
State Street School, Frankfort, 236
statehood for Kentucky, 41–44, 76–77, 125
states, 76
stations, 29
  map, 30
steamboats, 64
steel-rolling mills, 171
stereotypes of Kentucky, 61, 161, 200
Stewart, Cora Wilson, 233
Still, James, 184, 185
St. Joseph Cathedral, Bardstown, 118
St. Louis, Missouri, 212
stone axes, 9, 10
story telling, 111–12
Stowe, Harriet Beecher, *Uncle Tom's Cabin*, 133
Stringtown on the Pike (Lloyd), 249
strip mining, 60, 170–71
Stuart, Jesse, 184, 188
Stubblefield, Nathan, 194
Stumbo, Janet, 86
Sturgis, Union County, 218
Supreme Court of Kentucky, 85–87, 90
Supreme Court of the United States, 237
Surtees, Robert, 224

T

Taco Bell, 172
Tate, Allen, 184
Tate, "Honest Dick," 75, 76, 91–92, 162
Taylor, Caroline Burnam, 168
Taylor, Irene, 208
Taylor, Sarah Knox, 139–40
Taylor, Zachary, 139, 140, 144
Taylor County, 65, 240
teachers in early schools, 231–32, 235
technical schools, 239
technology, 248
Tecumseh (Indian chief), 137, 235
telephones, 94, 205, 206
television, 194, 195, 196, 205
Tennessee River, 51, 72
  and Jackson Purchase, 57
Tevis, Julia Ann H., 142, 227
Thomas More College, 62
Thrasher, Mattie Lou, 208
timber industry, 168, 169
Time of Man, The (Roberts), 182

timeline of history, 7, 8
tobacco, 164, 165, 166, 167
Todd County, 114, 139, 184
toilets, 96
toll roads, 203, 204
Tolliver family feud, 161
Tolson, Edgar, 197
tourist trade, 65, 72, 175
Toyota, 62, 64, 173, 174
Trabue, Daniel, 17, 26
traces or trails, 22–24
Trachoma, 109
trade and barter, 12, 16, 20
Trail of Tears, 43–44
Trail of the Lonesome Pine, The (Fox), 181
trails or traces, 22–24
transportation, 202
transportation revolution, 202–5
    air travel, 204–5
    boat travel, 202
    cars, 203–4
    horse or stagecoach travel, 202
    interstate highway system, 203
    parkways, 203
    railroads, 202
    space travel, 205
Transylvania University, 64, 239, 240
Trappist, 121
travel to Kentucky, 25–26
"Traveling Church," 118
Travis, Merle, 194
Trimble County, 134
Truman, Harry, 87, 222, 223
Tug Fork River, 51
    map, 52
Tumbleweed, 172
Tuttle, John W., 150–51, 154
twentieth-century changes, 201–24
    communication revolution, 205–6
    equal rights for all races, 216–20
    equal rights for women, 213–16
    New Deal, 206–9
    out-migration, 211–12
    politics, 221–24
    transportation revolution, 202–5
    wars, 209–11
two-year community colleges, 239
Twyman, Luska J., 219

U

"Uncle Peter," 118
Uncle Tom's Cabin (Stowe), 133
Underground Railroad, 133–34
Union, 145
    flag of, 146, 147
    Kentucky in, 146, 155
    Sixth Kentucky group, 157
    see also Civil War
Union College, 243
Union County, 167, 218, 222
United Parcel Service (UPS), Louisville,
    174, 178
"United we stand; Divided we fall," 73
universities, 64
University of Kentucky, 64, 188, 241
    basketball at, 115–16, 222
    dorm rooms, 244
    early times, 242
    Martin Luther King Center, 190
    segregation at, 237
    writers at, 185
University of Louisville, 70, 241
    basketball at, 116
University of Mississippi, 73
University of North Carolina, 217
University Press of Kentucky, 190
Unseld, Wes, 116
Urban League, 219
U.S. Congress, 76–77
U.S. Constitution, 67, 79
U.S. Military Academy, 155
U.S. Supreme Court, 87

V

Versailles, Kentucky, 74, 114,
    214, 222
veto, 89
Vietnam War, 157, 209, 211
villages, Native American, 12
Vinson, Fred, 87, 222
violence, 155, 159, 162,
    fueds, 61, 160–61
    on the frontier, 18, 27–28, 33, 34, 36, 37–38,
        39, 40
Virginia, and Kentucky, 76
Virginians, settling Kentucky, 15, 17
visual arts, 196–200

voting, 77–78, 84, 222
   African Americans, 158
voting machines, 77, 78

W

W-Hollow, Greenup County, 184
Wade, David, 123
wagon making, 168–69
Waiting Years, The (Jackson), 217
Walker, Daniel, 34
Walker, Frank X
   Affrilachia, 190
   "Kentucke," 190
Walker, Thomas, 20, 21
War of 1812, 35, 138, 146
Warren, Robert Penn, 184–85, 188, 192, 224
Warren County, 1, 65, 109, 125, 147, 168, 173,
   206, 214, 227, 241
wars, 209–11
   Gulf War, 209
   Korean War, 209
   Vietnam War, 209, 211
   World War I, 209
   World War II, 209, 210–11
Washington County, 89, 138, 182
Watterson, Henry, 191
Wayne County, 149, 150, 154, 184, 218
Wayne, John, 224
Webster, Delia, 134, 135
Webster County, 169, 218
Wendell Ford Western Kentucky Parkway, 203
Western Coal Fields, 59
Western Kentucky University, 65, 116
West Kentucky, 70–72
West Point, 155
wheat, 164
Wheeler, Mary, 192
"Whirlwind Campaign," 236, 238
whiskey, 67
White Castle (hamburgers), 217
White Hall, 136
Whitley, Esther, 35
Whitley, William, 35, 111
Whitley County, 60, 69, 103, 150, 174, 240
whoopflarea, 74
Wilcutt, Terry, 1–2
Wilderness Road, 34
   map of, 30

William Natcher (Green River)
   Parkway, 203
Williamsburg, 61
Willis, Bruce, 71
Winchester, 63, 184
Wolfe, George C., 187–88
women
   in basketball, 115
   black, 89, 126, 142
   in business, 168
   in church, 120
   clothes and fashion, 97–99
   colleges and universities, 241, 242
   equal rights for women, 213–16, 251
   the first non–Indian woman in, 18
   in health care, 109
   Ingles, Mary, 18
   Knott, Sarah Gertrude, 212
   Lynn, Loretta, 193
   Mason, Bobbie Ann, 71
   percent in Kentucky, 246
   Powers, Georgia Davis, 89
   schools for females, 227
   Stewart, Cora Wilson, 233
   on Supeme Court of Kentucky, 86, 87
   Taylor, Caroline Burnam, 168
   Tevis, Julia, 142
   voting, 77, 78
   and work, 104–5
Woodford County, 80, 114, 157, 214, 216, 222,
   229, 241
Woodland Indian, Mammoth Cave, 11
Woodland Period, 10–11
work, 103–6, 163–78
   industries, 171–75
   and play, 110
   see also coal mining; economy of Kentucky;
      farming
World War I, 209
World War II, 209, 210–11
Wright Brothers, 204
writing and writers, 180–90
   drama, 187–88
   early writing, 180–82
   history, 4–6, 188
   modern writers, 185, 187
   novels, 187
   poetry, 188–90

writing and writers, *cont.*
    twentieth-century writers, 182–85
    see also culture of Kentucky

Y

Yandell, Enid, 197
Yokam, Dwight, 194

York (slave), 131
Young, Charles, 155
Young, John, 132
Young, Whitney, Jr., 219
Yum!Brands, Louisville, 171, 172